JAMES LONGSTREET

JAMES LONGSTREET

The Man, the Soldier, the Controversy

Edited by

R.L. DiNardo
and
Albert A. Nofi

COMBINED PUBLISHING
Pennsylvania

For information, address:
Combined Publishing
P.O. Box 307
Conshohocken, PA 19428
E-mail: combined@dca.net
Web: www.dca.net/combinedbooks
Orders: 1-800-4-1860-65

"Petticoats, Promotions, and Military Assignments: Favoritism and the Antebellum Career of James Longstreet" by William Garrett Piston, oiginally appeared in *Military History of the West*, Vol. 22, No. 1 (Spring, 1992), copyright 1992, used with permission.

Chickamauga maps from Patrick Abbazia, *The Chickamauga Campaign*, copyright 1986, Combined Books,Inc., used with permission.

Gettysburg maps from Albert A. Nofi, *The Gettysburg Campaign*, copyright 1993 Albert A. Nofi, used with permission.

ISBN 0-938289-96-9

Printed in the United States of America

Contents

List of Maps

Acknowledgements

This book grew out of a conference on General Longstreet held at the Williams Club, in New York City, on 9 October 1993, under the auspices of the New York Military Affairs Symposium in cooperation with the Longstreet Memorial Fund.

The Symposium is an independent, not-for-profit educational body devoted to increasing public knowledge, awareness, and understanding of military history, arms control, defense policy, disarmament, civil-military relations, international security, veterans affairs, and the interrelationship of war, society, and culture, through the presentation and dissemination of diverse scholarly viewpoints. It began in the Fall of 1983 as an informal, occasional activity in which graduate students of military history and defense affairs could meet to assist each other in improving their knowledge and understanding of the phenomenon of war in history. Since its foundation, NYMAS has held more than 600 lectures on a variety of topics. In addition, since 1992 the Symposium has sponsored an annual scholarly conference and has presented the annual "Arthur Goodzeit Best Book Award."

Formed in the late 1980s because the people of the South had "turned our backs on one who devoted four years of his life to 'The Lost Cause,'" The General James Longstreet Memorial Committee is dedicated to the erection of a monument ot the General's memory at Gettysburg. The culmination of the Committee's efforts will be the erection of a life-size bronze equestrian statue of Longstreet in the Pitzer Woods, in the Gettysburg National Military Park on the 135th anniversary of the great battle.

By special arrangement with the contributors to this volume, all royalties from the sale of *James Longstreet: The Man, the Soldier, the Controversy* are to be donated to the General Jame Longstreet Memorial Fund and the New York Military Affairs Symposium.

In addition to the contributors to this volume, the editors would like to thank Professor Emeritus Hans Trefousse, of the City University of New York and noted biographer of Carl Schurz, who assisted in the organization of the Longstreet conference, to Professor David Syrett of Queens College, CUNY, President of NYMAS, for his support, as well as the members of both NYMAS and the Longstreet Memorial Committee, that odd combination of Northerners and Southerners who made this book possible.

A number of ahistorical conventions have been adopted in this work to facilitate the identification of military units. Except in direct quotes, Union formations have been italicized. In addition, Union brigades have been identified using the formula *3/1/XX*, which indicates the *Third Brigade, First Division, XX Corps*. In an additional ahistorical note, Roman numerals have been used for Federal army corps.

Quotes have generally not been edited.

R.L. DiNardo
Albert A. Nofi
Brooklyn
January 8, 1998

Foreword

by

Robert C. Thomas

When Dr. Nofi called to ask me to write the preface for this collection of essays on General James Longstreet, I must admit I was completely surprised and, needless to say, very honored. To be included in the company of the outstanding scholars who so kindly contributed to this historical inquiry is the ultimate compliment. As Chairman of the Longstreet Memorial Committee, I wanted to express my appreciation to these fine gentlemen and to the New York Military Affairs Symposium for their support and assistance on this very overdue project to honor a long forgotten figure of American history.

Thanks to parents who were proud of our history, I grew up in a home where our ancestors were honored and talked about. I remember how my father's eyes would glow with pride as he told us about his great-granddaddy, who fought for the Confederate Army and came home after being wounded in the foot in eastern North Carolina. The "Late Unpleasantness" has, since that time more than 30 years ago, always fascinated me. No matter how much I read about the war, I never tired of it and could never learn enough.

A few years ago, a friend, Gary Thompson, himself a student of military history, lent me a copy of Professor William Garrett Piston's work *Lee's Tarnished Lieutenant: James Longstreet and His Place in Southern History*. After reading the book, I found myself angered by the way my fellow-countrymen had treated General Longstreet because of his political preferences after the war. The fact that there was no monument to the General anywhere in the world was to me simply ludicrous. After talking to several of my brother members of the Sons of Confederate Veterans, we decided to attempt to remedy this historical oversight. We put a plan together which resulted in the adoption, unanimously, of a resolution by the National Sons of Confederate Veterans absolving General Longstreet of any blame for the loss of the Battle of Gettysburg and vowing support to the North Carolina Division, SCV, in its project to erect a monument to General Longstreet at the Gettysburg National Military Park.

Through Professor Piston, I had the opportunity to meet Professor Richard L. DiNardo in Raleigh, N.C., and another Longstreet supporter was found. Professor DiNardo, through his membership in the New York Military Affairs Symposium, arranged for the organization of the "Longstreet Reconsidered" symposium, held at the Williams Club, in New York City, in October of 1993, an event co-sponsored by the North Carolina Division, SCV. The symposium was a rousing success, enjoyed by everyone in attendance. This publication is the result of the symposium.

Again, I would like to express my appreciation on behalf of the Longstreet Memorial Committee to the authors and editors of this volume. An extra word of thanks should be given to Professor Richard DiNardo, for organizing the symposium, for encouraging me through slow times, and for being a good friend.

> Robert C. Thomas
> Chairman,
> General James Longstreet Memorial
> Committee
> North Carolina Division, SCV
> January 8, 1998

History, Politics, and James Longstreet

by

Albert A. Nofi

James Longstreet: The Man, the Soldier, the Controversy is part of an effort to right an historical wrong, the defamation of the military record of Confederate Lieutenant General James Longstreet. Regarded by some as having "no superior in either army as a battlefield tactician," during the Civil War Longstreet's reputation as a commander seemed unshakable.[1] Indeed, in the midst of the struggle Robert E. Lee several times called Longstreet "my old war horse." But after the war, or, more accurately, after Lee's death in 1870, Longstreet became the target of a vicious campaign to smear his reputation and loyalty to the "Cause." Former comrades-in-arms such as Jubal Early and William Nelson Pendleton sought to blame Longstreet for the Confederate defeat at Gettysburg, and, by extension, for the disastrous outcome of the war itself. Their campaign was so successful that even Douglas Southall Freeman, among the most devoted, careful, and hard working of Civil War researchers, treated Longstreet with much disdain.[2] By the mid-twentieth century Longstreet was at best considered a rather pedestrian commander, and at worst an incompetent and disloyal one.

Building upon important recent work by a number of Civil War scholars, some of whom are numbered among its contributors,[3] *James Longstreet: The Man, the Soldier, the Controversy* takes a fresh look at the general's war record, goes on to examine the nature of the charges brought against him, inquires into the motivations of those who worked so hard to deny him his niche in history, and reflects upon the large measure of success which attended their efforts.

The broad outlines of Longstreet's life and career may be readily summarized. A native of South Carolina, Longstreet (1821-1904) graduated from West Point in 1842, virtually at the bottom of his class, 54th out of 56.[4] Commissioned in the infantry, he served briefly against the Seminoles in Florida. During the war with Mexico, in which he was wounded, Longstreet received two brevets for gallantry. In March of 1848 he married Maria Louisa Garland, the daughter of Brigadier General John Garland, a connection which brought him a number of choice postings as he served on the frontier and in garrison over the next dozen years.[5] By the eve of the Civil War Longstreet was a major in the Paymaster's Department.

Longstreet resigned from the Old Army on May 9, 1861, nearly a month after Fort Sumter. Entering Confederate service, he was commissioned a brigadier general in the Provisional Army of the Confederate States to date from June 17, 1861. Longstreet commanded a brigade with some distinction at Blackburn's Ford and First Bull Run/Manassas the following month. On October 7, 1861 he was promoted to major general and given a division, which he led ably during the opening phases of the Peninsular Campaign in the Spring of 1862. But Longstreet performed poorly at Seven Pines, when he was given command of a "wing" (army corps not being formally instituted in the Confederate Army until later that year) in what would become the Army of Northern Virginia, and for a time he reverted to division command.[6] Nevertheless, when Robert E. Lee assumed the leadership of the army, Longstreet was given a command which totalled fifteen brigades. In his new capacity Longstreet performed well, redeeming his reputation during the Seven Days' Battles. When the Army of Northern Virginia was formed in the summer of 1862, shortly before the Second Bull Run Campaign, Longstreet was given command of the "Right Wing," comprising five divisions, which became the First Corps on November 6, 1862. He was ever after in Lee's confidence, as commander of the First Corps and as second-in-command of the Army of Northern Virginia.

Longstreet led his corps with considerable ability during the Second Bull Run Campaign, delivering the flank attack which very nearly proved fatal to John Pope's *Army of Virginia* on August 30, 1862. At Sharpsburg on September 17, his corps held the southern flank of Lee's line, blunting Ambrose Burnside's afternoon assault across Antietam Creek. That evening Lee called Longstreet "My old war horse," the first of several occasions on which he would use this phrase.[7] As a consequence of his distinguished conduct, Longstreet was promoted to lieutenant general on October 9, 1862, out-ranking Thomas J. Jackson and all other Confederate officers save the handful of full generals. At Fredericksburg on December 13, 1862, his front was the subject of repeated Union assaults, all of which were successfully repulsed. The following Spring Longstreet was given a critical assignment, taking two divisions of First Corps on an expedition in southeastern Virginia (the so-called Suffolk Campaign), with the dual mission of collecting supplies and detering Union forces ensconced along the coast. He thus missed the Chancellorsville Campaign. Longstreet took part in the planning for Lee's proposed invasion of Pennsylvania, although he seems to have believed that a reinforcement of the Confederate armies in the West would have been a better strategy.

Longstreet played a critical role in the Battle of Gettysburg (July 1-3, 1863), for most of which he commanded Lee's right wing. He conducted the massive attack which severely injured the *Army of the Potomac* on the afternoon on July 2. The next day Longstreet undertook the preparations for what has come to be known as "Pickett's Charge," about the wisdom of which he had serious reservations, reservations which have tended to be confirmed in retrospect. Despite the failure of this attack, he continued to be on cordial terms with Lee: During the retreat Lee once more called him "My old war horse."[8]

In September of 1863, Longstreet, long an advocate of a "Western Strategy," received permission to take the bulk of his corps across the Appalachian Mountains to support Braxton Bragg's Army of Tennessee against the Federal *Army of the Cumberland*, under William S. Rosecrans. The subsequent Confederate victory at Chickamauga on September 20, 1863 was largely the work of several brigades of Longstreet's troops and his leadership. Soon afterwards, following a personality clash with Bragg, a not unusual occurrence in the Army of Tennessee, Longstreet and his corps were sent to upper east Tennessee. The Suffolk Campaign aside, this was Longstreet's only experience of independent command. Although there were some bright moments, on balance the operation was a failure, and Longstreet was unable to wrest Knoxville from Union Major General Ambrose Burnside, whose forces greatly outnumbered his own.

Longstreet and First Corps returned to Virginia in early 1864. His corps joined the Battle of the Wilderness (May 5-6, 1864) on the afternoon of May 6, blunting a major Federal assault and then delivering a flanking counterattack which nearly collapsed the Union left. Late in this attack, as Longstreet was riding forward in the dusk, he found himself caught between the converging lines of Confederate troops, and was seriously wounded by men from Mahone's Brigade. It was an incident reminiscent of that which had cost Thomas "Stonewall" Jackson his life almost exactly a year earlier, in virtually the same area. Longstreet did not return to duty until October 16, 1864. Once back, however, he commanded First Corps, which comprised all Confederate forces in the trenches between Richmond and the James River, through the bitter winter of 1864-1865. On the night of April 2-3, 1865, Longstreet joined Lee's general withdrawal westwards from the Richmond-Petersburg lines. At Appomattox, a week later, he was the only senior officer to urge continued resistance should Ulysses S. Grant offer draconian terms, saying to Lee, "General, unless he offers us honorable terms, come back and let us fight it out."[9] When the war ended Longstreet was the senior lieutenant general in the Confederate Army, and second-in-command to Robert E. Lee in the Army of Northern Virginia.

After the war Longstreet settled in New Orleans. He became a Republican and advocated compliance with Reconstruction. Longstreet argued that the sooner the South acquiesced in the new system the sooner the old order could return in a different guise, a point which was apparently too subtle for some of his more ardent former comrades. For a time Adjutant General of Louisiana, Longstreet once ordered black militiamen to suppress a riot by an anti-Reconstruction white mob in New Orleans, during which he was himself briefly captured by the rioters.[10] Longstreet was afterwards made minister to Turkey by President Rutherford B. Hayes, served in a variety of other government posts, and attempted to answer the increasingly vituperative attacks on his character and reputation.

In 1896 Longstreet, for some years a widower, married Helen Dortch, a beautiful young woman over 40 years his junior. The new Mrs. Longstreet survived her husband by nearly sixty years, and was at the time of her death in 1962, the last surviving wife of a Civil War general.

Nicknamed "Old Pete" by his friends, Longstreet had been a merry, affable man before the war, but had become reserved and "cheerless" after three of his children (a girl and two boys) died of scarlet fever in Richmond in the Winter of 1861-1862. A man of considerable temper, he several times clashed with subordinates, such as Evander McIvor Law and Lafayette McLaws.[11] One of the best corps commanders of the war, if not the best, Longstreet had a good eye for ground and a fine tactical sense. Despite this, he appears to have had limited talent for independent command, based upon the evidence of his East Tennessee Campaign in late 1863 and early 1864. Nevertheless, the fact that on several occasions Longstreet urged a "Western" strategy on the Confederate command suggests considerable strategic vision, perhaps even greater than did Lee himself.

While Lee was alive, he had frequently praised Longstreet's abilities. But after Lee's death several of Longstreet's erstwhile comrades-in-arms undertook a campaign to belittle his reputation and blame him not only for the defeat at Gettysburg, but ultimately for the failure of the Confederacy's bid for independence. When Longstreet attempted to answer these charges, his writings were often done in a slipshod, abrasive, and egotistical fashion, thereby providing his enemies with yet more ammunition with which to attack him. As a result, within a few years of the end of the Civil War, his reputation as a soldier was in decline. It has been long in recovering.

James Longstreet: The Man, the Soldier, the Controversy is a further step in that recovery. The book comprises six essays, each of which addresses a different aspect of Longstreet's career.

R.L. DiNardo's "James Longstreet, the Modern Soldier" looks at Longstreet in terms of his comprehension of the critical changes which were occurring in the profession of arms at the time of the Civil War. Longstreet was a perceptive and original commander. His penchant for the tactical defensive followed by counterattacks, reflects an understanding of the power of modern firearms. The surprising efficiency of his staff work—when compared with that of other Civil War commanders—is also suggestive of a progressive thinker, as is his concern for logistics. Far from being a "sluggish" commander, we find Longstreet to be among the Civil War's most skilled generals, a small company indeed.

"Petticoats, Promotions, and Military Assignments" by William Garrett Piston examines Longstreet's early career, and points out the importance of his father-in-law, Brigadier General John Garland, in securing for him important assignments. The essay also is something of a call to action, for it suggests that an important dimension of life in the antebellum army has hitherto been very neglected, the effect of family ties on an officer's prospects for advancement, what people in eighteenth century England were wont to call "interest."[12]

Jeffry D. Wert's "No 15,000 Men Can Take that Position," is a careful look at Longstreet's role in the Battle of Gettysburg. It was Longstreet's performance at Gettysburg which lay at the heart of the post-war attacks upon his character, loyalty, and professional skill. Yet Longstreet's achievements on the second day of the battle were outstanding, and his preparations on the morning of the third day for what is traditionally known as "Pickett's Charge" were about as thorough as could possibly have been, given the circumstances. In short, of the Confederate corps commanders at

Gettysburg, Longstreet by far turned in the most impressive performance.

"The Bull of the Woods: James Longstreet and the Confederate Left at Chickamauga," by James R. Furqueron, deals with one of the most spectacular victories of the Civil War, the defeat of the Union *Army of the Cumberland* by the Confederate Army of Tennessee. In a careful analysis, Mr. Furqueron not only examines the course of events, but also looks at the state of the command in the Confederacy's main western army in mid- and late-1863, and addresses various criticisms of Longstreet's performance, concluding that it was a victory in which James Longstreet's handling of his hastily assembled wing played a decisive role.

"Longstreet and Jackson Compared: Corps Staffs and the Exercise of Command in the Army of Northern Virginia," also by Professor DiNardo, looks at a surprisingly neglected aspect of command and administration during the Civil War, the organization and functioning of higher level staffs. In the process the essay permits the development of a better understanding of Longstreet's professional competence as a soldier, a commander who gave his staff officers considerable authority to interpret his orders in the light of tactical developments, rather than merely using them as glorified messengers.

In many ways, William Garrett Piston's "Marked In Bronze: James Longstreet and Southern History " is the most comprehensive essay in this volume. Building on the sort of evidence such as is presented in the earlier articles, and in such works as his own *Lee's Tarnished Lieutenant* and Jeffry D. Wert's *General James Longstreet*, Professor Piston examines the development of what may be termed the "Anti-Longstreet Cabal." An essential element in the rise of their school of Confederate historiography—if the often scurrilous assaults on "Old Pete" may be so dignified—was his post-war "collaboration" with the forces of Reconstruction. Further fuel for Longstreet's enemies was provided by his refusal to subscribe to the elevation of Lee to the status of a demigod, an apotheosis which may be said to have reached its peak with Douglas Southall Freeman's massive *R.E. Lee*, in 1934. Then too, there was Longstreet's rather abrasive approach in his writings on the subject of his war experiences. However, it is important to recall that it was not until Lee was safely dead that the assault on Longstreet's role in the war really began. Clearly, Longstreet's enemies understood that Lee's opinion of the man who had been his principal subordinate and adviser, not to mention a personal friend, was considerably higher than theirs. It is an enlightening, if sad tale, of the ways in which the historical record can be manipulated for political purposes.[13]

James Longstreet: The Man, the Soldier, the Controversy is by no means the final word on the subject. Much work remains to be done. One important area of inquiry which suggests itself immediately is the motivations of the principal leaders of the anti-Longstreet movement. The two men most dedicated to the assassination of Longstreet's professional standing, Jubal Early and William Pendleton, themselves had much to answer for in terms of their own professional performance in the course of the war.

Jubal A. Early (1816-1894) a native Virginian, graduated 18th in the West Point class of 1837,[14] entering the artillery. After a tour of duty in Florida against the Seminoles, he resigned from the army. Over the next few years he practiced law and engaged in politics in his native state with considerable success, becoming a member of the House of Burgesses and commonwealth's attorney. He served as a major of Virginia volunteers in the Mexican War. In 1861, Early was a delegate to the Virginia secession convention, at which he voted against secession. Nevertheless, he became an ardent Confederate, entering the army as colonel of the 24th Virginia. Early commanded a brigade under Beauregard during the First Bull Run/Manassas Campaign and was promoted brigadier general shortly thereafter. He led his brigade during the opening phases of the Peninsular Campaign in 1862, until wounded. He returned to duty in time to command a brigade in the Second Bull Run Campaign. Early received a division during the Antietam Campaign, which he led at Fredericksburg, and he was promoted major general in January of 1863. The following spring he demonstrated some skill as a rear guard fighter when he commanded the forces which defended Marye's Heights during the Chancellorsville Campaign.

During the Gettysburg Campaign Early commanded a division in Lieutenant General Richard Ewell's Second Corps of the Army of Northern Virginia. His performance during the campaign was at best a mixed one. On the first day of the Battle of Gettysburg his division played an important role in the devastating flank attack which unhinged the Union position north and west of Gettysburg.[15] However, at a commanders' conference that night, Early helped convince Lee that a major attack on the Union right was likely to be unprofitable.[16] The next day, July 2, Early advised Ewell to delay his scheduled diversionary attack on Culp's Hill, originally to have been simultaneous with Longstreet's attack in the south, and then performed poorly during the actual assault.[17]

At Spotsylvania in May of 1864 Early assumed command of the Second Corps when Ewell went on sick leave, and was soon after promoted to lieutenant general. He commanded the corps at Cold Harbor. On June 13 Early took the Second Corps and began his famous "raid" down the Shenandoah Valley and into Maryland with the intention of putting pressure on Washington, in the hope of causing troops to be pulled away from Richmond. He achieved some success in this venture, but allowed Union Major General Lew Wallace with about 6,000 green troops to delay his 14,000 veterans for nearly a day at Monocacy (July 9, 1864), thereby permitting strong reinforcements to reach Washington before he could. Faced with superior numbers of Union troops, Early fell back from the Washington area on July 12th. Returning to the Valley, Early had some success against the Union forces initially sent against him, but the arrival of Union Major General Philip Sheridan resulted in his defeat in a series of battles, and his command was finally dispersed by Brigadier General George Armstrong Custer early in 1865. Early's performance was so poor, and public outcry so great, that he was relieved, the only commander Lee ever sacked for ineptitude.[18] Early spent the last months of the war on the shelf.

After the war Early fled to Mexico, thinking to take service with the forces of the Emperor Maximilian, but then went to Canada. He eventually returned to Virginia, where he resumed his law practice and became involved in the corrupt Louisiana Lottery. Early became the first president of the Southern History Society, wrote a number of books on the war, and engaged in a rather successful campaign to place all blame for the Confederate reverse at Gettysburg on Longstreet, and by implication the outcome of the war itself.[19]

Early's close collaborator in his campaign against Longstreet was William N. Pendleton (1809-1883). Like Lee and Early a Virginian, Pendleton graduated from West Point in 1830, fifth in a class of 42.[20] He resigned from the Army in 1833 and became a teacher, while studying for the ministry. In 1838 he was ordained a Episcopal priest, eventually becoming the rector of Grace Church, Lexington, Virginia. On the outbreak of the Civil War he entered Confederate service as an artilleryman, serving on General Joseph E. Johnston's staff during the First Bull Run Campaign. Promoted brigadier general in March of 1862 (one of only three Confederate artillerymen to attain a generalship), Pendleton was shortly appointed effective chief of artillery in the Army of Northern Virginia, a post in which he served for most of the war. Despite this, although a fair administrator, he seems to have lacked the necessary tactical skill for the post. Lee "cannot have been wholly satisfied with Pendleton,...because he never gave Pendleton real control of the artillery in action."[21] At Chancellorsville Pendleton was criticized for what was regarded as poor handling of the artillery on Marye's Heights, a matter which appears to have rankled for some time.[22] One apparent result of his limited abilities was that at Gettysburg preparations for the artillery bombardment which preceded "Pickett's Charge" on July 3, 1863 were entrusted to Edward Porter Alexander, a colonel. However, Pendleton meddled with the preparations for the bombardment. Without consulting or informing Alexander, or anyone else, Pendleton ordered to the rear several howitzers which had been assigned to accompany the attacking infantry. By the time the error was discovered it was too late to correct it, and the troops advanced without the benefit of artillery support.[23] Perhaps as a result of his carelessness at Gettysburg, although Pendleton retained his titular position as chief of artillery under Lee, he was relegated to purely administrative duties for the final two years of the war.

Shortly before Appomattox, Pendleton acted as the spokesman for a group of senior officers who believed that the game was up, asking Longstreet to convey their sentiments to Lee. Longstreet, citing Confederate regulations which equated talk of surrender with treason, refused.[24]

Considering their own war records, both Early and Pendleton had much to gain by attacking Longstreet's professional competence and loyalty, a matter which should merit further inquiry.[25]

There are some important lessons to be learned from the abuse to which James Longstreet's memory has been subject in the literature, both professional and popular. The deliberate campaign to turn an authentic champion of Confederate arms into a villain is a sobering reminder of what can happen to the historical record when it is manipulated for personal or political purposes. It also demonstrates that, despite conventional wisdom, it is very often the losers, rather than the winners, who write the histories.[26]

Notes to the Introduction

1. Ezra J. Warner, *Generals in Gray* (Baton Rouge: Louisiana State University Press, 1981), 193, a statement which, considering that it was penned in the 1950s, is one of the most generous to Longstreet in the entire literature of the Civil War.

2. Consider the following sampler of comments from Freeman's four volume *R.E. Lee: A Biography* (New York: Scribner's, 1934-1935),

   "Longstreet...was eating his heart away in sullen resentment that Lee had rejected his long-cherished plan of a strategic offensive and a tactical defensive," III, 85.

   During the Gettysburg Campaign, Longstreet displayed "temper and antagonism," towards his commander, III, p. 89.

   "Usually Lee had to ride with Longstreet to accomplish even as much as was credited to the slow moving commander of the First Corps," IV, 173.

   Yet Freeman was a careful enough researcher to spot an obvious lie. Thus, regarding the claim by Charles S. Venable, of Lee's staff, to have witnessed an unseemly incident between Lee and Longstreet on the morning of July 2nd, Freeman wrote "it seems almost certain that Longstreet did not arrive until after Venable had left" (III, 87, note 5). Later Freeman would revise his view of Longstreet, a matter much overlooked in the literature, on which see Note 3, below.

3. See, for example, William Garrett Piston's *Lee's Tarnished Lieutenant: James Longstreet and his Place in Southern History* (Athens: University of Georgia Press, 1987), Jeffry D. Wert's *General James Longstreet: The Confederacy's Most Controversial Soldier, A Biography* (New York: Simon & Schuster, 1993), and Thomas L. Connelly's and Barbara Bellow's even earlier *God and General Longstreet: The Lost Cause and the Southern Mind* (Baton Rouge: Louisiana State, 1982). Nor should Ezra Warner's 1959 comment cited in Note 1, above, be ignored,

one of the first rounds in the battle to rescue Longstreet's reputation.

In this regard it is interesting to note that in later life Douglas Southall Freeman himself had clearly begun to revise his opinion of Longstreet. In *Lee's Lieutenants* (New York: Scribner's, 1942-1944), published a decade after *R.E. Lee*, Freeman was far less critical of the general's abilities, and went so far as to say that Longstreet was "...always at his best in battle, a reliable lieutenant" (III, xxiv), and expressed some sympathy for the fate which befell him, saying "he received at the hands of some of his former military associates far less than justice as a soldier." (III, 769). An examination of causes of Freeman's change of heart would seem useful.

4. Longstreet's classmates included the future Union generals Napoleon J. T. Dana (29th), Abner Doubleday (24th), Henry L. Eustis (1st), John Newton (2nd), John Pope (17th), William S. Rosecrans (5th), George Sykes (39th), and Seth Williams (23rd), as well as the Confederates Richard H. Anderson (40th), Daniel H. Hill (28th), Mansfield Lovell (9th), Lafayette McLaws (48th), Gustavus W. Smith (8th), Martin Luther Smith (16th), Earl Van Dorn (52nd), and James Monroe Goggin, who left the Academy at the end of his third year.

5. On this see Chapter II of this volume, "Petticoats, Promotions, and Military Assignments: Favoritism and the Antebellum Career of James Longstreet," by William Garrett Piston.

6. In this regard it should be noted that Thomas "Stonewall" Jackson did not perform with particular brilliance when first given a corps command either, leading to jokes about "Jackson of the Valley" being a better general than "Jackson of the Chickahominy." See the discussion in Freeman, *Lee's Lieutenants*, I, 655-669.

7. Wert, 200.

8. See Confederate Brigadier John D. Imboden, "The Confederate Retreat from Gettysburg," *Battle and Leaders of the Civil War*, edited by Robert Underwood Johnson and Clarence Clough Buel (Reprint, New York: Thomas Yoseloff, 1956), III, 428.

9. Edward Porter Alexander, *Military Memoirs of a Confederate: A Critical Narrative* (New York: 1907), 609; see also Freeman, *Lee*, IV, 131-132.

10. An interesting discussion of the circumstances of this incident can be found in Jim Dan Hill, *The Minute Man in Peace and War* (Harrisburg: Stackpole, 1964), 113-116.

11. During Longstreet's operations in Eastern Tennessee in late 1863, McLaws was relieved by his commander for lack of cooperation. Subsequently cleared of all charges, McLaws' relations with Longstreet were stormy thereafter and he was sent to an administrative command in the Carolinas, and later directed the defense of Savannah. A man of considerable character, despite his personal differences with Longstreet McLaws supported the latter when Jubal Early and William N. Pendleton combined to smear his reputation after the war.

12. Consider, if you will, the possibilities which prosopography may offer to the student of the Civil War. The study of family and personal relationships and their effects on history, prosopography has been a useful tool in elucidating the obscurer aspects of things like the politics of the later Roman Republic or of the British parliament of 1910. It has not been used much as a tool in examining American history. This is unfortunate, for, as Prof. Piston's essay suggests, there appears to be a whole new dimension to be explored.

It is today sometimes difficult to recall that its earliest period, the United States was an extremely small place, and a remarkable number of people turn out to have sometimes surprisingly interesting family relationships. Family ties connected many of the principal political and military leaders in the war: By one accounting there were at least 52 families with two or more generals among their kinsmen, accounting for well over 10 percent of the generals in the war, both sides taken together. Consider the ties of blood and marriage which linked Robert E. Lee with many of the other prominent political and military leaders of his times.

Lee himself, of course, was a full general in the Confederate Army. His sons George Washington Custis Lee and William

Henry Fitzhugh Lee, were both Confederate major generals, and his nephew, Fitzhugh Lee, was a lieutenant general. A cousin, Richard L. Page, the son of Lee's maternal aunt, was a Confederate brigadier general. Samuel Cooper, the seniormost Confederate general, was Fitzhugh Lee's father-in-law. Union Brigadier General Frank Wheaton was married to another daughter of Samuel Cooper's, and hence Fitzhugh Lee's brother-in-law.

Confederate Brigadier General Edwin G. Lee, another distant cousin, was the son-in-law of Confederate Brigadier General William N. Pendleton, one of Longstreet's persecutors. Union Rear Admiral Samuel P. Lee was yet another cousin. Robert E. Lee was also a cousin, at some remove, to Confederate Brigadier General James Terrill and his brother Union Brigadier General William R. Terrill, both of whom died in the war.

Confederate Lieutenant General Richard P. Taylor was a fourth cousin to the general: his father, the late President Zachary Taylor, and his uncle, Union Brigadier General Joseph P. Taylor, were being kin to Lee's mother. Confederate Major General Lafayette McLaws, one of Longstreet's ablest subordinates, was Zachary Taylor's nephew by marriage, and hence Dick Taylor's cousin-in-law, and thus tied to Robert E. Lee as well. Confederate Brigadier General Allen Thomas was a brother-in-law of Dick Taylor's uncle, Union Brigadier General Joseph P. Taylor. And, of course, Dick Taylor's sister had been Jefferson Davis' first wife.

So Robert E. Lee appears to have been linked by ties of blood or marriage to more than a dozen men who attained generalcies during the war, both sides taken together, as well as to the President of the Confederacy. This strongly suggests that a systematic study of such relationships among the higher levels of political and military leadership in the war may be of some value.

13. Professor Piston's remark about the South being a land "rich in bronze," reminds this writer of the statue of Confederate hero Lieutenant General Thomas J. Jackson which stands on the Bull Run/Manassas battlefield. Dedicated between the

World Wars, at the height of sympathy for the Confederate "Cause" not only in the popular culture but even among historians, the statue has a splendidly uniformed "Stonewall" sitting gallantly astride a noble stallion. In reality, Jackson was very careless of his dress, and had a seat so poor that he was several times thought by casual observers to be drunk in the saddle, while Little Sorrel was a small, ugly, inelegant mare, albeit intrepid and imperturbable under fire.

14. Early's more distinguished classmates included the future Confederate General Braxton Bragg (1st), Lieutenant General John Pemeberton (27th), and Brigadier General Lewis A. Armistead, who was dismissed from the Academy in his junior year after breaking a plate over Early's head in a mess hall quarrel (see Warner, *Generals in Gray*, 11), as well as the future Union Major Generals William H. French (22nd), John Sedgwick (24th), and Joseph Hooker (29th), in addition to several other generals of lesser fame.

15. David G. Martin, *Gettysburg July 1* (Conshohocken, PA: Combined Books, Inc., 1995); Harry W. Pfanz, *Gettysburg: Culp's Hill and Cemetery Hill* (Chapel Hill: The University of North Carolina Press, 1993), 77-80.

16. *Ibid.*, 83-84.

17. *Ibid.*, 235-236 and 281-282, contains a discussion of Early's influence on the second day's fighting, and his attempt to blame others for the failure of the belated assault on Culp's Hill, most notably Major General Robert E. Rodes, who commanded one of the other divisions in Ewell's corps.

18. Lee had relieved Lieutenant General Richard Ewell of the command of Second Corps on June 1, 1864, officially on grounds of poor health, though performance probably was a factor. Considering his usual courtesy and sensitivity, Lee used unusually strong language in sacking Early, telling the latter that his performance had "shaken the confidence of the troops and of the people" and that "the public and the army judge chiefly by result"; Freeman, *Lee*, IV, 507-508.

19. *Cf.*, "Early was one of General Lee's most faithful defenders," Freeman, *Lee*, IV, 509. Interestingly, Early's *War Memoirs*

(Bloomington: Indiana University Press, 1960) devote very few pages to Gettysburg (266-275), none of which are particularly controversial nor critical of Longstreet. In contrast, his treatment of Chancellorsville is much more extensive (193-235), and he devotes several pages (199-201) to the defense of William N. Pendleton against charges that he mismanaged the artillery on Marye's Heights during the latter battle, a matter which Early attributes to Colonel Robert H. Chilton, Lee's chief-of-staff, ignoring the fact that Chilton, was almost certainly acting under orders, which Early could not say without explicitly criticizing Lee.

20. Pendleton was one of three men in his class to attain a generalship, the others being Confederate Major General John B. Magruder (15th) and Union Brigadier General Robert C. Buchanan (31st). An even more famous classmate washed out in his second year, Edgar Allan Poe. While at the academy, Pendleton appers to have begun his lifelong friendships with Jefferson Davis (Class of 1828) and Robert E. Lee (1829). See Jennings C. Wise, *The Long Arm of Lee* (New York: Oxford University Press, 1959), 742.

21. Freeman, *Lee*, III, 230. In the same place Freeman cites Lee's *Dispatches*, No. 242, in which the general wrote of Pendleton, "I do not say he is not competant, but from what I have seen of him I do not know what he is." There is some evidence that Lee would have happily dispensed with Pendleton's services, see Wise, *The Long Arm of Lee*, 745.

22. Wise, *The Long Arm of Lee*, 743-744.

23. The absence of the howitzers was not discovered until literally the last moment: "...I decided to send for the nine howitzers and take them ahead of Pickett up nearly to musket range, instead of following close behind him as at first intended; so I sent a courier to bring them up in front of the infantry....The courier could not find them....I afterward learned that General Pendleton had sent for a part of them...," E. Porter Alexander, "Artillery Fighting at Gettysburg," Johnson and Buell, *Battles and Leaders*, III, 363. Although it probably had no effect on the outcome of the attack, Longstreet made much of this

incident in his *From Manassas to Appomatox: Memoirs of the Civil War in America* (Reprint, Secaucus, N.J.: Blue and Gray Press, 1988), 392.

24. Freeman, *Lee's Lieutenants*, III, 721.

25. Indeed, Early seems to have had a penchant for blaming others: Chilton for Pendleton's apparent failure at Chancellorsville (*Cf.*, Early, *War Memoirs*, 199-201); Rodes for the failure of Ewell's attack on Culp's Hill on July 2, 1863 at Gettysburg (*Cf.*, Pfanz, 235-236 and 280-281); and, of course, Longstreet for the failure of "Pickett's Charge," the defeat at Gettysburg, and ultimately the loss of the war.

26. Aside from the American Civil War, a short list of events for which the popular—and frequently the professional—historical judgment has been shaped largely by, from, or in favor of, the perspective of the losers must inevitably include the English Civil War, the Napoleonic Wars, the Mexican-American War, the Spanish *Reconquista*, the Spanish Civil War, the First World War during the 1920s and early 30s, and, in some professional circles, the Cold War as well. Indeed, it is only with some effort that a similar trend has not affected the history of the Second World War, considering the degree to which the German perspective has affected treatment of operations on the Eastern Front, the prevelance of Holocaust Denial, and recent attempts to accuse Eisenhower of genocide and to place the blame for the Pacific War on the U.S.

CHAPTER 1

James Longstreet, the Modern Soldier

A Broad Assessment

by

R.L. DiNardo

*T*he American Civil War has long been seen as a transitional phase from the Napoleonic period to modern warfare. In the use of field fortifications, for example, the later stages of the war, perticularly the operations around Richmond and Petersburg in late 1864 were seen clearly as the progenitors of the trench systems that dominated much of World War I.[1] More recently Edward Hagerman has argued, by and large correctly in my estimation, that the American Civil War marked the beginning of modern warfare, especially in the realms of communications, the employment of railroads, and staff operations.[2] The campaigns of William T. Sherman in Georgia and the Carolinas and Philip Sheridan in the Shenandoah Valley in 1864 have long been regarded as the beginning of what would come to be called "Total War" in the twentieth century.[3]

If we look at the American Civil War in this broad context, it is clear that a very important commander in this regard was James Longstreet. An examination of his operations reveals a commander who displayed a splendid grasp of the elements of modern command, and an intuitive understanding of the developing trends in tactics, as well as a fine instinct for strategy.

Strategically, Longstreet understood the importance of the western theatre in a way many of his contemporaries did not. His requests to be sent west, even if motivated in part by his desire for independent or semi-independent command, displayed an understanding of the strategic issues that were all too lacking in the highest levels of the Confederate command.[4] When he arrived in the west he saw the opportunity which glittered before the Army of Tennessee and he executed the decisive attack at Chickamauga. Some have dismissed his plaintive letter to Confederate Secretary of War James Seddon asking for Robert E. Lee to be sent to Tennessee, as being disingenuous, motivated by his desire to replace Braxton Bragg with himself as commander of the Army of Tennessee.[5] Even though there may be some truth to this, it should be added that Bragg was eminently dislikeable, and that it should not obscure the clarity of Longstreet's thinking. He appreciated that some positve action had to be undertaken if Chickmauga were to be something other than a pyrrhic victory. This was something Longstreet was not about to get from Braxton Bragg, who in the aftermath of Chickamauga proved himself a master of waffling and indecision.[6]

Longstreet's ideas on strategy showed some flair, but were deficient in considering the bane of Confederate strategy, logistics. During the lull between Chancellorsville and Gettysburg, Longstreet urged the transfer of two of his divisions from Virginia to Tennessee. Once united with the Army of Tennessee and the troops from Joseph E. Johnston's command in Mississippi, an offensive would be undertaken to "break up" William S. Rosecrans' *Army of the Cumberland* in Tennessee, thus relieving the pressure on Vicksburg.[7] Although a good plan on paper, it was ignorant of the logistical problems that confronted Braxton Bragg, who at the time was having all kinds of trouble maintaining the Army of Tennessee in its position covering the highland rim of the Cumberland Plateau.[8]

After Chickamauga, Longstreet proposed that the Army of Tennessee cross the Tennessee River east of Chattanooga, with the idea of flanking Rosecrans' army out of Chattanooga, and then moving on Knoxville.[9] It was certainly an interesting idea, but at the time Longstreet suggested it, he was ignorant of state of the Army of Tennessee's supply situation, which was near breaking down even before Chickamauga.[10] His proposal for a Confederate offensive in the spring of 1864 showed imagination, but again failed to take logistical problems into account.[11] These flaws, however, do not obviate the fact that Longstreet, very much in the manner of a Henry Halleck or a Ulysses Grant, saw the war in its totality, going well beyond the parochial concerns of so many of his contemporaries.

Longstreet's record in independent command was very mixed. The Suffolk campaign was a supply gathering operation pure and simple. Longstreet's critics, especially his biographers Hamilton J. Eckenrode and Bryan Conrad, have seen this campaign as part of a devious scheme by Longstreet to get away from Lee, leaving Lee in a perilous situation facing the *Army of the Potomac.* Robert Krick, never to be outdone in deriding Longstreet, called the campaign "an embarrassment."[12] Such criticism can only be described as nonsense. Longstreet was not supposed to involve his command in any major fighting, and he did not.[13] The operation netted two months' worth of supplies for the Army of Northern Virginia. Lee himself considered the operation a success.[14]

The East Tennessee campaign was another matter. To be sure, the campaign itself was ill-conceived. More than anything, it was an attempt by Jefferson Davis to prevent the already burgeoning feud between Longstreet and Bragg from getting any more out of control than it already was. Bragg supported the idea as it was consonant with his program after Chickamauga of purging the upper echelons of command of the Army of Tennessee of any real or suspected dissident elements. Longstreet approved of the idea as it would leave him independent of Bragg.[15] All of this was done in complete awarness of the fact that the Union forces in Chattanooga were being heavily reinforced. Moreover, Union supply difficulties in Chattanooga had been eased by the opening of the "Cracker Line" by Joseph Hooker's troops after the battle of Wauhatchie, arguably the poorest showing by Longstreet as a combat commander during the war.[16]

Once dispatched, the expedition ran into a series of problems, some avoidable and some not. Longstreet's first error was to underestimate the size of the force needed to take Knoxville, believing that he required only the services of his two divisions, one of which had been heavily engaged at Chickamauga, altogether a total of about 15,000 men.[17] This was far too small a force to take Knoxville, a heavily fortified city defended by Ambrose Burnside's *IX* and *XXIII Corps*, a total force of about 30,000 men supported by 111 guns.[18] Longstreet's only real chance to take Knoxville would have been provided only if Burnside chose to engage in open battle. Given that Burnside, according to Charles Dana, estimated Longstreet's strength at anywhere from 20,000 to 40,000, as well as his cautious nature and his recent battle-field disaster at Fredericksburg, he was not about to come out from his strong fortifications and risk a battle.[19]

Longstreet's force was poorly supplied to begin with, owing to the general shortage of transport that was affecting the Army of Tennessee even before Chickamauga. Once Longstreet's force reached East Tennessee, it found itself operating in an almost barren countryside. That he kept his troops supplied at all was due largely to the efforts of his quartermaster, Raphael Moses.[20]

Longstreet conducted the campaign poorly. He launched a half-hearted attack on Fort Sanders, an attack that should not have been made in the first place. Aside from that, Longstreet spent most of his time engaging in a squabble with some of his subordinate division and brigade commanders that can only be described as unutterably petty.[21] The entire operation was brought to a halt by Bragg's disaster at Missionary Ridge. Once informed of this, Longstreet abandoned his positions around Knoxville and moved east to Bristol in early 1864 and received definitive orders to return to Virginia on April 7 1864.[22]

Many of Longstreet's critics have held the East Tennessee adventure against him as proof of his incompetence.[23] Although poorly conducted, one cannot make too much out of it. A general's record must be looked at in its totality. Here Longstreet's critics are guilty of having a rather selective memory. While they focus attention on East Tennessee, they conveniently ignore Chickamauga, where Longstreet played the decisive role in securing the only victory won by the Army of Tennessee during the war.[24] This would be very much like considering Stonewall Jackson a great general simply on the basis of the Shenandoah Valley campaign.[25] It might also be pointed out that, for an incompetent general, Longstreet was welcomed back to the Army of Northern Virginia with open arms. As Walter H. Taylor wrote to his wife on April 24, 1864, "Old Pete Longstreet is with us and all seems propitious."[26]

Longstreet also comes in for heavy criticism in his treatment of some of his subordinate commanders during this campaign, especially LaFayette McLaws, Jerome Robertson, and Evander Law. To be sure, such criticism is justified. The treatment of McLaws and Law as it took its course, was extremely shabby. Some of McLaws' letters, written in a white-hot rage, have often been used by Longstreet's critics against him.[27]

It is grossly unfair, however, to hold Longstreet to such a standard, while letting his contemporaries off the hook. Krick, for example, criticizes Longstreet's behavior as having "outstripped the record of the notoriously litigious Stonewall Jackson, who, though harsh and fond of courts, had no need of scapegoats."[28] Such an airy opinion would have surprised Richard Garnett, whose career was almost destroyed by a vindictive Jackson after Garnett's understandable retreat at First Kernstown. While A.P. Hill certainly ranked as one of the Army of Northern Virginia's most prickly personalities, and played his part in the infamous Hill-Jackson feud, he was also the subject of some shabby treatment by Jackson as well.[29] Other well known cases of such treatment would include Ulysses Grant's treatment of Rosecrans, William T. Sherman's of Joseph Hooker, and finally Braxton Bragg and almost every one of his senior officers. In this regard, Longstreet proved neither better nor worse than his contemporaries.

At the operational level, Longstreet clearly understood the importance of speed. Contrary to his detractors, who have accused him of being slow at Second Manassas and the Wilderness, his marches on both of those occasions were models of celerity. Each time he moved his corps at rates as high as 36 miles a day.[30] His performance at Second Manassas becomes even more impressive when one realizes that before moving, his part in Lee's plan involved fixing John Pope's attention on the position along the Rapidan, while Jackson made his march down the Shenandoah Valley around the

Union right flank. Once Jackson reached his objective, Longstreet then had to come up to his support, while having to fight through a Union covering force at the very defensible Thoroughfare Gap.[31] It is also worth pointing out that his marches, while every bit as rapid as Jackson's, were not attended with the same level of straggling that at times drove Jackson to distraction.

Longstreet also understood the ancillary aspects of command at this level. While he was rarely in a position where he could command cavalry, he was clearly aware of the importance of good intelligence. This was exemplified by his use of the actor Harrison as a scout during the Gettysburg campaign. With Lee virtually blinded by Jeb Stuart's absence while on his controversial ride around the *Army of the Potomac*, Harrison's information may have saved the Army from a serious defeat on July 1.[32] As Douglas Southall Freeman pointed out, "corps commanders usually employed spies, but Longstreet, with his usual care for detail, saw to it that his spies were well-chosen and diligent."[33]

Tactically, Longstreet clearly grasped the principles of good battlefield tactics, and saw with equal clarity the growing importance of the combination of fire power and field fortifications. Lee's victory at Fredericksburg greatly influenced Longstreet's thinking in this regard.[34] Thereafter, he generally showed a healthy (and sensible) respect for Union forces fighting from either strong natural or fortified positions. Hence his reluctance to attack at Gettysburg, as well as his reticence to launch a direct assault on the strongly fortified *Army of the Cumberland* in Chattanooga following Chickamauga. It is worth pointing out here that Longstreet was not alone in his belief of the superiority of the tactical defense over the tactical offense. No less a figure than Helmuth von Moltke, the premier soldier of the period in

Europe, advocated the tactical offensive only after several enemy attacks had been defeated by the tactical defense.[35]

Offensively, Longstreet tried to make his attacks as powerful as possible. Thus, "Old Pete's" attacks were masterpieces of concentration. His decision to delay his attack at Second Manassas on August 30, 1862, seconded by Lee, ultimately allowed him to put four divisions into an assault which swept away John Pope's left flank. The much debated attack on July 2 at Gettysburg, while perhaps delivered later than desired, had about as much punch behind it as Longstreet could muster.[36] At the battle of Chickamauga Longstreet, faced with a well-positioned Union force to his front, launched an attack—something of a miracle in itself, given the situation Longstreet found himself in after his arrival—after assembling an assault force that was five brigades deep. Even without the so-called "fatal order" which opened a gap in the Union front, Longstreet's attack had sufficient depth that it would have severely dented, if not broken, the Union line. In some ways Longstreet's attack at Chickamauga anticipated the equally innovative but much better known assault engineered by Union general Emory Upton against the Mule Shoe at Spotsylvania the following year.

Longstreet's best tactical moment, however, was at the Wilderness. Coming off a long and rapid march, he was able to launch an attack with his own two divisions plus several brigades from A.P. Hill's Third Corps which, according to Union *II Corps* commander Winfield Scott Hancock, "rolled me up like a wet blanket."[37] Equally interesting here were Longstreet's actions after he was wounded in a manner eerily reminiscent of Jackson a year earlier. Whereas Jackson could only tell his immediate successor, Jeb Stuart, that he must "do what he thinks best," Longstreet, while on a stretcher, was able to blow the blood from his mouth and explain clearly to the ranking officer present, Major General Charles

Field, the state of affairs and the objective of the attack.[38] The Wilderness must rank as the best moment of one of the war's best battlefield tacticians.

It was in his style of command, however, that Longstreet most clearly showed himself to be a modern soldier. If anyone understood the impact of tactical dispersion on command, it was James Longstreet. This was especially true when it came to his staff. Longstreet's selection and employment of his staff was markedly different from that of many of his contemporaries, especially in the Confederacy. Many Confederate generals manned their staffs with friends, relatives and cronies, a practice which led Braxton Bragg to complain that too many important staff positions were filled by grossly unqualified men.[39] With but two exceptions, Longstreet's staff was quite different in this regard.[40] Generally, the only quality that Longstreet sought was intelligence, regardless of background or social status, best exemplified by officers such as Thomas Goree and G. Moxley Sorrel.[41]

Longstreet's employment of his staff and headquarters could definitely be described as modern. The Kirkwood Rangers, a South Carolina cavalry company, provided a large pool of men for courier service, thus giving Longstreet's corps an efficient communications system.[42] By means of these men, Longstreet's staff was generally kept informed of his pending plans and operations. Perhaps the most significant statement in this regard comes from Longstreet's report on the Second Manassas/Sharpsburg campaign, where he credits his staff with giving "direction to the commands such as they saw fit."[43] In his report on Fredericksburg, Longstreet again saw fit to mention the "intelligent" nature of the service rendered by his staff.[44] It is reasonable to assume that Longstreet's staff could best render "intelligent" service if their chief gave them some general idea as to his plans.

Longstreet's staff officers were promoted rapidly. They were also given a wide degree of latitude in dealing with the units under the general's command. A good minor example of this occurred when Osman Latrobe redeployed a gun of the Donaldsonville Artillery at Fredericksburg on his own initiative.[45]

It was in this regard, however, that Moxley Sorrel came into his own. A review of his activities can easily lead one to the conclusion that he was Longstreet's alter ego, and as such fulfilled the role of a modern chief of staff. Sorrel's description of his duties in his memoirs certainly indicate that he had the authority to speak in Longstreet's name and to use his own initiative and Longstreet's authority as circumstances required, as was amply demonstrated at Chickamauga and the Wilderness.[46] Here again it is important to point out that Longstreet's employment of Sorrel was fairly close to the much more highly developed command system used by the Prussian Army under Moltke.[47]

James Longstreet showed himself to be a modern soldier in numerous ways. How can we account for this? Certainly there was nothing in Longstreet's educational background to give any indication of his future prowess as a general. Born on January 8, 1821, he received a better education at the hands of his uncle, Augustus Baldwin Longstreet, and at a preparatory school near Augusta, Georgia, than most people in the South of that period.[48] He entered West Point in 1838, graduating 54th in his class of 56 in 1842.[49] In the Mexican War he served as a company commander in the 8th Infantry, and gained valuable experience in both the administrative and practical sides of soldiering.[50] There is no way to tell whether or not he pursued the study of military matters between his graduation from West Point in 1842 and his resignation from the U.S. Army in 1861. Given his educational background, however, and the fact that he makes no mention of any such an undertaking in his memoir, it is reasonable that he did not.

A clue to Longstreet's conduct as a general comes, I think, from his personality. Some successful generals derive their success from a streak of brilliance which can surface at critical moments. Two such commanders who would fall into this category would be Stonewall Jackson and Erich von Manstein. Other commanders, while only occasionally brilliant, are generally very steady performers, owing primarily to the fact that they are endowed with a healthy dose of common sense. Some famous commanders who would be included in this category would be Ulysses Grant, George Meade, William T. Sherman, and Dwight Eisenhower. Finally, there are those commanders who combine both brilliance and common sense. This would apply to Horatio Nelson, Napoleon, the Elder Moltke, and Robert E. Lee, to name but a few.

Where does Longstreet fit into this? Like his kinsman Sam Grant, Longstreet seemed to be endowed with a healthy dose of common sense. This particular quality would suggest to Longstreet the advantage of combining the defensive firepower of Civil War weaponry with field fortifications at a battle such as Fredericksburg, while the same set of circumstances suggested nothing of the sort to the brilliant but often erratic Stonewall Jackson. It is worth noting that after the battle, Jackson asked Longstreet for instructions on how to construct field fortifications.[51] Consequently, if one looks at Longstreet's record, one sees the occasional flash of brilliance, however, were long stretches of days marked by good, solid, steady performance and growth. In his biography of Braxton Bragg, Grady McWhiney remarked that one of Bragg's greatest defects as a combat commander was his failure to improve over time. The Bragg of Shiloh was also the Bragg of Chickamauga.[52] In contrast to this, the Longstreet of Chickamauga and the Wilderness was immeasurably better than the Longstreet of Seven Pines.[53] After those initial missteps, he grew in the job, aided by his innate ability to adapt to the differing conditions on battlefields ranging from the plains of Manassas to the fields of Gettysburg to the heavily wooded terrain of Chickamauga and the Wilderness.[54] By 1864 he was certainly the best corps commander in the Confederacy and one of the best on both sides.

Before concluding this brief overview of Longstreet as a general, an excursion into the realm of comparison, some of it speculative, may be profitable. Civil War commanders are often compared to their contemporaries—allies or enemies. By this standard, Longstreet comes off very well. At the corps level, Longstreet was simply better than almost every one of his contemporaries. He was a better battlefield commander than every other corps commander in the Confederacy, including Jackson.[55] For those who would characterize Longstreet as disloyal, insubordinate and even traitorous would do well to compare Longstreet's record to those of such luminaries as William J. Hardee, D.H. Hill, Joseph Hooker, Dan Sickles, and the inimitable Leonidas Polk.[56]

Longstreet comes off even better when compared to those who occupied comparable levels of command during the Mexican War. One can can only consider commanders such as Winfield Scott and Zachary Taylor veritable saints for putting up with such recalcitrant and incompetent subordinates as David E. Twiggs, William J. Worth, and the eternal butt of bad puns, Gideon J. Pillow.[57]

Placing Longstreet in the context of the contemporaneous art of war in Europe is admittedly problematic, owing to the fact that there is little in the way of operational history in English of the Franco-Austrian, Austro-Prussian, and Franco-Prussian Wars.[58] Nonetheless, some general observations may be made. First, I think it reasonable to assert that Longstreet, and this would probably hold true for Jackson as well, would have fit quite well into the Prussian system. This was largely because the manner in which Robert E. Lee commanded the Army of Northern Virginia was very similar to Moltke's style of command.[59]

In terms of responsiveness to a commander's orders, Moltke would probably have regarded Longstreet as a model subordinate. The great Prussian leader had to contend with army and corps commanders who were princes of the blood, monarchs of minor German states, or old court favorites such as General Karl Friedrich von Steinmetz, who had served with William I of Prussia when both were young officers in 1814. All of these men had the right of direct access to the King, and did not hesitate to use it. They also, with Steinmetz being the most notorious, were willful enough to completely wreck Moltke's plans by ignoring orders or doing the exact opposite of what they were ordered to do.[60] Some of the corps commanders were at times so uncommunicative as to make even Stonewall Jackson at his most laconic seem a positive fountain of information, a problem Moltke took great pains to correct.[61] Thus Longstreet would have stacked up well against his peers in the Prussian Army.

Longstreet looks even better compared to his counterparts in the French and Austrian armies. The French system of command was so centralized that it completely stifled initiative. French officers, from corps level down, were often told almost nothing of their immediate superior's intentions. The result was to wait until the order arrived in writing. The action of Longstreet at Second Bull Run, in anticipating Lee's decision to finally launch the attack on Pope, and sending his four divisions in even before Lee's order arrived, would have been almost unthinkable for a French officer in the Army of Napoleon III.[62] Likewise, Longstreet's staff ran much more efficiently than that of a corresponding French organization. French staff organization and procedures in

1870 can only be described as chaotic.[63] Much of what has been said about the French here can also be said of the Austrians.

How then, can we conclude this brief examination of the generalship of Lee's "Old Warhorse?" With regard to the tactical and operational trends that were beginning to emerge in the middle of the nineteenth century, Longstreet clearly understood them and their implications for the future of warfare. His notions of combining the operational offensive with the tactical defensive showed an understanding of those realms of warfare that would have impressed even a Clausewitz or a Moltke. His grasp of the elements of command in an age of increasing tactical dispersion was instrumental in his selection and employment of a staff that made him the envy of many Civil War commanders, and probably not a few Austrian, French, and Prussian commanders as well. In an age where war was being modernized in all its facets, James Longstreet truly emerges as the modern soldier.

Notes to Chapter 1

1. Major General J.F.C. Fuller, *Grant and Lee* (Bloomington, 1957), pp. 45-49.

2. Edward Hagerman, *The American Civil War and the Origins of Modern Warfare* (Bloomington, 1992).

3. J.B. Walters, "General William T. Sherman and Total War," *Journal of Southern History*, Vol. 14, No. 4 (November 1948): pp. 447-480. For a more recent work, see Hagerman, *The American Civil War and the Origins of Modern Warfare*, pp. 207-208.

4. William Garrett Piston, *Lee's Tarnished Lieutenant* (Athens, 1987), p. 41. See also General E. Porter Alexander, *Fighting For the Confederacy* (Gary W. Gallagher ed.) (Chapel Hill, 1989), pp. 219-220, and Jeffry D. Wert, *General James Longstreet* (New York, 1993), pp. 227-228, 240-241, 243-246, and 300-303.

5. United State War Department, *Official Records of the War of the Rebellion* (Washington, 1880-1902), Series I, Vol. XXX, Part 4, pp. 705-706. (Hereafter cited as *OR*. All references unless otherwise noted are from Series I.) See also Wert, *General James Longstreet*, pp. 325-326, and Steven E. Woodworth, *Jefferson Davis and His Generals* (Lawrence, 1990), p. 239.

6. Braxton Bragg to Joseph E. Johnston, September 26 1863, James Power Smith Collection, Library of Congress, Washington, D.C. (Hereafter cited as LOC.), and Bragg to Jefferson Davis, September 29 1863, Braxton Bragg Papers, Special Collections Library, Duke University. (Hereafter cited as DU.)

7. Gen. James Longstreet, *From Manassas to Appomattox* (Reprint, New York, 1991), p. 327.

8. Thomas L. Connelly, *Autumn of Glory* (Baton Rouge, 1971), p. 114.

9. *OR*, Vol. XXX, Part 2, p. 290.

10. George W. Brent Diary, Braxton Bragg Papers, Western Reserve Historical Society, Cleveland Ohio. (Hereafter cited as WRHS.)

11. Wert, *General James Longstreet*, pp. 371-372.

12. Hamilton J. Eckenrode and Bryan Conrad, *James Longstreet: Lee's War Horse* (Chapel Hill, 1936), p. 165-166. Robert K. Krick, "If Longstreet...Says So, It is Most Likely Not True," Gary Gallagher (ed.), *The Second Day at Gettysburg* (Kent, Ohio, 1993), p. 81.

13. *OR*, Vol. XVIII, pp. 922, 966.

14. Raphael J. Moses Manuscript, pp. 62-63, Southern Historical Collection, University of North Carolina, Chapel Hill, North Carolina. (Hereafter cited as SHC). Wert, *General James Longstreet*, p. 238.

15. Connelly, *Autumn of Glory*, pp. 262-264, Woodworth, *Jefferson Davis and His Generals*, p. 248 and Wert, *General James Longstreet*, p. 339.

16. Piston, *Lee's Tarnished Lieutenant*, p. 75.

17. *OR*, Vol. XXXI, Part 1, p. 474.

18. *OR*, Vol. XXXI, Part 1, p. 267.

19. *OR*, Vol. XXXI, Part 1, p. 258. See also William Marvel, *Burnside* (Chapel Hill, 1991), pp. 316-325.

20. Raphael J. Moses Manuscript, pp. 66-67. Moses Manuscript, SHC.

21. For details, see Wert, *General James Longstreet*, pp. 360-365, and Piston, *Lee's Tarnished Lieutenant*, p. 81.

22. Wert, *General James Longstreet*, p. 371.

23. See for example, Krick, "If Longstreet Says So...," p. 81, and Judith Lee Hallock, *Braxton Bragg and Confederate Defeat*, Vol. II (Tuscaloosa, 1991), pp. 108, 126.

24. Krick, in his article, simply skips from Gettysburg to East Tennessee. Krick, "If Longstreet Says So...," p. 81. Hallock takes the approach of damning Longstreet with faint praise.

Hallock, *Braxton Bragg and Confederate Defeat*, Vol. II, pp. 74-75.

25. To be absolutely fair, Jackson does deserve high marks for his conduct of the campaign. It must be noted, however, the he operated with several enormous advantages. First, he was operating in an area in which he was intimately familiar. He also had the aid of a very friendly and supportive local populace. Finally, Jackson was fortunate in being opposed in the field by three of the most incompetent generals who ever took the field wearing the Federal uniform. It should be added that after the Valley campaign, Jackson put in a performance in the Peninsula campaign that was as bad as any put in by any general in the war on either side.

26. R. Lockwood Tower ed., *Lee's Adjutant: The Wartime Letters of Colonel Walter Herron Taylor*, 1862-1865 (Columbia, 1995), p. 155. See also Piston, *Lee's Tarnished Lieutenant*, p. 87.

27. Krick, "If Longstreet Says So...," pp. 82-84, and Freeman, *Lee's Lieutenants*, Vol. 3, p. 301. See also Eckenrode and Conrad, *James Longstreet*, p. 279.

28. Krick, "If Longstreet Says So...," p. 82.

29. Garnett's case went to a court-martial in August 1862. Fortunately for Jackson, as the case was proving to be an embarrassment, it was cut short without resolution by the press of events. Garnett was able to escape Jackson when he went to Pickett's newly formed division. Krick, "Armistead and Garnett," Gary Gallagher ed., *The Third Day at Gettysburg & Beyond* (Chapel Hill, 1994), p. 114. For the origins of the Hill-Jackson feud, see James I. Robertson, *General A.P. Hill* (New York, 1987), pp. 110-111.

30. For the Wilderness, see Alexander, *Fighting For the Confederacy*, p. 350, and Gallagher, "The Army of Northern Virginia in May 1864: A Crisis of High Command," *Civil War History*, Vol. 36, No. 2 (June 1990): pp. 101-118. For the Second Manassas campaign see Hennessy, *Return to Bull Run* (New York, 1992), p. 460, and Gallagher, "Scapegoat in Victory: James Longstreet and the Battle of Second Manassas,"

31. Hennessy, *Return to Bull Run*, p. 154. It must be pointed out also that Longstreet's efforts here were aided by Pope's incompetence in failing to cover Thoroughfare Gap as strongly as he might have.

32. Edwin B. Coddington, *The Gettysburg Campaign* (New York, 1984), pp. 180-181, 186.

33. Freeman, *Lee's Lieutenants*, Vol. 3, p. 49.

34. Piston, *Lee's Tarnished Lieutenant*, pp. 31-32, and Freeman, *Lee's Lieutenants*, Vol. 2, p. 368.

35. *Generalfeldmarschall Helmuth, Graf von Moltke, Ausgewählte Werke*, F. von Schmerfeld ed. (Berlin, 1925), Vol. I, p. 335. Ordinarily, citations of Moltke's military writings should be from his *Militärische Werke*, which run to some 14 volumes. Unfortunately, at the time this was being written I do not have quick access to Moltke's *Militärische Werke*, and had to rely on the four volumes of selected works edited by Schmerfeld. For those unfamiliar with German, a valuable source here is Daniel J. Hughes ed., *Moltke on the Art of War: Selected Writings* (Novato, 1993).

36. One main reason Longstreet delayed the attack was to await the arrival of Law's Brigade of Hood's Division, so he could put in every man available. Wert, *General James Longstreet*, p. 265. Alexander felt that an even wiser move would have been to wait until Pickett's Division arrived, thus allowing Longstreet to launch a three division assault on the Union left. Alexander, *Fighting For the Confederacy*, p. 242. The matter of Longstreet's delay is a controversial one. Some traditionally minded authors have argued that this delay cost the Confederates the battle. See, among others Eckenrode and Conrad, *James Longstreet*, p. 199, Freeman, *Lee's Lieutenants*, Vol. 3, p. 173, Krick, "If Longstreet Says So...," pp. 70-73, and Emory Thomas, *Robert E. Lee: A Biography* (New York, 1995), p. 297. On the other hand, some authors have argued that Longstreet's attack profited from the delay as it allowed Dan Sickles to deploy the Union *III Corps* along an untenable line from the Peach Orchard to Devil's Den, which Longstreet's attack

overran. For this argument, see Coddington, *The Gettysburg Campaign*, p. 406, and Wert, *General James Longstreet*, p. 279.

37. Robert Garth Scott, *Into the Wilderness With the Army of the Potomac* (Bloomington, 1988), p. 160.

38. Frank E. Vandiver, *Mighty Stonewall* (New York, 1957), pp. 484-485 and Freeman, *Lee's Lieutenants*, Vol. 3, p. 366.

39. *OR*, Series IV, Vol. III, p. 316.

40. The two exceptions were Thomas Walton and Peyton Manning. Walton was one of Longstreet's in-laws, while Manning may have been acquainted with Longstreet from before the war. Wert, *General James Longstreet*, pp. 62-63, 225.

41. For the manner in which Longstreet selected and used his staff, see this writer's "Longstreet and Jackson Compared: Corps Staffs and the Exercise of Command in the Army of Northern Virginia," later in this volume.

42. *OR*, Vol. XII, Part 2, p. 567. Sorrel, *Recollections of a Confederate Staff Officer* (New York, 1905), p. 118.

43. *OR*, Vol. XII, Part 2, p. 567.

44. *OR*, Vol. XXI, p. 571.

45. *OR*, Vol. XXI, pp. 620-621, 628. See also this writer's "Longstreet and Jackson Compared: Corps Staffs and the Exercise of Command in the Army of Northern Virginia," later in this volume.

46. For details see this writer's "Longstreet and Jackson Compared: Corps Staffs and the Exercise of Command in the Army of Northern Virginia," later in this volume.

47. Gunther E. Rothenberg, "Moltke, Schlieffen and the Doctrine of Strategic Envelopment," Peter Paret ed., *Makers of Modern Strategy* (Princeton, 1986), p. 301, and Hughes, *Moltke on the Art of War*, p. 221.

48. Piston, *Lee's Tarnished Lieutenant*, pp. 2-3.

49. Wert, *General James Longstreet*, p. 30. Longstreet, working from memory, stated that he graduated sixtieth in a class of sixty-two. Longstreet, *From Manassas to Appomattox*, p. 16.

50. Piston, *Lee's Tarnished Lieutenant*, p. 5. For a more detailed examination of Longstreet's pre-war career, see Piston, "Petticoats, Promotions, and Military Assignments: Favoritism and the Antebellum Career of James Longstreet," elsewhere in this volume, and Wert, *General James Longstreet*, pp. 33-55.

51. Piston, *Lee's Tarnished Lieutenant*, pp. 34-35. Undoubtedly, characterizing Jackson as "erratic" will make some people cringe. However, a thorough examination of Jackson's record, stripped of heroic myth, shows that he had as many bad days as he had good days.

52. Grady McWhiney, *Braxton Bragg and Confederate Defeat* (New York, 1969), Vol. I, p. 390.

53. For Longstreet's performance at Seven Pines, see Stephen W. Sears, *To the Gates of Richmond* (New York, 1992), pp. 119-133, and Wert, *General James Longstreet*, pp. 110-126.

54. Wert, *General James Longstreet*, pp. 321-322.

55. Hennessy points out that while Jackson excelled in conducting operational movements, his record as a battlefield tactician was "mediocre." Hennessy, *Return to Bull Run*, p. 459.

56. See for example Hardee's letter to Polk of July 1 1863, in *OR*, Vol. XXIII, Part 1, p. 623.

57. See for example John S.D. Eisenhower, *So Far From God* (New York, 1989), p. 269, and K. Jack Bauer, *The Mexican War 1846-1848* (New York, 1974), p. 267. Pillow has been the recipient of any number of puns, especially at the hands of students of famed Civil War scholar Frank Vandiver. Thomas Connelly described Pillow as "overstuffed": Connelly, *Army of the Heartland* (Baton Rouge, 1967), p. 32. Emory Thomas thought Pillow "soft on maps and directions": Thomas, *Robert E. Lee*, p. 126.

58. As far as I know, there is no good work in English on the Franco-Austrian War of 1859. For the Austro-Prussian War, Geoffrey Wawro, *The Austro-Prussian War: Austria's War with Prussia and Italy, 1866* (Cambridge: 1996) is excellent, though Gordon A. Craig, *The Battle of Königgrätz* (New York, 1964) is still quite useful. For the Franco-Prussian War, the best work

remains Michael Howard, *The Franco-Prussian War* (New York, 1961). The issue of the impact of technology is brilliantly covered in Dennis E. Showalter, *Railroads and Rifles* (Hamden, Ct., 1975). There is a good deal more material in German. The historical sections of both the Austrian and German General Staffs compiled multi-volume studies of the Austro-Prussian War. The German General Staff's historical section turned out a large number of works on the Franco-Prussian War, the most notable of which is *Der deutsch-französische Krieg*, 5 Vols. (Berlin, 1872-1881). Much material on the Austro-Prussian and Franco-Prussian Wars can be found in Moltke's *Militärische Werke*. Finally, aside from memoirs, a number of excellent articles can be found in two of the leading military periodicals of the time, *Militär Wochenblatt*, and the *Österreichische Militärische Zeitschrift*.

59. Compare Lee's statement to Prussian observer Justus Scheibert in "General Robert E. Lee, Ober-Commandeur der ehmaligen Sudstaatlichen Armee im Nord Amerika," *Jahrbucher für die Deutsche Armee und Marine*, Vol. XVI (September 1875): pp. 208-209 with Moltke, *Ausgewählte Werke*, Vol. I, p. 260.

60. Craig, *The Battle of Königgrätz*, p. 58, and Howard, *The Franco-Prussian War*, pp. 82-85.

61. Hughes, *Moltke on the Art of War*, p. 228.

62. *OR*, Vol. XII, Part 2, p. 557. Arthur T. Coumbe, "Operational Command in the Franco-Prussian War," *Parameters*, Vol. XXI, No. 2 (Summer 1991): p. 97.

63. Coumbe, "Operational Command in the Franco-Prussian War," p. 89.

CHAPTER 2

Petticoats, Promotions, and Military Assignments
Favoritism and the Antebellum Career of James Longstreet

by

William Garrett Piston

James Longstreet is best known as a Confederate general, but he spent most of his twenty-three year military career as an officer in the United States Army. A significant portion of that career was spent on garrison duty in the Southwest following the Mexican War. Longstreet's peacetime years on the frontier brought no glory, but they are not without interest. His experiences shed light on a much neglected subject: the degree to which marriage, and kinship through marriage, affected promotions and military assignments in the Old Army.

Longstreet's personal papers perished in a fire in 1889, forcing the historian to rely largely on military records and secondary sources rather than family letters for the details of his early career. But enough information exists to suggest

that Longstreet, whose skill was such that four army commanders—P. G. T. Beauregard, Joseph E. Johnston, Robert
E. Lee, and John Bell Hood—requested him as second-in-
command, owed part of his success in the antebellum period
to his marriage to the daughter of a high-ranking officer. For
on March 8, 1848, in an Episcopal church in Lynchburg,
Virginia, he wed Maria Louisa Garland, the daughter of
brevet Brigadier General John Garland.[1]

By all accounts the marriage was an especially happy one.
The couple had ten children, five of whom lived to adult-
hood. When Louise (as she was called) died in 1890,
Longstreet was devastated with grief.[2] Nothing suggests a
reason other than romance for their match, yet it undeniably
worked to Longstreet's advantage, and advantages were something he was not in a position to scorn.

Born in South Carolina in 1821, but raised in Georgia
and Alabama, Longstreet was the son of a prosperous but
undistinguished farmer. He owed his early education largely
to his famous planter uncle, the humorist, clergyman, and
educator Augustus Baldwin Longstreet. He capped his education with an appointment to West Point. Because he
graduated a disappointing 54th out of 56 in the West Point
Class of 1842, Longstreet was not allowed to choose his
assignment, as were distinguished cadets. He was sent to the
infantry, where prospects for advancement were minimal
except in wartime. Actually, the infantry suited him. Longstreet had little use for the elite branches of service such as
the engineers. Courtly and well-mannered when the occasion
demanded, his rustic upbringing left some rough edges which
never entirely disappeared, and he was quite at home with
the common foot soldiers.[3]

Nevertheless, this brevet second lieutenant was handsome
and charming enough to catch the eye of a raven-haired
teenager at Jefferson Barracks, Missouri, the home of his

assigned unit, the 4th Infantry. Louise had been born at Fort Snelling, Minnesota, and spent her childhood at the various army posts to which her father was assigned. Longstreet's fellow Second Lieutenant Richard S. Ewell considered Louise and her older sister Elizabeth to be the only attractive girls in the entire state of Missouri. While this was doubtless an exaggeration, it is not surprising that Louise and Bessie were much sought after.[4] As Edward M. Coffman notes in *The Old Army:*[5]

> Second lieutenants seemed to be always falling in love....To marry beneath oneself meant risking the censure of friends and the ostracism of wives....The question of a potential bride's wealth frequently subordinated the fancies of love when bachelors talked of matrimony.

The Garland family was apparently quite well off, thanks to investments in Detroit real estate and the American Fur Company. But it was Louise Garland's father's position, rather than his money, which made her an especially attractive catch for a young second lieutenant like Longstreet. Up to that time John Garland, a Virginia native, had enjoyed a highly creditable, if not particularly distinguished, military career. During the War of 1812 many civilians received officers' commissions because the United States Military Academy at West Point could not produce a sufficient number of junior officers. One of these was John Garland, who in March of 1813 was commissioned a first lieutenant in the newly-organized 35th Infantry.[6]

Garland's regiment did not see combat, but he remained in the Army after the war ended. Transferring to the 3rd Infantry, he was promoted to captain on May 31, 1826, and served as assistant quartermaster until July, 1832. During these years, the 3rd Infantry was usually stationed in the Old Northwest Territory.[7] Garland received rapid promotions for a peacetime officer. He reached the rank of major in 1836 and was transferred to the 1st Infantry. In 1839 he became a lieutenant colonel and was transferred to the 4th Infantry. When young Longstreet first began to take an interest in his daughter, Garland was second-in-command to Josiah H. Vose at Jefferson Barracks. The rank and position of lieutenant colonel may not seem exalted, but at that time there were fewer than 750 officers in the Army and Garland out-ranked almost seven hundred of them.[8]

According to one account, Colonel Garland informed Louise that she could not marry anyone who did not hold at least the rank of captain. The story is almost certainly apocryphal, as her sister Bessie became engaged to Second Lieutenant George Deas, 5th Infantry, shortly after Louise and James Longstreet began seeing each other.[9] Although many women married quite young in the nineteenth century, age seems to have been the main factor in Garland's reservations. Longstreet was twenty-three, but Louise only seventeen, and the Colonel insisted they wait until they were older. The young couple enjoyed the limited social life of Jefferson Barracks until Longstreet's regiment was transferred to Louisiana in 1844. On Longstreet's departure, he and Louise sealed their relationship with their first kiss.[10]

Longstreet did not see Louise Garland for almost three years, but during that time he distinguished himself as a soldier. Transferred to the 8th Infantry in 1845, Longstreet participated in most of the important actions of the Mexican War. He saw combat at Palo Alto, Resaca de La Palma, Monterrey, Vera Cruz, Churubusco, El Molino del Rey, and Chapultepec. Cited repeatedly for conspicuously bravery and gallantry, he survived a grievous wound to the leg and returned from the war on medical furlough as a brevet major (his substantive rank was first lieutenant). Moreover, he held the trusted position of regimental adjutant. Garland, who was himself now a full colonel and brevet brigadier general as a result of wartime service, quickly consented to Louise's marriage to this apparently up and coming young soldier.[11]

But the exhilaration of combat was followed by the realities of peacetime service. Between 1848 and 1861, the U.S. Army held few adventures which could compete with the wild charges and hand-to-hand combat Longstreet had experienced during the fighting in Mexico. Promotions in peacetime were agonizingly slow. Longstreet had the honor of being addressed by his brevet rank of major, but he retained the pay of a first lieutenant. Initially, at least, the postwar Army provided few opportunities for Longstreet and his bride. After a brief honeymoon in March, 1848, the Longstreets were sent to Poughkeepsie, New York, where James served as a recruiting officer. This was a make-work assignment, for his regiment was still in Mexico. As Longstreet remained adjutant of the 8th Infantry, he was probably anxious to rejoin his comrades. This did not happen quickly, although the Army kept him moving. The Longstreets were barely settled in New York when they were transferred to Carlisle Barracks, Pennsylvania. One of James's first assignments was to escort recruits to Jefferson Barracks. Louise accompanied him and they were able to be present in St. Louis, Missouri, for the wedding of Ulysses S. Grant and Julia Dent. "Sam" Grant was Longstreet's close friend since West Point. Julia was distantly related to Longstreet through his mother's family. In December, back in Pennsylvania, the Longstreets' first child was born. Christened John Garland Longstreet, he was barely four months old when his parents took him on an arduous overland journey to San Antonio, Texas. There, in May, 1849, James Longstreet rejoined his regiment and resumed his duties as adjutant.[12]

Longstreet now began twelve years of service on the frontier, rising from the rank of first lieutenant to major. For almost eleven of those twelve years he served with or near his father-in-law under circumstances which suggest Longstreet benefitted from favoritism.

Upon reaching Texas, Lieutenant Longstreet was assigned to Company G of the 8th Infantry. This made him a subordinate of Captain Joseph Selden, a Virginia native commissioned directly into the Army from civilian life in 1838. Like Longstreet, Selden was a brevet major thanks to service in Mexico.[13] When Longstreet resumed his duties as adjutant, he did not become Selden's superior, but he was responsible for transmitting orders to Selden from the regimental commander. There was nothing unusual about this arrangement. But in May, 1849, the 8th received word that it would soon have a new commander: John Garland. It would have been awkward, to say the least, for Longstreet to retain the adjutancy. Working directly for his father-in-law would almost certainly have provoked jealousies among the regiment's other subalterns. Apparently for this reason, he was relieved as adjutant in July.[14]

Longstreet's reaction to this development is not known. Few men would have found it pleasant to exchange a position as chief administrative officer of a regiment, with all its prestige, privileges, and de facto power, for that of sub-commander of a single company. Longstreet spent the summer of that year on detached duty at Fort Lincoln, a post almost two days' ride west of San Antonio, and did not rejoin his family until the fall.[15] By accident or design, however, he did not have to endure a subordinate position for long.

Although appointed in May, Colonel Garland did not arrive in San Antonio with his wife Harriet until December. They were forced to reside in a boarding house until suitable quarters were found. On January 8, 1850, San Antonio officials made the most of the regimental commander's belated appearance by holding a grand ball and supper for the officers and wives of the 8th Infantry. George McCall, a young subaltern, recalled this as "quite a stylish affair."[16] The Longstreets could cite an additional reason for celebrating, for within days of his father-in-law's arrival, James had received a new assignment.

On January 1, 1850, Brevet Major General George Mercer Brooke named Longstreet chief of commissary for Military Department No. 8. As Brooke's headquarters was in San Antonio, the assignment must have seemed ideal from the Longstreet/Garland point of view. Longstreet's duties were now increased substantially beyond even those he had exercised as adjutant. He was responsible for feeding every person and animal the Army employed in southeastern Texas.[17]

Longstreet probably owed this new position to his father-in-law. Both Garland and Brooke were natives of Virginia. Brooke had once served as lieutenant colonel of the 8th Infantry and may have been well disposed toward assisting young officers from his old unit. But without Garland's presence in Texas, Brooke would have had little reason to select Longstreet as his departmental commissary officer. Longstreet had an excellent record and was well-qualified for the post, but his regiment possessed three officers who by virtue of rank, service, or both were just as fit: Lieutenants John Donnell Clark, Alfred St. Amand Crozet, and Thomas Gamble Pitcher. Moreover, the 8th was only one of several regiments under Brooke's command; he had a surplus of officers from whom to choose.[18]

However Longstreet obtained the position as commissary officer, he evidently disliked the job. As great lover of the outdoors and any sort of strenuous exercise, Longstreet probably found his desk assignment tedious, for he soon sought a transfer to the cavalry. In June, 1850, he solicited the help of Georgia congressman Thomas Butler King:[19]

> I have just learned that there is a strong possibility of an
> increase of one Regiment of Cavalry to the Army in this

Session of Congress. If such be the case I would like very much to get an appointment as Major in it. If you are in Washington I have no doubt you can procure it for me. To make sure, Senators Brien [sic] and Dawson will (I think) willingly render any assistance that may be necessary.

General Garland presumably endorsed his son-in-law's request, but as Congress failed to create the new regiment, nothing came of Longstreet's efforts. He remained as commissariat with the rank of first lieutenant. All career officers are concerned with rank, and Longstreet was no exception. He was irritated by the Army's failure to award him another brevet promotion for his wartime conduct at Chapultepec, as it had his friends George Pickett and Daniel Harvey Hill. But his desire was not entirely selfish. Promotion would mean a pay raise and Longstreet's scant forty dollars per month as a first lieutenant now had to support an additional son, Augustus Baldwin, born in October, 1850.[20]

Longstreet performed his commissary duties so well that General Mercer recommended him for permanent assignment to the Subsistence Department, which existed as a separate organization under Commissary General George Gibson. Longstreet, however, declined.[21] His reasons are not known, but in addition to a dislike of desk work, they may have included the realization that his most immediate prospects for advancement and preferential treatment lay in the hands of his father-in-law. This is suggested by the fact that when General Mercer died in March, 1851, Longstreet did not continue as commissariat under Mercer's replacement, Brevet Brigadier General William S. Harney, but returned instead to field duty.[22]

Longstreet was assigned to Fort Martin Scott, Fredericksburg, Texas. Within a few weeks, Garland went on a prolonged sick leave. During this time, Longstreet was primarily occupied with routine scouting duties. Garland returned to active duty in March, 1852, and eventually took up his duties as commander of the 8th Infantry with headquarters at Camp Johnston, on the North Concho River. Longstreet was re-assigned to the same post. When Garland transferred to Fort Chadbourne, in Coke County, his son-in-law followed.[23]

During this period Longstreet was promoted to captain, to date from December 7, 1852. While there is no evidence that Garland's influence was required to secure this, Garland clearly liked to have Longstreet and his family close at hand whenever possible. Once Garland was named commander of the Military Department No. 9 in July of 1853, with headquarters at Albuquerque, he apparently used the prerogatives of his office to secure desirable appointments for his son-in-law. The first apparent result of this, however, was tragic.[24]

During the summer of 1854 Longstreet was sent east temporarily, perhaps as a dispatch courier, and he took the family with him. In addition to Louise, Garland, and Gus, there was now an infant, William Dent. Tragically, William contracted an illness and died while the Longstreets were in Washington, D.C.[25]

By August the family was back in Texas. While this meant little respite for grief, Longstreet's assignment was a source of joy. He was named commander of Company I, 8th Infantry, at Fort Bliss, Texas. Located at El Paso, along the Rio Grande in extreme western Texas, this small post had been established only seven months earlier.[26] It consisted of nothing more than a series of low, dirt-floored, thatched roofed buildings arranged around a parade ground. Nevertheless, Fort Bliss "was considered by army officers and their families as one of the most desireable posts in the country."[27] Although isolated and sparsely populated, the area around El Paso was noted for its well-kept orchards and vineyards, and game abounded in the well-watered region. An army officer's wife who lived there in the 1850s remembered it as "the most delightful station we ever had."[28]

Longstreet found himself second-in-command to Major Edmund B. Alexander, a Virginian with a highly creditable record in the Mexican War. The garrison's four companies averaged only forty men apiece, half of whom were assigned mules or horses to act as mounted infantry. One of Longstreet's first responsibilities was to lead a lengthy expedition against allegedly marauding Mescalero Apaches. His column, and another consisting of the 2nd Dragoons, failed to trap the Native Americans, but during the campaign Longstreet met young J.E.B. Stuart, then a second lieutenant, for the first time.[29]

In his history of Fort Bliss, Donald Bridgman Sanger notes that Longstreet's "pretty wife was soon the center of a gay circle."[30] As daughter of the department commander, Louise Garland was in a position to wield considerable behind-the-scenes power, and as a life-long "Army brat" (to use modern terminology), she probably knew how to do so. In the spring of 1855, Major Alexander was promoted and transferred to the 10th Infantry. This left Longstreet in command of Fort Bliss and made Louise the focus of social life there.[31]

In the Army, social status for both men and women followed rank and command responsibilities. The position occupied by a female's father, brothers, or husband placed her on a specific rung on the social ladder, and she was blessed to rise or doomed to fall with her menfolks. In small frontier outposts the garrison functioned like an extended family. Consequently, women often developed fierce loyalties to "their" regiment or company.[32]

The close proximity of garrison life meant that almost nothing could remain secret. With everyone knowing almost everything about everyone else's affairs, whether or not life was pleasant for all concerned often depended upon how well the distaff got along. Louise Longstreet's activities at Fort Bliss are not known, but Lydia Spencer Lane, who lived there shortly after the Longstreets left, recalled: "There was a good deal of social visiting among us all, and an occasional formal entertainment, to which everybody was invited."[33]

Louise may have helped to establish the social traditions of Fort Bliss, and she probably promoted her husband's interests at the same time. In June, John T. Sprague returned from leave. Like Longstreet, Sprague was a captain and brevet major, but by holding an earlier date of commission he was the senior of the two and took command of Fort Bliss. Within six months, Garland transferred Sprague and Company E of the 8th Infantry to the less desirable, newly-established Fort Stanton in New Mexico. While this was an important move in the "pacification" of the Mescaleros, and Garland took pains to visit Fort Stanton himself, his actions nevertheless made his son-in-law an independent post commander once more. Quite soon after Sprague's departure, Garland descended upon Fort Bliss with a large staff and escort in order to spend the Christmas season with his daughter and grandchildren.[34]

Captain John G. Walker arrived at Fort Bliss with a company of mounted riflemen in March, 1856, assuming command by right of seniority. He lasted only two months longer than had Sprague. By October, Longstreet once again ruled Fort Bliss. Due to attrition, the post's garrison was down to a mere 111 men. Walker's company had constituted badly needed reinforcements and its transfer sparked rumors of favoritism on Longstreet's behalf. Garland's actions seemed particularly suspicious as the transfer was one of the last orders he issued before taking six month's leave. But whatever the benefits of General Garland's largess, the year was not a happy one for the Longstreets, as it witnessed the birth and death of a daughter, Harriet Margaret.[35] Longstreet retained command at Fort Bliss from October 1857 until the beginning of 1858. His duties were entirely routine, although his visitors included a detachment of the new United States Camel Corps, an experiment dear to the heart of Secretary of War Jefferson Davis. Louise traveled to Santa Fe, now the headquarters of Garland's re-named Department of New Mexico, where she gave birth to another son, christened James. Garland detached Longstreet for service at Santa Fe from January to May, 1858. The family accompanied him and enjoyed something of a reunion, as Louise's brother-in-law, Captain William A. Nichols, was then serving on General Garland's staff.[36]

As spring returned to the desert southwest, Longstreet submitted to Washington a request that he be "put on Recruiting or other service in the east." He took pains to note that his application did not stem from dissatisfaction with his current assignment "on the frontier." Rather, he desired "to have time, and opportunity, for setting my children at some good school." He hoped for a position in Philadelphia.[37]

In May, Longstreet was granted a six month's leave of absence. Although the length and timing raise the question of favoritism, long leaves of absence were quite common in the antebellum Army. Robert E. Lee, for example, took twenty-seven months leave in order to settle his father-in-law's estate. Longstreet's respite was well earned, as it was his first leave in ten years.[38] Nor was his purpose frivolous, for Longstreet was not willing to wait for, or rely upon, a transfer in order to facilitate his children's education. The family journeyed to Columbia, South Carolina, where Augustus Baldwin Longstreet had recently been installed as president of the College of South Carolina. Captain Longstreet was particularly concerned about his eldest child, ten-year-old

Garland, and discussed with his uncle the possibility of leaving him in Columbia. Garland remained with the family, however, as they visited New York and New Jersey. While in Burlington, New Jersey, Longstreet learned that he had been transferred to the Pay Department with a promotion to major. He took immediate advantage of his increase in salary to place Garland at a boys' school in Yonkers.[39]

As a paymaster, Longstreet was now part of the Army's staff rather than its line establishment. The rank went with the position; if Longstreet were to transfer back to the line, his rank might revert to captain. Longstreet had, of course, declined a similar staff assignment upon General Mercer's recommendation in 1851. But at that time he had been only thirty years old and the Mexican War was a recent memory. Little wonder he sought a cavalry assignment rather than a desk. With the passing of years, however, his priorities changed. At the end of a year of his new duties, he informed his Uncle Augustus: "I am now able to save enough of my pay to give me some hope of being able in time to educate my boys as they should [be]. That itself will reconcile me to living anywhere on the continent."[40] At thirty-eight Longstreet was not only approaching middle age, he had also seen two of his children die. He was now willing to place his career second to the welfare of his remaining three sons.

In addition, General Garland would not be in a position to assist his career much longer. Aged and infirm, he left Albuquerque for an extended sick leave in the East.[41] On his own amid the 950-odd officers in the Army in 1858, Longstreet could not expect the law of averages to provide him with the sort of independence or preferential assignments his father-in-law had apparently arranged. This may have made the Pay Department more attractive. Even so, it must at times have seemed quite a come down for the former commander of Fort Bliss. Independent command, on whatever scale, is immensely attractive to almost all soldiers.

There were compensations, however. Longstreet was assigned to Ft. Leavenworth in the volatile Kansas Territory. While hardly on par with Philadelphia, the adjacent town of Leavenworth provided good schools for his younger children. For Louise, the officers' quarters meant a pleasant change from the all-too-familiar adobe. Meanwhile, Paymaster Longstreet spent much of his time in the saddle, or at least on a wagon seat. In theory the Army paid its soldiers every two months. Longstreet rode an extended circuit. Soldiers were doubtless glad to see the paymaster, and he was freed from the gossip and petty jealousies of frontier garrison duties. If Longstreet followed common procedure, once he reached a post he would set up a table and spread out his records. As the garrison filed past he would check these against the records of each company commander to deduct anything a soldier owed the post sutler. Then he would proceed to the next post, sleeping under canvas in snow or rain, camping under the stars in good weather, working his way along his circuit, back toward Leavenworth, home, and family.[42]

During the fall season in 1859 the Longstreets moved once again, to Albuquerque. General and Mrs. Garland had returned to New Mexico, and if the old soldier could not place his son-in-law in charge of anything he could at least have him by his side. The family reunion was brief, however. Sometime in the spring of 1860, the Garlands departed for Saratoga Springs, New York, for reasons of health. Mrs. Garland died there in August. Thereafter, General Garland resided in New York with one of his sons. He passed away on June 5, 1861. An elaborate military funeral was held, and the Adjutant General of the Army ordered flags flown at half-staff.[43]

Longstreet's reaction to his father-in-law's death is not known. During the spring of 1860 he purchased over fifty acres of land at the site of Fort Mason, Texas, north of San Antonio.[44] This may have been a simple economic investment of the sort Army officers made all the time to supplement their modest incomes. Indeed, Longstreet may have made others of which no record has survived. The timing of the purchase, however, suggests that he may have been planning a homestead, a place to live as a civilian if Army life became intolerable without the mediating influence of General Garland. Such an interpretation is supported by the fact that at the end of the Civil War Longstreet intended to live in Texas. On the other hand, Longstreet remembered his pre-Civil War service as the happiest period of his life, and there is no direct evidence that he ever considered leaving the Army before the secession crisis impelled him to fight for the South. He resigned on May 9, 1861.[45]

How then, did marriage and kinship through marriage affect the antebellum career of James Longstreet? In a tribute written after his death in 1904, Longstreet's second wife, Helen Dortch, wrote of his antebellum service: "He considered it his duty and made it his delight, as do all good soldiers, to go willingly where he was sent."[46] It appears, however, that as General John Garland's son-in-law Longstreet was sent where the General wanted him to be sent. He frequently received preferential treatment.

During the Mexican War Longstreet rose to the rank of brevet major and the position of regimental adjutant of the 8th Infantry. Without question, these resulted entirely from his talent and courage. But shortly after his marriage to Louise Garland in 1848, Longstreet began to obtain assignments that cannot be easily explained on the basis of his own accomplishments. He became chief of commissary for the Department of Texas despite the presence of dozens of officers who, based on rank or length of service, had greater claims to the office. Longstreet was frequently assigned to the same post as General Garland. The main exception to this pattern was his extended posting at Fort Bliss. But here the evidence suggests that Garland manipulated personnel assignments in order to ensure his son-in-law an independent command, even if it meant reducing the garrison there to dangerously low levels.

If Longstreet's connection with Garland affected his assignments, the same cannot be said for promotion. The key step to consider is Longstreet's promotion from first lieutenant to captain, as this was his only promotion within the line, rather than staff, after the time he married Louise.

Of the fifty-six members in the West Point Class of 1842, twenty-six reached the rank of captain prior to 1861, but six of these were via staff appointments. The remaining twenty averaged eighty-nine months between the rank of first lieutenant and captain, significantly higher than the seventy months Longstreet took to achieve promotion. Moreover, if one considers the bottom ten cadets from Longstreet's class, he rose much more quickly than all but one of his peers, Lafayette McLaws, who was promoted after only fifty-four months. On the other hand, if one defines Longstreet's "peers" more broadly to be the bottom ten cadets of the West Point classes from 1840 through 1844, the average time spent in the rank of first lieutenant was seventy-one months—a figure not significantly different from Longstreet's.[47]

In summary, Longstreet's career stands as an example of both the benefits and limits of the sort of preferential treatment an officer in the antebellum Army might receive if he had the right connections. From the time he was a mere lieutenant, he would have enjoyed social status beyond his rank as the husband of the daughter of one of the Army's relatively few generals. John Garland greatly influenced the nature, scope, and location of his son-in-law's assignments. Thanks to Garland's intervention, Longstreet served in more pleasant places, and enjoyed greater responsibilities, than he would have otherwise.

But these things were possible only because Longstreet was posted within Garland's bailiwick. In the larger scheme of things, Garland could offer no help. For example, Longstreet did not get the transfer to the cavalry he sought in 1850 because Congress failed to create the regiment. The question of rank is more important, however, for rank means everything in the armed services. Yet kinship to Garland apparently had no effect on Longstreet's rate of promotion. He was forced to transfer from the line to the staff to get the pay raise he needed to provide for his children's education. Moreover, Garland's influence did not produce the assignment in the East which Longstreet desired. As a paymaster he was sent to the West. Garland's influence was probably responsible for Longstreet's transfer from Leavenworth to Albuquerque. Death made this the General's final bit of patronage. How Longstreet would have fared after 1860 without his father-in-law's help one cannot say, for like all officers in the Army, Longstreet was soon swept up in the larger national crisis.

Analysis of Longstreet's antebellum military career confirms the assessment of historians on the issue of promotions.[48] The Army had no retirement policy and promotion within line service was strictly according to seniority. Kinship, marriage, and political connections therefore had no impact on promotions between the ranks of second lieutenant and colonel. Politics usually entered the question only when new units, such as the cavalry regiment Longstreet anticipated, were created. The staff services, such as the paymaster department Longstreet finally entered, were far more politicized, as these were under the control of the

Secretary of War rather than the Army's general-in-chief. Nevertheless, there is no evidence that Longstreet owed his transfer and promotion to politics.

In terms of military assignments, Longstreet's experience demonstrates the need for a systematic study of the way in which nepotism, favoritism, and other social relationships affected the antebellum Army. A model for this type of approach would be the Civil War study *The Politics of Command* by Thomas L. Connelly and Archer Jones.[49] Historian Robert M. Utley notes that due to the power struggles between the general-in-chief and the secretary of war, department commanders such as Garland possessed a degree of freedom which allowed them to shape the military's frontier policies.[50] A broad examination of department-level commanders is needed to determine how Garland's treatment of his son-in-law stands in relation to others who possessed the power and opportunity to effect military assignments.

Finally, Longstreet's experiences raise questions concerning the division of power by gender. How much de facto power did Louise Garland Longstreet possess and how did she use it? The absence of surviving letters makes it impossible to answer this question. In a recent bibliographic essay, Sandra L. Myres notes that while the study of women has been integrated into much of the socially-conscious "new" military history, historians have yet to "look closely at the role of family connections in nineteenth century military and political life" or the role wives played in "power struggles and internal military politics."[51] A comprehensive exploration of the way women who were connected with the military used power, and the degree to which soldiers sought by marriage or other gender relationships to tap into and utilize such women's power, would add greatly to our understanding of the military as a social organization.[52]

Notes to Chapter 2

1. Helen D. Longstreet, *Lee and Longstreet at High Tide: Gettysburg in Light of the Official Records* (Gainesville, Ga.: By the author, 1904), 160.

2. For complete details of Longstreet's marriage, see Donald Bridgman Sanger and Thomas Robson Hay, *James Longstreet: Soldier, Politician, Officeholder, and Writer* (Baton Rouge: Louisiana State University Press, 1952), 9-10, 12-16, 288, 317-318, 367, 402-404; and William Garrett Piston, *Lee's Tarnished Lieutenant: James Longstreet and His Place in Southern History* (Athens: University of Georgia Press, 1987), 3-4, 95, 99, 111, 153.

3. Piston, *Lee's Tarnished Lieutenant,* 2-3; for a fuller discussion, see William Garrett Piston, "Lee's Tarnished Lieutenant: James Longstreet and His Image in American Society" (Ph.D. dissertation, University of South Carolina, 1982), 5-18, 33-34.

4. Percy Gatlin Hamlin, ed., *The Making of a Soldier: Letters of General R.S. Ewell* (Richmond: Whittet & Shepperson, 1935), 53.

5. Edward M. Coffman, *The Old Army: A Portrait of the American Army in Peacetime, 1784-1898* (New York and Oxford: Oxford University Press, 1986), 108-109.

6. Francis B. Heitman, *Historical Register and Dictionary of the United States Army from Its Organization, September 29, 1789, to March 2, 1903* (2 vols.; Washington: Government Printing Office, 1903), 1:447; hereinafter cited as Heitman, *Historical Register*; Sanger and Hay, *James Longstreet,* 13.

7. Francis Paul Prucha, *The Sword of the Republic; The United States Army on the Frontier, 1783-1846* (Lincoln and London: University of Nebraska Press, c. 1969), 127, 186, 235, 256, 257.

8. Heitman, *Historical Register,* Vol. 1, 447; Vol. 2, 588-589.

9. Sanger and Hay, *James Longstreet*, 9.

10. *Ibid.*, 9; Percy Gatlin Hamlin, *"Old Bald Head" (General R.S. Ewell): The Portrait of a Soldier* (Strausburg, Va.: Shenandoah Publishing House, Inc., 1940), 51-54; Lloyd Lewis, *Captain Sam Grant* (Boston: Little, Brown and Company, 1950), 107-108; Helen Longstreet, *Lee and Longstreet at High Tide*, 109.

11. The fullest account of Longstreet's Mexican War service is in Piston, "Lee's Tarnished Lieutenant." See also Sanger and Hay, *James Longstreet*, 10-12; Heitman, *Historical Register*, Vol. 1, 447, 640-641.

12. James Longstreet to J. B. Crane, 21 July 1848, James Longstreet Papers, Duke University; Sanger and Hay, *James Longstreet*, 13; Thomas Wilhelm, *A Synopsis History of the Eighth U.S. Infantry and the Military Record of Officers Assigned to the Regiment From Its Organization July, 1838, to Sept. 1871* (New York: Eighth Infantry Headquarters, 1871), 193, 288; hereinafter cited as Wilhelm, *Eighth U.S. Infantry*.

13. Heitman, *Historical Register*, Vol 1, 873; Wilhelm, *Eighth U.S. Infantry*, 155-156.

14. Heitman, *Historical Reqister*, Vol 1, 640.

15. Sanger and Hay, *James Longstreet*, 13.

16. George B. McCall, *Letters From the Frontiers* (Philadelphia: J.B. Lippincott & Co., 1868), 489; Wilhelm, *Eighth U.S. Infantry*, 193.

17. Raphael P. Thian, comp., *Notes Illustrating the Military Geography of the United States, 1813-1880* (Washington: Adjutant General's Office, 1881; reprint, Austin and London: University of Texas Press, c. 1979), 47; hereinafter cited as Thian, *Military Geography*; Wilhelm, *Eighth U.S. Infantry*, 155-156.

18. Heitman, *Historical Register*, Vol 1, 248, 304, 342, 793; Robert M. Utley, *Frontiersmen in Blue; The United States Army and the Indian, 1848-1865* (Lincoln and London: University of Nebraska Press, c. 1967), 71-72.

19. James Longstreet to Thomas Butler King, 12 June 1850, Thomas Butler King Papers, Southern Historical Collection,

University of North Carolina-Chapel Hill. King represented Waynesville. Longstreet wrongly identified Repersentative J. Macpherson Berrien of Savannah as a senator. Senator William C. Damson was from Greensboro, Georgia. See *Biographical Directory of the United States Congress, 1744-1989* (Washington: Government Printing Office, 1989), 147.

20. James Longstreet to Thomas Butler King, 12 June 1850, King Papers; pay voucher, Brevet Major James Longstreet, 10 November 1852, James Longstreet Papers, Chicago Historical Society Library; Oliver Knight, *Life and Manners in the Frontier Army* (Norman: University of Oklahoma Press, 1978), 40, 43.

21. James Longstreet to George Gibson, 11 January 1853, James Longstreet Papers, Harvard University; Heitman, *Historical Register*, Vol 1, 40.

22. Heitman, *Historical Register*, Vol 1, 248; Thian, *Military Geography*, 48.

23. Wilhelm, *Eighth U.S. Infantry*, 193, 288; Heitman, *Historical Register*, Vol 2, 487, 513, 543.

24. Thian, *Historical Geography*, 48, 50; Heitman, *Historical Register*, Vol 2, 640; Wilhelm, *Eighth U.S. Infantry*, 288.

25. Sanger and Hay, *James Longstreet*, 14.

26. Wilhelm, *Eighth U.S. Infantry*, 155; Richard K. McMaster, *Musket, Saber, and Missile: A History of Fort Bliss* (El Paso, Tx.: Complete Letter and Printing Service, 1963), 18; Donald Bridgman Sanger, *The Story of Old Fort Bliss* (El Paso, Tx.: Buie Company, Printer, 1933), 9.

27. W. W. Mills, *Forty Years at El Paso, 1858-1898* (El Paso, Tx.: Carl Hertzog, 1962), 10.

28. Lydia Spencer Lane, *I Married a Soldier: or, Old Days in the Old Army* (Albuquerque: Horn & Wallu, Publisher, 1964), 68-69.

29. Sanger, *The Story of Old Fort Bliss*, 9-11; McMaster, *Musket, Saber, and Missile*, 10; Emory M. Thomas, *Bold Dragoon: The Life of J.E.B. Stuart* (New York: Harper & Row, Publishers, 1986), 38; Heitman, *Historical Register*, Vol 1, 156.

30. Sanger, *The Story of Old Fort Bliss*, 10.

31. McMaster, *Musket, Saber, and Missile*, 19.

32. Lane, *I Married a Soldier*, 68-69, 83-84; Knight, *Life and Manners in the Frontier Army*, 34-43, 59-61, 110-111; Coffman, *The Old Army*, 104-105.

33. Lane, *I Married a Soldier*, 68-69.

34. Utley, *Frontiersmen in Blue*, 88, 152, 174; McMaster, *Musket, Saber, and Missile*, 20; Heitman, *Historical Register*, 1:912.

35. McMaster, *Musket, Saber, and Missile*, 20; Sanger and Hay, *James Longstreet*, 14; Heitman, *Historical Register*, Vol 1, 996.

36. Sanger and Hay, *James Lonqstreet*, 14-15; McMaster, *Musket, Saber, and Missile*, 21.

37. James Longstreet to I. McDowell, Assistant Adjutant General, 29 March 1858, James Longstreet Papers, The Historical Society of Pennsylvania.

38. Sanger and Hay, *James Longstreet*, 15; Hoffman, *The Old Army*, 83.

39. W. R. Drinkwater, Acting Secretary of War, to James Longstreet, 19 July 1858, Longstreet Papers, Chicago; James Longstreet to Augustus Baldwin Longstreet, 19 November 1859, Augustus Baldwin Longstreet Papers; John Donald Wade, *Augustus Baldwin Longstreet: A Study of the Development of Culture in the South* (Athens: The University of Georgia Press, 1969), 314-317.

40. James Longstreet to Augustus Baldwin Longstreet, 19 November 1859, Augustus Baldwin Longstreet Papers.

41. Utley, *Frontiersmen in Blue*, 169.

42. W. S. Burke and J. L. Roch, *The History of Leavenworth, the Metropolis of Kansas* (Leavenworth: The Leavenworth Times Book and Job Printing Establishment, 1880), 11-12, 17, 29; Percival Lowe, *Five Years a Draqoon ('49 to '54) And Other Adventures on the Great Plains* (Norman: University of Oklahoma Press, 1965), 24-26; Sanger and Hay, *James Longstreet*, 15;

43. Sander and Hay, *James Longstreet*, 16; *Washington National Intelligencer*, 8 June 1861; 11 June 1861.

44. Sander and Hay, *James Longstreet*, 15-16.

45. The details of Longstreet's abortive postwar journey to settle in Texas are described in the diary of his staff officer Thomas J. Gorge, Department of Archives and History, Louisiana State University.

46. Longstreet, *Lee and Longstreet at High Tide*, 111.

47. Calculations are based on data in George W. Cullum, *Biographical Register of the Officers and Graduates of the U.S. Military Academy at West Point*, N.Y. (3 vols.; Boston and New York: Houghton, Mifflin and Company, 1891), Vol 2, 53-59, 104-109, 146-152, 183-192, 200-208.

48. For the best discussion of these issues see Coffman, *The Old Army*, 48-49, 60; Utley, *Frontiersmen in Blue*, 31-33, 48-49.

49. Thomas Lawrence Connally and Archer Jones, *The Politics of Command: Factions and Ideas in Confederate Strategy* (Baton Rouge: Louisiana State University Press, 1973).

50. Utley, *Frontiersmen in Blue*, 50.

51. Sandra L. Myres, "Frontier Historians, Women, and the 'New' Military History," *Military History of the Southwest*, XIX (Spring 1989), 34.

52. Coffman, *The Old Army*, Sandra L. Myres, *Westering Women and the Frontier Experience, 1800-1915* (Albuquerque: University of New Mexico Press, 1982), and Glenda Riley, *Women and Indians on the Frontier, 1825-1915* (Albuquerque: University of New Mexico Press, 1984) are excellent on most topics, but they do not treat systematically the issue of women's influence on promotions and assignments. Grady McWhiney, *Southerners and Other Americans* (New York: Basic Books, Inc., Publishers, 1973), 45, states that some men probably sought advantages by marrying the daughters of higher ranking officers, offers no data. Patricia Y. Stallard's study of the post Civil War Army, *Glittering Misery: Dependents of the Indian Fighting Army* (San Rafael: Presidio Press, 1978), 103, notes that women could help advance their husbands' careers, but provides only a few examples.

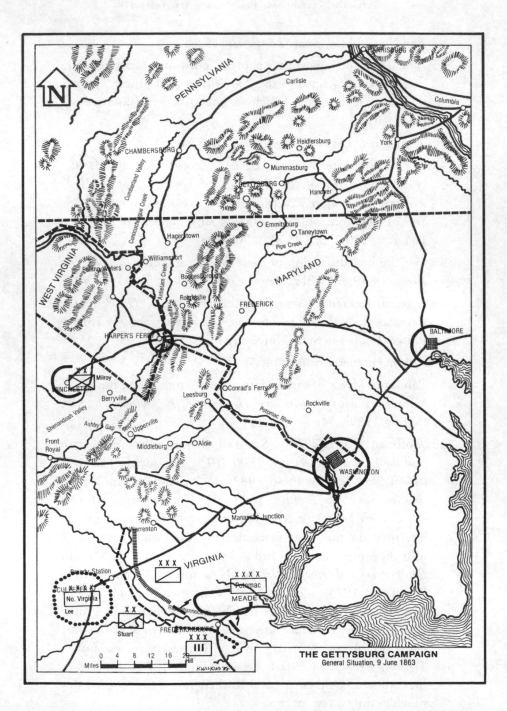

THE GETTYSBURG CAMPAIGN
General Situation, 9 June 1863

CHAPTER 3

"No Fifteen Thousand Men Can Take That Position"
Longstreet at Gettysburg

by

Jeffry D. Wert

Confederate Lieutenant General James Longstreet, commander of the First Corps, Army of Northern Virginia, rode on to the battlefield of Gettysburg about five o'clock on the afternoon of July 1, 1863. As he arrived, infantry units of the army's other corps were sweeping Gettysburg's streets of the broken elements of two Union corps. Neither army had expected such a collision on this day, but once it occurred, the combat escalated as commanders on the field fed more men into the fighting. The Confederates had earned a decisive victory with the possibility of greater gains before nightfall.

Longstreet halted near the buildings of the Lutheran Theological Seminary on Seminary Ridge. Dismounting, he walked toward General Robert E. Lee, who "was engaged at the moment." For several minutes, Longstreet viewed through field glasses the ground east and south of the town, where the Federals were rallying. The terrain appeared naturally strong—a long ridge terminated at each end by one or two hills. From his brief survey, from his experience and from his tactical preferences, Longstreet concluded that assaults on the enemy position should be avoided. He lowered his glasses, turned toward Lee, and spoke—the greatest controversy of Gettysburg, perhaps of the Civil War, had begun.[1]

James Longstreet was forty-two years old on that July day. An 1842 graduate of the United States Military Academy, a veteran of the Mexican War and the antebellum army, he was Lee's senior subordinate officer. Since Lee had taken command of the Army of Northern Virginia exactly thirteen months earlier, Longstreet and Thomas J. "Stonewall" Jackson had served as the army's wing or corps commanders. Lee brilliantly exploited their talents and the combat prowess of the officers and men under them to alter the course of the war in the East. The Confederates marched to a drumroll of success—the Seven Days, Second Manassas, Fredericksburg, and Chancellorsville. Although the Southern raid into Maryland ended unfavorably, Lee's men held the field at Sharpsburg or Antietam before returning to Virginia.[2]

During these months, Longstreet's performance equaled or exceeded that of all the generals in the army, including Jackson. At the conclusion of the Seven Days Campaign, Lee described Longstreet as "the staff in my right hand," and on the field of carnage at Sharpsburg, Lee called him "my old war-horse." Lee rewarded Longstreet by appointing him the senior lieutenant general in the army. Likewise, a close relationship developed between the two men, one Longstreet described later as "affectionate, confidential, and even tender, from first to last." Lee sought and valued Longstreet's counsel, and the subordinate shared his opinions.

Longstreet and two divisions were on detached duty in a supply operation in southeastern Virginia when Lee and Jackson scored a stunning victory at Chancellorsville, May 1-5, 1863. The battle was arguably Lee's most brilliant, spearheaded by Jackson's assault on the evening of May 2. It was also arguably his costliest, as Jackson fell mortally wounded, dying eight days later. Chancellorsville gave Lee the second opportunity to carry the war into Northern territory.

Longstreet rejoined Lee outside of Fredericksburg on May 9. While en route back to the army, Longstreet had conferred with Secretary of War James Seddon in Richmond, recommending the dispatch of two divisions from Virginia to Tennessee to reinforce Braxton Bragg's Confederate forces there. Three months earlier, Longstreet had proposed a similar concentration, but now with Vicksburg, Mississippi, threatened by Union Major General Ulysses S. Grant's operations, it seemed more urgent to him for some offensive maneuver in Tennessee that might relieve pressure on the vital river city. Such an operation had been under discussion within the administration for weeks.[3]

On the day Longstreet reached Fredericksburg, he established his headquarters and shared a meal with Lee. The next day, Sunday, May 10—the day Stonewall Jackson died—Lee and Longstreet began a series of private meetings that continued to the 13th. In published, postwar writings Longstreet recounted the discussions between himself and the commanding general. Most likely at the initial meeting, Longstreet reiterated the strategic plan he had presented to Seddon—a concentration in Tennessee, followed by an offensive thrust into Kentucky which would, as Longstreet speculated, force U.S. Grant to detach troops from the Vicksburg operation to support Federal forces in Kentucky.

"I laid it before him [Lee] with the freedom justified by our close personal and official relations," wrote Longstreet.[4]

Lee, however, opposed Longstreet's plan, voicing objections to a division of the army similar to those that he had already offered to the administration in Richmond when it proposed such an operation. Lee outlined his plan for a large-scale offensive or raid into Pennsylvania that would maintain the strategic initiative secured at Chancellorsville and temporarily relieve the Old Dominion of the war's terrible grip. Longstreet agreed to Lee's operation, or as he stated in his memoirs, [5]

> it became useless and improper to offer suggestions leading to a different course. All that I could ask was that the policy of the campaign should be one of defensive tactics; that we should work so as to force the enemy to attack us, in such good position as we might find in his own country, so well adapted to that purpose—which might assure us of a grand triumph. To this he readily assented as an important and material adjunct to his general plan.

Such was Longstreet's subsequent published version of the meetings, written years later, when he seemingly wanted to distance himself from the campaign and to justify his advocacy of a defensive battle at Gettysburg. Undoubtedly much of Longstreet's retelling was accurate, but his views at the time the discussions were concluded were significantly different on critical points. At the time, he revealed his ideas to Senator Louis T. Wigfall, one of his confidants in the government in Richmond. In a letter of May 13, the day he and Lee concurred upon a summer offensive, Longstreet wrote Wigfall,[6]

> There is a fair prospect of forward movement. That being the case we can spare nothing from this army to re-enforce in the West. On the contrary we should have the use of our own and the balance of our Armies if we could get them.

If we could cross the Potomac with one hundred & fifty thousand men, I think we could demand Lincoln to declare his purpose. If it is a Christian purpose enough of blood has been shed to satisfy any principles. If he intends extermination we should know it at once and play a little at that game whilst we can.

Knowing that Wigfall was an advocate of a so-called "western concentration" policy, Longstreet addressed the issue of detaching troops from Lee's army. Reinforcements sent to Mississippi would be of little worth, Longstreet asserted, because one or two divisions would not be enough manpower as it seemed from Virginia that Grant was "a fighting man," while John Pemberton, Confederate commander at Vicksburg, "seems not to be a fighting man." If Vicksburg fell, the Confederacy could continue, as the states west of the Mississippi were already cut off from those east of the great waterway. "In fact," Longstreet stated, "we should make a grand effort against the Yankees this summer, every available man and means should be brought to bear against them." Finally, added the general: [7]

When I agreed with the Secy & yourself about sending troops west I was under the impression that we would be obliged to remain on the defensive here. But the prospect of an advance changes the aspects of affairs to us entirely. Gen. Lee sent for me when he recd the Secy's letter. I told him that I thought that we could spare the troops unless there was a chance of a forward movement. If we could move of course we should want everything, that we had and all that we could get.

In this contemporary private letter, then, Longstreet endorsed Lee's strategic offensive across the Potomac River, contrary to his later published assertions. Furthermore, Longstreet did not indicate to Wigfall that his concurrence with Lee was contingent upon the adoption of defensive tactics once a battle was joined. After the war, when someone asked Lee if he had acquiesced to the proposal of such an engagement, the old warrior termed the idea as "absurd." Lee surely "never made any such promise," but the evidence from other officers, besides Longstreet, support the premise that it was expected or understood that the army would wage a defensive fight unless compelled to do otherwise by circumstances. In his own post-battle report, Lee stated, "It had not been intended to fight a general battle at such a distance from our base, unless attacked by the enemy."[8]

The discussions between Lee and Longstreet about strategy and tactics did not end at Fredericksburg but continued for weeks as the army reorganized and refitted for the operation, and as it marched northward into Pennsylvania. According to Longstreet in a letter that was written in 1873, a decade later, but before the Gettysburg controversy flamed across the South, he and Lee talked "almost every day from the 10th May 63 until the Battle." The two generals analyzed previous campaigns—First and Second Manassas, the Seven Days, and Fredericksburg—and, in Longstreet's words, "concluded even victories such as these were consuming us, and would eventually destroy us." In time, the pair of officers agreed on "the ruling idea of the campaign." According to Longstreet, this was "Under no circumstances were we to give battle, but exhaust our skill in trying to force the enemy to do so in a position of our own choosing. The 1st Corps to receive the attack and fight the battle. The other corps to then fall upon and try to destroy the Army of the Potomac."[9]

For Longstreet, "the ruling idea of the campaign," as he described it, reflected his strategic and tactical views.

Although the letter was written ten years after the battle, it accurately stated his ideas in the summer of 1863. To him, the Confederacy could no longer drain away manpower in tactical offensives, or as he put it in the letter, "Our losses were so heavy when we attacked that our army must soon be depleted to such extent that we should not be able to hold a force in the field sufficient to meet our adversary." While Chancellorsville may have been the supreme achievement of Lee's brilliant generalship, Longstreet saw it as a hollow victory, a battle won at losses not commensurate with the results. He found Lee's masterpiece nearly a year earlier, at Second Manassas, a campaign which had been a perfect blend of the strategic offensive and tactical defensive that nearly destroyed the Federal army. Like Lee, Longstreet knew a collision had to come on Northern soil, but when it occurred, he wanted it to be the enemy that sacrificed its young men in assaults.[10]

The collision with the Union forces ultimately came on Wednesday, July 1st, west of Gettysburg. Without J.E.B. Stuart's cavalry to screen the army and to locate the Federal corps, the Confederates stumbled into a battle Lee neither expected nor wanted. In the words of Douglas Southall Freeman, Lee was "a blinded giant" as he rode toward the sounds of combat. But on that first day of the battle his infantry and artillery units at Gettysburg routed two Union corps and held the tactical initiative. To Lee, the day's outcome altered previous designs to avoid an engagement unless assailed, or as he noted in his report, "a battle thus became, in a measure, unavoidable. Encouraged by the successful issue of the engagement of the first day, and in view of the valuable results that would ensure from the defeat of the army of General Meade, it was thought advisable to renew the attack."[11]

Longstreet rode on to the field in the wake of the initial success, located Lee, surveyed the Federal position, and said to his commander, "We could not call the enemy to position better suited to our plans. All that we have to do is file around his left and secure good ground between him and his capital."

The words either surprised or angered Lee, who pointed a fist toward the ridge beyond the town and exclaimed, "If the enemy is there tomorrow, we must attack him."

"If he is there," rebutted Longstreet, "it will be because he is anxious that we should attack him—a good reason, in my judgment, for not doing so."[12]

By his subsequent admission, Longstreet "was not a little surprised" at Lee's reaction, his evident "impatience" with Longstreet's advice. In a postwar letter to Lafayette McLaws, one of his former division commanders, Longstreet expanded, "Lord will not understand my surprise at finding all of our previously arranged plans so unexpectedly changed, and why I might wish and hope to get the Gen. to consider our former arrangements." Longstreet believed from his cursory examination that the enemy held favorable ground and to drive him from it would entail casualties that the South could not afford. The limited manpower resources of the Confederacy necessitated the avoidance of assaults. "Our losses were so heavy when we attacked," Longstreet explained to McLaws, "that our army must soon be depleted to such extent that we should not be able to hold a force in the field sufficient to meet our adversary."[13]

In Lee's defense, the commanding general could only react to what he saw and knew. Without intelligence about the location of the other corps of the Union army, he could not approve a vague movement beyond an unknown flank. Lee held the tactical initiative, was reluctant to relinquish it to George Meade, and perhaps most importantly, believed, as he said weeks earlier, that his men, "if properly led...will go anywhere, never fail at the work before them." A sense of invincibility permeated the ranks of the Army of Northern Virginia, and the day's victory reaffirmed it. If anything, Lee was audacious, a general who weighed possibilities and confronted risks. The Federals were on Cemetery Hill and

Cemetery Ridge, and "if properly led," the Confederates could drive them from the heights. For the next two days, Lee fashioned his tactical schemes upon this belief.[14]

Before nightfall on July 1, Lee endeavored to coordinate a final push against the regrouped Federals. On the army's left, Lieutenant General Richard S. Ewell, Jackson's successor in command of the Second Corps, had orders to assault the enemy if practicable. Ewell hesitated and sought support from Lieutenant General A. P. Hill's Third Corps. When Lee could not promise assistance from Hill, Ewell abandoned the effort. Lee later joined Ewell for discussions about plans for the 2nd, but again nothing was finalized. Meanwhile, to the west of Gettysburg, along Chambersburg Pike, Longstreet lay down for a few hours sleep. At an evening meal with his staff, he had been unable to hide his displeasure with Lee's proposals for the next morning's work.[15]

Longstreet rejoined Lee on Seminary Ridge in the pre-dawn darkness of July 2. When the generals met, Longstreet once again suggested a broad turning movement around the Federal left flank, and once again Lee rejected the idea. Lee told Longstreet that he would need the services of the First Corps divisions of Major Generals Lafayette McLaws and John Hood for an attack, and ordered a reconnaissance of Meade's flank along the southern section of Cemetery Ridge. After the reconnaissance party started, other generals and staff members joined Lee and Longstreet.[16]

Sometime between seven and eight o'clock, the reconnaissance party, led by Captain Samuel Johnston of Lee's staff, returned. Johnston described his route, stating that they had reached the bases of Little and Big Round Top, the southern anchors of Meade's line, and had discovered no Federal troops in the area. The report surprised Lee, who asked Johnston if he indeed had ridden to where he had indicated on the map.

Johnston repeated that they had gone there, and Lee fashioned his attack scheme upon that assurance.[17]

Lee summoned McLaws to his side, and pointing to the map, directed that officer to align his division perpendicular to the Emmitsburg Road for an attack up the road, and to get into position without being detected. McLaws told Lee that he knew "of nothing to prevent me." Listening to the conversation, Longstreet stepped forward and indicated on the map that he wanted the division placed parallel to the road. "No, General," objected Lee, "I wish it placed just perpendicular to that." McLaws asked twice if he could conduct a personal reconnaissance of the terrain, and twice Longstreet refused. For the present, the matter had been settled.[18]

About nine o'clock, Lee departed for Ewell's headquarters to discuss the situation on the army's left and the Second Corps' role in the offensive. Lee had not issued specific orders to Longstreet to begin the movement, but undoubtedly Longstreet understood that McLaws' and Hood's divisions and First Corps' artillery batteries would be involved in an assault along the Emmitsburg Road. Lee too undoubtedly expected Longstreet to begin preparations, if not to begin the march, while he conferred with Ewell. Longstreet, however, did little during the two hours of Lee's absence, except order Colonel E. Porter Alexander to assume command of the corps artillery on the field and find a route the batteries could follow to get into position without detection from a Union signal station on Little Round Top.[19]

Whether Longstreet agreed with Lee's plans or not—and he did not—duty required that he attend to the details of the movement. He "failed to conceal some anger," according to his chief of staff, Major Moxley Sorrel, and allowed his displeasure to affect his conduct. The hallmarks of his generalship on previous battlefields—careful planning, current intelligence, and attention to details—were lacking. He neither ordered another, more timely reconnaissance, scouted a route of march, spoke with McLaws and Hood, nor learned if Alexander had succeeded in locating a secure route for the artillery. "There was apparent apathy in his movements," remembered Sorrel. "They lacked the fire and point of his usual bearing on the battlefield." For this, Longstreet deserves censure. His instincts and judgment about Lee's decision to resume the offensive may have been correct, but the commanding general had determined otherwise, with the responsibility given to Longstreet.[20]

When Lee returned to Seminary Ridge about eleven o'clock, he ordered Longstreet forward. The latter requested that the march be delayed until Brigadier General Evander Law's brigade of Hood's division arrived from New Guilford, where it had been posted, and Lee assented. With this, Longstreet joined McLaws and Hood. Law arrived about noon, and sometime before one o'clock the divisions started. Before long the columns came to a rise, and if the men crossed it, they would be seen from Little Round Top. Longstreet countermarched the units, and it was not until nearly three o'clock that McLaws's leading brigade cleared Seminary Ridge. Before the Confederates, however, was an unexpected scene—the Union *III Corps* was moving forward into the area of the Peach Orchard and the ground between it and the Round Tops. The attack formations were adjusted; Hood argued for a movement around the hills, which Longstreet rejected, and at about four o'clock the Rebels advanced to the attack.[21]

The eight Confederate brigades entered the fighting *en echelon*, with Longstreet personally ordering McLaws's two final brigades forward. The combat enveloped the southern end of the field in places henceforth famous—Peach Orchard, Wheatfield, Valley of Death, Devil's Den, Little

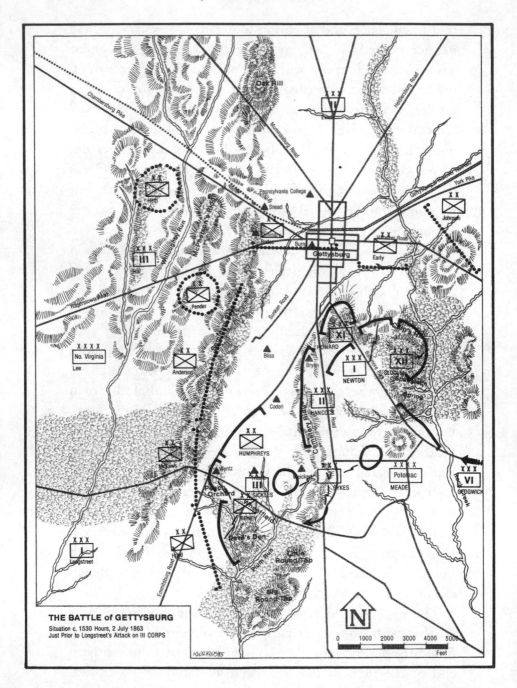

THE BATTLE of GETTYSBURG

Situation c. 1530 Hours, 2 July 1863
Just Prior to Longstreet's Attack on III CORPS

Round Top, and Trostle's Woods. The fury consumed men, and the Confederates nearly attained a victory. In time, Longstreet described his men's efforts as "the best three hours' fighting ever done by any troops on any battlefield." He may have been correct.[22]

The coordination of assaults that Lee had directed never occurred, however: Hill had only one division engaged, and Ewell's attacks on Cemetery and Culp's Hills came too late to assist Longstreet. As Major Walter Taylor of Lee's staff noted later, "The whole affair was disjointed. There was an utter absence of accord in the movements of several commands, and no decisive results attended the operations of the second day." To Lee, this breakdown, if rectified, could bring decisive pressure against Meade's lines, and after dark he ordered a renewal of the offensive for daylight on July 3.[23]

Lee was in the saddle before sunrise on the 3rd, and rode to Longstreet's position near the Peach Orchard, where he expected to find preparations underway for the day's assault. Instead, he found neither the units stirring for the attack nor Major General George E. Pickett's division with Longstreet. (By some unexplained oversight, neither general had informed Pickett of the planned daylight offensive.) Lee located the corps commander, seeking an explanation.[24]

"General," began Longstreet, "I have had my scouts out all night, and I find that you still have an excellent opportunity to move around to the right of Meade's army and maneuver him into attacking us."

Lee bristled at the suggestion, and Longstreet saw it at once. Then, pointing toward Cemetery Ridge, the commanding general replied firmly, "The enemy is there, and I am going to strike him."

As Longstreet recounted it later, "I felt then that it was my duty to express my convictions: I said, 'General, I have been a soldier all my life. I have been with soldiers engaged in fights by couples, by squads, companies, regiments, divisions, and armies, and should know, as well as any one, what soldiers can do. It is my opinion that no fifteen thousand men ever arranged for battle can take that position."[25]

Longstreet probably did not reply in the precise manner in which he remembered it, but he said something very similar to it. His words defined the difference between the two generals. Lee's proposal for an assault on the Federal position made no sense to Longstreet, for it entailed enormous sacrifice of life with no chance of success. "He was a trained soldier," James I. Robertson, Jr. has written of Longstreet, "who dealt in human life with a conservatism lacking in most military men. In the intangibility of battles he took no chances. Life was too precious to gamble needlessly." That "conservatism," his preference for the tactical defensive, and his assessment of the Confederacy's draining pool of manpower, moved Longstreet to oppose Lee for a third time in three days. Longstreet could not accept, without objection, "the sacrifice of my men," as he argued afterward.[26]

Lee's assault nevertheless went forward, with Longstreet given the responsibility for it. Preparations consumed the morning, and following a thunderous artillery bombardment, infantrymen of Pickett's division and of Hill's Third Corps advanced. When Pickett came to his old friend for the order to charge, Longstreet could not speak, but only nodded. Valiantly, the Confederates went forward into what one of the brigade commanders described as "the cul-de-sac of death." Union infantry and artillery erased the serried Rebel ranks, until only the bravest of Southerners—perhaps several hundred—breached the Federal line before being engulfed by overwhelming numbers of Yankees. "Pickett's division was gone," said Longstreet. On the field, Lee rode

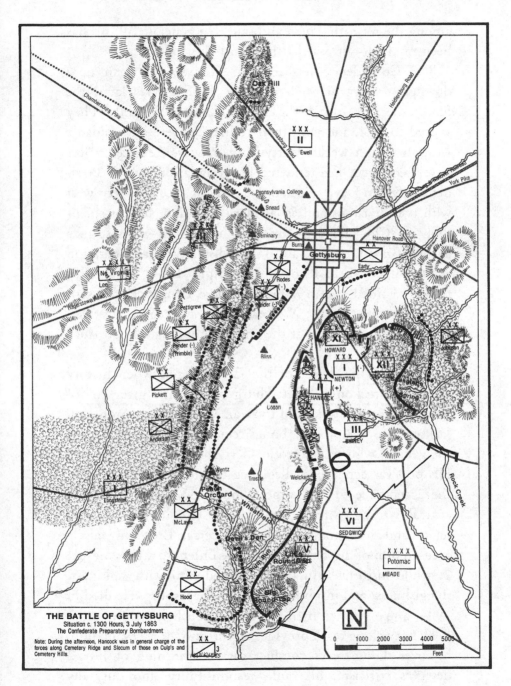

THE BATTLE OF GETTYSBURG
Situation c. 1300 Hours, 3 July 1863
The Confederate Preparatory Bombardment

Note: During the afternoon, Hancock was in general charge of the forces along Cemetery Ridge and Slocum of those on Culp's and Cemetery Hills.

among the retreating men and said to a general, "all this has been my fault—it is I that have lost this fight."[27]

The Confederate retreat from Gettysburg began in a downpour after nightfall on July 4. Ten days later, the Southerners recrossed the Potomac into Virginia. They started to heal, and with their resiliency, were a formidable weapon within weeks. Gettysburg, however, exacted a loss never recouped. Lee tendered his resignation, which President Jefferson Davis rejected. Later, Longstreet was sent west with two divisions and an artillery battalion, fought splendidly at Chickamauga, involved himself in a conspiracy against Braxton Bragg, and failed dismally in an operation against Union-held Knoxville. In April 1864, he and his troops rejoined Lee in Virginia, where Longstreet fell seriously wounded at the Wilderness on May 6. Longstreet, however, was with Lee at the end, at Appomattox, on April 9, 1865.[28]

Following the defeat of the Confederacy, when history offered its reckoning, Gettysburg became the great "if" of Southern interpretations of the war. With Lee and Stonewall Jackson above reproach, Longstreet became the scapegoat, the general who had failed at Gettysburg and lost the war. His postwar activities—allegiance to the Republican Party, the acceptance of government jobs, and his intemperate, critical writings—made him an apostate in the defeated region and an easy target. Former officers in Lee's army falsely accused him of disobeying a "sunrise order" to attack on July 2, while historians, in time, charged him with sulkiness, sluggishness, and insubordination at Gettysburg. He died in 1904, a man vilified by many fellow Southerners.[29]

History's long reach provides opportunity for reevaluation, however. Longstreet's conduct on the morning of July 2 deserves criticism, his rank, responsibility, and duty demanded more of him. Yet once the march began and the combat ensued, Longstreet did his duty. On July 3, despite his objections to the attack and his depression at the idea of sending his men to certain defeat, he saw to the deployment of the units, passed in front of the men during the bombardment in a demonstration of personal bravery, and issued the order to attack. He, Lee, and A. P. Hill should have been more careful in the alignment of the left wing of the assault force, an oversight reflective of the Confederate effort at Gettysburg. The climactic battle was not Longstreet's finest performance of the war, but it was not his failings there that resulted in Confederate defeat.[30]

E. Porter Alexander, Longstreet's artillery commander and steadfast friend, who, after the war, became perhaps the most astute student of the army's operations among former members, argued subsequently that Lee "never paid his soldiers a higher compliment than in what he gave them to do" at Gettysburg. Like Longstreet, Alexander thought that Lee made a grievous mistake in resuming the offensive. "I think it is a reasonable estimate to say," wrote Alexander, "that 60 per cent of our chances for a great victory were lost by our continuing the aggressive. The Union position could never have been successfully assaulted." To Alexander, Lee should have prepared a defensive position on Seminary Ridge and forced Meade to assault him. Lee dismissed the idea of a defensive stance in his report, but Alexander argued that Meade would have had to attack with the Confederates in Pennsylvania.[31]

As for Longstreet's objections to Lee's plans and his evident reluctance to undertake the offensive, Alexander believed that they could be justified. In a private, postwar letter Alexander claimed, "It is true that he obeyed reluctantly at Gettysburg, on the 2nd & on the 3rd, but it must be admitted that his judgment in both matters was sound & he owed it to Lee to be reluctant, for failure was inevitable do it soon, or do it late, either day."

By the summer of 1863, James Longstreet saw the war as a struggle of endurance, with the Confederacy confronted by crippling shortages in manpower and materiel. There could be no more defeats like Malvern Hill or victories like Chancellorsville. Of the war's third spring he would later write,[33]

> The only hope we had was to outgeneral the Federals. We were all hopeful and the army was in good condition, but the war had advanced far enough for us to see that a mere victory without decided fruits was a luxury we could not afford....The time had come when it was imperative that the skill of generals and the strategy and tactics of war should take the place of muscle against muscle. Our purpose should have been to impair the morale of the Federal army and shake Northern confidence in the Federal leaders.

When Longstreet rode on to the field that July Wednesday in 1863, "the time had come" once again. When it passed two days later, he viewed Gettysburg not as a great if, but as a great mistake for the Confederacy.

Notes to Chapter 3

1. Jeffry D. Wert, *General James Longstreet: The Confederacy's Most Controversial Soldier—A Biography* (New York: Simon & Schuster, 1993), 257.

2. James Langston Goree, V, Ed., *The Thomas Jewitt Goree Letters*, Vol I, *The Civil War Correspondence* (Bryan, Texas: Family History Foundation, 1981), 164; G. Moxley Sorrel, *Recollections Of A Confederate Staff Officer*, edited by Bell Irvin Wiley (Jackson, Tennessee: McCowat-Mercer Press, 1958), 108; William Miller Owen, *In Camp And Battle With The Washington Artillery* (reprint, Gaithersburg, Maryland: Butternut Press, n.d.), 157; *The Annals Of The War Written By Leading Participants North And South* (reprint, Dayton, Ohio; Morningside House, 1988), 433.

3. James Longstreet, *From Manassas To Appomattox*, edited and with an Introduction and Notes by James I. Robertson, Jr. (Bloomington: Indiana University Press, 1960), 327, 328; Wert, *Longstreet*, 240, 241.

4. *Annals*, 415-416; James Longstreet-Lafayette McLaws, July 25, 1873, Lafayette McLaws Papers, Southern Historical Collection, University of North Carolina (SHC/UNC).

5. Longstreet, *Manassas to Appomattox*, 331.

6. James Longstreet-Louis T. Wigfall, May 13, 1863, Louis T. Wigfall Papers, Library of Congress.

7. *Ibid.*

8. Robert K. Krick, "'I Consider Him a Humbug...'—McLaws on Longstreet at Gettysburg?" *Virginia Country's Civil War Quarterly*, Vol 5, 28-29; Walter H. Taylor, *Four Years With General Lee*, edited by James I. Robertson, Jr. (Bloomington: Indiana University Press, 1962), 91; U. S. War Department, *The War of the Rebellion: Official Records of the Union and Confederate*

Armies (Washington, D. C.: U. S. Government Printing Office, 1880-1901), Vol 27, Pt. 2, 308, hereafter *OR*; for a fuller discussion see Wert, *Longstreet.* 244-246.

9. James Longstreet-Lafayette McLaws, July 25, 1873, McLaws Papers, SHC/UNC.

10. *Ibid.*: Longstreet, *Manassas to Appomattox*, 197, 198, 329, 330; *Washington Post*, June 11, 1893.

11. Douglas Southall Freeman, *R.E. Lee: A Biography* (New York: Charles Scribner's Sons, 1934-1935), Vol III, 68; *OR*, Vol 27, Pt. 2, 308.

12. Longstreet offered various versions of the conversation. See Robert Underwood Johnson and Clarence Clough Buel, Eds., *Battles and the Leaders of the Civil War* (reprint, New York: Thomas Yoseloff, 1956), Vol III, 359, hereafter *B&L*; *Annals*, 421; Longstreet, *Manassas to Appomattox*, p. 358-359.

13. Longstreet, *Manassas to Appomattox*, 358; James Longstreet-Lafayette McClaws, July 25, 1873, McClaws Papers, SHC/UNC.

14. For an analysis see Wert, *Longstreet*, 258-259.

15. *Ibid.*, 259.

16. *Ibid.*, 260, 261; Longstreet, *Manassas to Appomattox*, 362; Fitzgerald Ross, *Cities And Camps of the Confederate States*, edited by Richard Barksdale Harwell (Urbana: University of Illinois Press, 1958), 48; *Annals*, 422, 439; Harry W. Pfanz, *Gettysburg: The Second Day* (Chapel Hill: University of North Carolina Press, 1987), 104; Freeman, *Lee*, Vol III, 86; John B. Hood, *Advance and Retreat: Personal Experiences in the United States and Confederate States' Armies*, edited and with an Introduction and Notes by Richard N. Current (Bloomington: Indiana University Press, 1959), 57: James Longstreet-John F. Nicholson, July 15, 1877, James Longstreet Papers, The Henry E. Hunington Library.

17. Samuel R. Johnston-Lafayette McLaws, July 27, 1892: Samuel R. Johnston-Fitz Lee, February 11 & 16, 1878; Samuel R. Johnston-George Peterkin, December 26, [?], Samuel R. Johnston Papers, Virginia Historical Society; Pfanz, *Gettysburg*,

106, 107; Roger J. Greezicki, "Humbugging the Historian: A Reappraisal of Longstreet at Gettysburg," *Gettysburg Magazine*, No. 6 (January 1992), 64.

18. Pfanz, *Gettysberg*, 110-112; Wert, *Longstreet*, 262, 264.

19. Longstreet, *Manassas to Appomattox*, 364, 365; *Annals*, 422; Pfanz, *Gettysburg*, 112-114; Wert, *Longstreet*, 264-268.

20. Sorrel, *Recollections*, 157; for a fuller analysis see Wert, *Longstreet*, 269-274.

21. Pfanz, *Gettysburg*, 114-121; Wert, *Longstreet*, 269-274.

22. *Annals*, 424; an excellent detailed description of the July 2 action can be found in Pfanz, *Gettysburg*, Chapters 8 through 14.

23. *Annals*, 311; *OR*, Vol 27, Pt. 2, 320.

24. Wert, *Longstreet*, 282-283.

25. Longstreet, *Manassas to Appomattox*, 385-386; *Annals*, p. 429; *B&L*, Vol 3, 342-343.

26. Longstreet, *Manassas to Appomattox*, xxiv-xxv; *Annals*, 429.

27. Wert, *Longstreet*, 284-292; James L. Kemper—W. H. Swallow, February 4, 1886, typed copy, John B. Bachelder Papers, New Hampshire Historical Society; *Annals*, 431; Walter Lord, Ed., *The Fremantle Diary* (Boston: Little, Brown & Co., 1954), 215.

28. For Longstreet's career after Gettysburg, see Wert, *Longstreet*, Chapters 15 through 19.

29. For an excellent examination of Longstreet's place in Southern history, see William Garrett Piston, *Lee's Tarnished Lieutenant: James Longstreet and His Place in Southern History* (Athens: University of Georgia Press, 1987), *passim*.

30. Wert, *Longstreet*, 286-287.

31. Gary W. Gallagher, Ed., *Fighting for the Confederacy: The Personal Recollections of General Edward Porter Alexander* (Chapel Hill; University of North Carolina Press, 1989), 233, 234, 277; E.P. Alexander-Frederick Colston, October 28, 1903, Campbell-Colston Family Papers, SHC/UNC.

32. E.P. Alexander-Mr. Bancroft, October 30, 1904, James Longstreet Papers, Duke University.

33. *B&L*, Vol 3, 246-247.

CHAPTER 4

The Bull of the Woods
James Longstreet and the
Confederate Left at Chickamauga

by

James R. Furqueron

*W*hen Lieutenant General James Longstreet and six members of his staff detrained at Catoosa Platform near Ringgold, Georgia on the afternoon of Saturday, September 19, 1863, the much debated western strategy of the Confederacy had been largely effected. A reinforcement of General Braxton Bragg's Army of Tennessee had been advocated by many in the Confederate High Command and government as well as Longstreet himself in order to retrieve the deteriorating situation in Tennessee.[1]

The Federal *Army of the Cumberland* under the command of Major General William S. Rosecrans had maneuvered Bragg out of the Duck River and Tullahoma position in late June and on August 16 began moving against Bragg's position around Chattanooga. Diverting Confederate attention by threatening a crossing of the Tennessee River above Chattanooga (which is what Bragg expected), Rosecrans crossed the bulk of his army well below Chattanooga. Poorly served by the Confederate cavalry under Major General Joseph Wheeler, who had the responsibility for picketing that area, Rosecrans' crossing of the Tennessee was reported to Bragg by a civilian. This offensive coincided with a move by Major General Ambrose E. Burnside's *Army of the Ohio* from its camps south of Lexington, Kentucky.[2]

In response to the moves by Rosecrans and Burnside, Major General Simon B. Buckner, commanding the Department of East Tennessee, evacuated Knoxville on August 25 and began a slow movement to the southwest toward the main army. On September 3, elements of Burnside's force entered Knoxville. The day before, Bragg wired Confederate Secretary of War, James A. Seddon, and reported that Rosecrans had crossed the Tennessee River below Chattanooga. Bragg also wired General Joseph E. Johnston, who commanded the Department of Mississippi and East Louisiana and asked for more help, which was approved by Richmond.[3]

Rosecrans' strength when his move began was about 80,000 against which Bragg could only oppose with some 40,000. The necessity to garrison an ever lengthening line of communications, however, gradually reduced the *Army of the Cumberland*, while Bragg's numbers grew substantively. Just prior to Buckner's arrival, Major General John C. Breckinridge's Division (4,500 total) and Major General William H. T. Walker's Division (5,400 total), less Brigadier General John Gregg's Brigade, arrived in late August from Mississippi. Gregg's and Brigadier General Evander McNair's Brigades were the last arrivals from Mississippi. These two Brigades, totaling 3,400, moved north out of Atlanta on September 12.[4]

The loss of Knoxville convinced President Jefferson Davis that additional reinforcements were needed for the Tennesse Theater, and by September 6, the President, in consultation with General Robert E. Lee, decided to send the Army of Northern Virginia's First Corps under Longstreet to Tennessee. On September 8, orders went out to Longstreet's Corps camped along the Rapidan River to break camp for Richmond. Major General George E. Pickett's Division was left behind because it had not, in Longstreet's opinion, recovered sufficiently from Gettysburg. Brigadier General George T. Anderson's Brigade of Major General John B. Hood's Division was ordered to Charleston, South Carolina, to reinforce General Pierre G. T. Beauregard's defense, thus further reducing the number of First Corps troops available for the move. Longstreet asked that the brigades of Brigadier Generals Micah Jenkins and Henry A. Wise be assigned to his command for the Tennessee move, but withdrew his request for Wise's Virginians when he learned that the brigade had not been in a major engagement since Seven Pines. In the end, eight brigades and six batteries were dispatched with "Old Pete" to the Tennessee theater.[5]

Years later, Longstreet recorded his last meeting with General Lee before departing. Longstreet recalled that he left Lee's tent and as he was mounting, the commanding General said: "Now, General, you must beat those people out in the West." Longstreet wrote that he withdrew his foot from the stirrup to a respectful position and promised, "If I live; but I would not give a single man of my command for a fruitless victory." Lee replied that it should be so. James Longstreet could not have known that in ten days he and his First Corps troops would contribute to the only substantive victory that the Army of Tennessee would ever win. There was a personal touch, as well, for Longstreet, as the Federal commander, Rosecrans, had been Longstreet's roommate at West Point and "Old Pete" and "Rosey" had developed a lasting affection for one another.[6]

After crossing the Tennessee River, Rosecrans determined to operate against Bragg's lifeline, the Western and Atlantic Railroad which connected Chattanooga and Atlanta, in order to "...compel him to quit his position by endangering his line of communication." The *XXI Corps* under Major General Thomas L. Crittenden moved just south of Chattanooga to the vicinity of Lookout Mountain; to the south and west operated the *XIV Corps* under Major General George H. Thomas, whose orders directed him toward McLemore's Cove; and on the far right of the line moved the *XX Corps* under Major General Alexander M. McCook who was ordered to support the *Cavalry Corps* under Major General David S. Stanley in their move toward Alpine, Georgia. It was the presence of the Federal cavalry with the *XX Corps* that alerted Bragg to the fact that the main Federal body was advancing against his supply line. On September 8, the same day that Longstreet's troops left their camps in Virginia, Bragg evacuated Chattanooga and began to fall back to the vicinity of Lafayette, Georgia.[7]

While Bragg's army retreated, the *Army of the Cumberland* continued to advance in accordance with Rosecrans' plan: the *XXI Corps*, after taking possession of Chattanooga, pushed south to Rossville; the *XIV Corps* crossed Sand Mountain and Lookout Mountain and entered McLemore's Cove (15 miles south southwest of Rossville); and the *XX Corps* moved to the vicinity of Alpine, Georgia (25 miles south southwest of the McLemore's Cove area). It was against this attenuated line that Bragg attempted to strike: first against a part of Thomas' *XIV Corps* in McLemore's Cove on September the 10th and three days later against the *XXI Corps* at Lee and Gordon's Mill on the West Chickamauga Creek. Both attempts to defeat the *Army of the Cumberland* in detail failed, the former due largely to the inexperience and over-caution of the newly arrived Major General Thomas C.

Hindman, and the latter because of Lieutenant General Leonidas Polk's disobedience. Both failures, however, had deeper roots in the deterioration of command confidence and cooperation that had developed in the Army of Tennessee.[8]

These abortive strikes alerted Rosecrans that Bragg, instead of being in demoralized retreat as he had hoped, was dangerously close and aggressive. The Federal commander, therefore, issued orders for the three corps to unite by having the *XIV Corps* and the *XX Corps* march northeast and join the *XXI Corps* at Lee and Gordon's Mill.

As Rosecrans and Bragg maneuvered, Longstreet's men were on their way from Virginia. The loss of Knoxville had interrupted the direct rail line between Virginia and Chattanooga, and the route of Longstreet's veterans was a circuitous one using the railroads of seven different companies to complete the journey. By Tuesday, September 15, three brigades under Brigadier Generals Jerome B. Robertson (1,300 strong), Henry L. Benning (1,200 strong), and Evander M. Law (2,000 strong) all from Hood's Division, had arrived in Atlanta and were being forwarded north to Catoosa Platform.[9]

By hard marching, the *Army of the Cumberland* managed to concentrate along the Chickamauga Creek in Catoosa and Walker Counties, Georgia, before Bragg could attack on Friday, September 18. Bragg's plan called for a crossing of the creek and a strike against the federal left in order to interpose his army between Rosecrans and Chattanooga. Robertson's Texas Brigade from Longstreet's command crossed the Chickamauga on the afternoon of the 18th as part of Brigadier General Bushrod R. Johnson's Division and was joined that evening by the brigades under Benning and Law. Hood arrived that afternoon and assumed command of his division as well as Johnson's Division and was designated

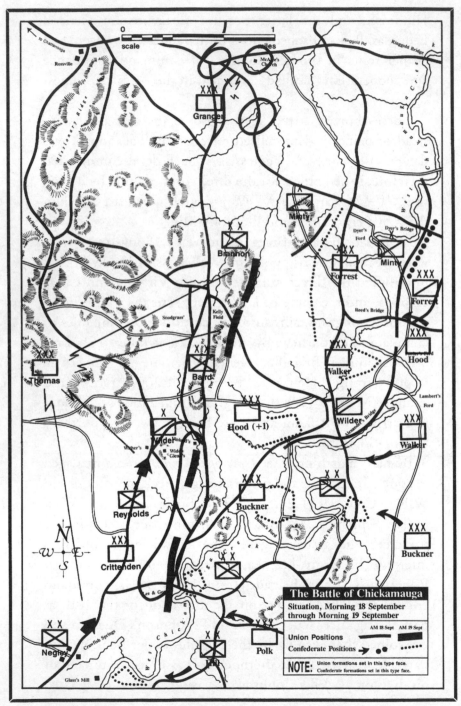

The Battle of Chickamauga
Situation, Morning 18 September
through Morning 19 September

Union Positions

Confederate Positions

AM 18 Sept   AM 19 Sept

NOTE: Union formations set in this type face.
Confederate formations set in this type face.

a corps commander that evening by Bragg. Hood, whose arm
was in a sling from his Gettysburg wound, led this "corps"
(six brigades) in the fight on Saturday (September 19) as the
Army of Tennessee hammered against Federal forces along
the north-south Lafayette to Chattanooga road. The Confederate assaults managed some headway; but at the cost of
severe casualties, and at the close of the fighting on the 19th,
the Federal line was still intact with a line of communication
north to Chattanooga. Ambrose Bierce, then a lieutenant on
the staff of Federal Brigadier General William B. Hazen,
wrote years after the event that the Battle of Chickamauga
was fought for possession of a road. It was indeed.[10]

Bragg clung to his plan to turn the Federal left and cut
Rosecrans off from Chattanooga. Having failed in his com-
binations on the 19th, Bragg would strike the enemy again
on the 20th. It was into a beleaguered command in the
middle of a battle that James Longstreet arrived.

The Army of Tennessee, in September of 1863, was an
organization plagued with more than its share of dissension,
in-fighting, and sectional discord that attended the semi-pro-
fessional, citizen armies that fought the American Civil War
(particularly those of the South). In formal existence since
November 20, 1862, the Confederacy's main army west of
the Appalachians had been beset with command problems
since its fight at Perryville in October, 1862. Officered from
the corps down to the brigade command level with men of
strikingly uneven qualifications and records (not to mention
temperaments), the Army of Tennessee's record had been one
largely of disappointment and retreat. Whereas the aforementioned characteristics were present to a lesser degree in its
eastern counterpart, these problems in the western army were
aggravated by the fault-finding attitude, acerbity, poor
health, and general tactlessness of its commanding general,
Braxton Bragg. A severe disciplinarian, Bragg was never able

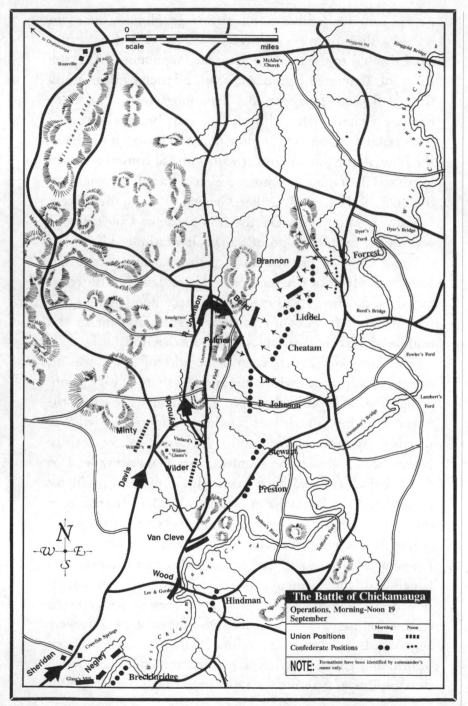

or willing to compromise his notion of command with the fiercely independent qualities of the southern soldier. A competent organizer, Bragg's relationship with too many of his subordinates was poor, and a mistrust had arisen, mutually harbored by the army commander and key lieutenants alike. Brigadier General St. John R. Liddell wrote: "It struck me that Bragg did not know whom to trust. He was not popular with his generals; hence I feared that zealous cooperation on their part was wanting." Major James W. Ratchford, Assistant Adjutant General on D.H. Hill's staff, concluded that Bragg "possessed the faculty of alienating every able man whom he came in contact." Bragg's poor health accounted for some of this command discord, but failure upon failure and retreat upon retreat had eroded morale. This, coupled with Bragg's tactless, officious attitude, left many subordinates surly and uncooperative. Robert E. Lee's comment concerning the Army of Northern Virginia is instructive: "I cannot do many things that I could do with a trained army. The soldiers know their duties better than the general officers do, and they have fought magnificently. You'll have to do what I do: when a man makes a mistake, I call him to my tent, talk to him, and use the authority of my position to make him do the right thing the next time." Unfortunately for the Confederacy, Bragg's temperament was not suited to this command philosophy.[11]

Bragg's command problems were compounded by troublesome subordinates such as Lieutenant General Leonidas Polk, a charismatic but incompetent commander who was, nevertheless, the senior lieutenant general in the Army of Tennessee. Furthermore, the rapid reinforcement of the army introduced into an already fractious command structure disparate organizations and officers who would have tried the most tactful and flexible army commander. Major General Thomas C. Hindman joined the army from the Trans-

Mississippi Department in August, 1863. A politically influential officer, Hindman's combat experience was limited, having last commanded troops in the field at Prairie Grove in December, 1862. Other new arrivals included Major General William H. T. Walker, who arrived from Mississippi in late August, and Lieutenant General Daniel Harvey Hill, who came from Richmond in July. Liddell wrote that Walker "...was well known to be a crackbrained fire-eater, always captious or cavilling about something whimsical and changeable and hardly reliable." Hill was a proven combat officer but had, as General Robert E. Lee described, "...such a queer temperament he could never tell what to expect from him, and that he croaked." Hindman took command of Major General Jones M. Withers' Division in Polk's Corps, while Hill assumed command of Lieutenant General William J. Hardee's Corps. Walker and his division were initially posted to Hill's Corps, but in early September, Bragg expanded Walker's command to five brigades and designated it as the Reserve Corps. As reinforcements arrived, Bragg was continually rearranging the organization of his army, and the commanding general's penchant for command tinkering continued into the Battle of Chickamauga.[12]

The news of James Longstreet's arrival on the field prompted Bragg to reorganize his force on the evening of the 19th. The army was divided into two wings, with Polk taking command of the northern Right Wing, and Longstreet taking command of the Left Wing to the south. Bragg did not meet with Longstreet until about 11:00 p.m. that evening at army headquarters near Thedford's Ford where Bragg informed him of the arrangement and the battle plans for the following day's attack. This last command reshuffle, while it gave the reputable and experienced Longstreet command of over half of the infantry, held difficulties. It was effected in the middle of a battle in which Bragg planned to

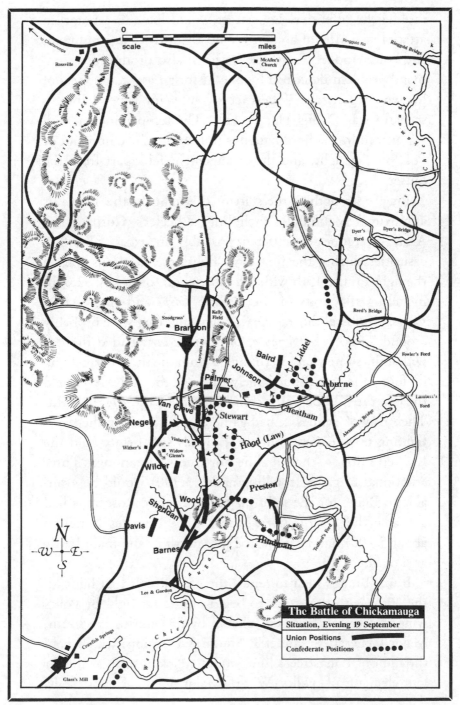

The Battle of Chickamauga
Situation, Evening 19 September
Union Positions
Confederate Positions

resume the offensive. Longstreet would have to arrange an attack in a matter of hours with mostly unfamiliar commands and commanders. Longstreet's arrival also produced a command problem described by one historian as "...an excess of lieutenant generals." The excess lieutenant general in this scenario was Daniel Harvey Hill. The temperamental Hill was placed in a subordinate position under the command of Polk on the right, and the arrangement fell apart from the outset.[13]

Bragg's strength at the start of the fight on the 19th was approximately 63,000 (including Wheeler's Corps). The Army of Tennessee suffered probably in excess of 8,000 casualties during the first day's fighting. Rosecrans started the fight on the 19th with a total strength of nearly 62,000, including the units of the *Reserve Corps* and the *Cavalry Corps*. His losses during the first day's fighting were probably around 7,000. The *Army of the Cumberland* ended the day with units somewhat intermingled from the three corps along its four mile front, but largely units of the *XIV Corps* held the left, the *XXI Corps* the center, and the *XX Corps* the right. The Army of Tennessee had gained ground during the fierce fighting on the 19th, but the Federals still firmly held the Lafayette Road—their lifeline north to Chattanooga. Three additional brigades (totalling about 3,900) would be available to Bragg for the fight on Sunday, while Rosecrans had available the *Reserve Corps* whose three brigades (totalling about 5,700) had been posted just north of the main battle area on the 19th.[14]

It was Bragg's plan to renew the offensive at first light on the 20th, with the attack to begin on the far right by Polk's wing and be taken up en echelon by division to the south. Major General Alexander P. Stewart's Division, which held the right of Longstreet's line, would attack as soon as the far left element of Polk's Wing (Major General Patrick R.

Cleburne's Division) began its assault. After conferring with Bragg for about an hour, Longstreet and his staff "...took to the leafy ground under the tall oaks and hickories for some sleep." Little time for rest was available, however, and at first light (5 a.m.), they rode to the front and set about familiarizing themselves with their order of battle and arranging for the attack.[15]

Longstreet's wing comprised the divisions of Brigadier General William Preston, T.C. Hindman, Bushrod Johnson, and A.P. Stewart, so deployed from south to north; Hood's Division, commanded now by Brigadier General Law, deployed behind Johnson; and a two brigade division under Brigadier General Joseph B. Kershaw formed in the rear of Law. The deep column of troops, which included Johnson's division as well as the five brigades which had arrived from Virginia, constituted Hood's Corps. The final two of these brigades, those of Kershaw and Humphreys, did not arrive on the field until after midnight on the 20th. Law moved up to command of Hood's Division comprising Benning's, Robertson's, and Law's brigades (the latter commanded by Col. James L. Sheffield on the 19th and Col. William F. Perry on the 20th), and Kershaw assumed command of the two brigade force from Major General Lafayette McLaw's Division from Virginia. Johnson's division was a provisional one that comprised Gregg's and McNair's brigades from Mississippi and Johnson's own brigade now led by Colonel John S. Fulton. Johnson himself had only recently stepped up from brigade command in Stewart's Division. The two divisions of Buckner's Corps occupied opposite ends of the Left Wing's line: Stewart on the right and Preston on the left, the latter having recently arrived with Buckner from East Tennessee. The final division in Longstreet's order of battle was that of Hindman, whose division belonged to Polk's Corps, and was included in Longstreet's wing because of its position at the close of the fighting on the 19th. Longstreet also had at his disposal twenty-one batteries including the Army Reserve Battalion under Major Felix Robertson. The task of organizing this force for an offensive was a formidable one.[16]

After reaching the front a little past first light, Longstreet met with his subordinate commanders and began arranging his wing for the attack. Longstreet ordered each division "to form with two brigades in the front line, and one supporting where there were but three brigades, and two supporting where there were more than three." This was a sound disposition which provided depth for the attacking force. The divisions assumed a brigade alignment from Confederate left to right (south to north) as follows: Gracie's and Kelly's brigades (Preston's Division) were recessed in the vicinity of Thedford's house; Trigg's brigade (Preston's Division) was up on the left of Patton Anderson's brigade (Hindman's Division), both being in the rear of Arthur Manigault's and Zachariah Deas' brigades (Hindman's Division) north of the Viniard Farm; Bushrod Johnson's Division connected with Deas, having the 7th Texas and the 50th Tennessee and the 1st Tennessee Battalion on Deas' right with Johnson's brigade (under Col. John S. Fulton) and Evander McNair's brigade forming the rest of Johnson's front rank; behind this line was formed the brigade of John Gregg (less the 7th Texas, 50th Tennessee, and 1st Tennessee Battalion), the command having devolved upon Col. Cyrus Sugg after the wounding of Gregg on the 19th; behind Sugg's line was deployed the front rank of the Virginia contingent; Evander Law's brigade under Col. William Perry forming the front rank while Henry L. Benning's and Jerome Robertson's brigades formed the fourth rank behind Perry; the brigades of Humphreys and Kershaw formed the fifth and last rank in what Longstreet termed the "main column of attack", this formation being just opposite the Brotherton house which stood on the west

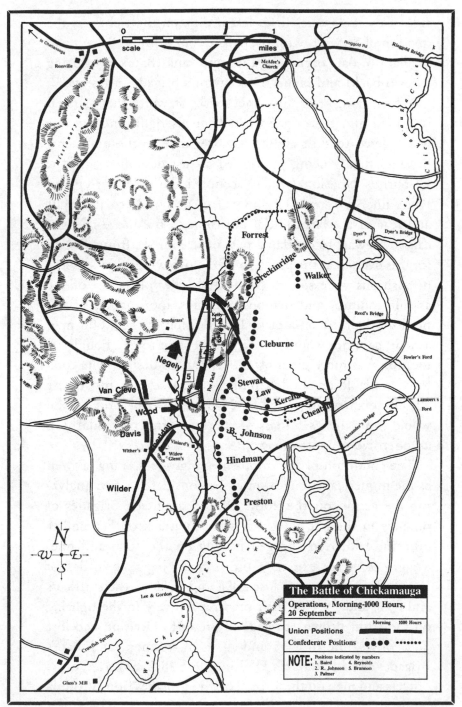

The Battle of Chickamauga

Operations, Morning-1000 Hours,
20 September

Union Positions

Confederate Positions

NOTE: Positions indicated by numbers
1. Baird   4. Reynolds
2. R. Johnson   5. Brannon
3. Palmer

side of the Lafayette Road; last in line on the right was the division of Stewart, with the brigades of John C. Brown and William B. Bate occupying the front rank (Bate's right being thrown back) and Henry D. Clayton's brigade in reserve.[17]

When Longstreet first met with Stewart, that general informed him that a gap existed on his right, and Stewart was ordered to shift about a quarter mile to the north, his brigades finally being positioned as just described. In fact, Cleburne's Division (which occupied the southern end of Polk's line) was recessed about a quarter mile to the right and rear of Stewart's initial position, so the move to right caused Stewart to overlap a part of Cleburne's front. Except for this overlap at the junction of the two wings, Longstreet's dispositions were sound, particularly the formation of the assault column, and demonstrated his appreciation of the need for depth in an attack. The position of the 9,600-man assault column would prove quite fortuitous, though its location was more circumstantial than by design. The total force available on the left under Longstreet was just under 23,000 infantry supported by 21 batteries, albeit the terrain would limit the usefulness of the long arm, particularly in an offensive support capacity.[18]

The condition of the troops in Longstreet's Wing, as well as the numerical strength, must be considered when analyzing the action on the 20th. Of the seventeen brigades of infantry in the left wing that were to attack on September 20, nine had been engaged heavily on the 19th and one, Trigg's, to lesser extent. Fulton's and Gregg's brigades of Johnson's Division had lost 43% and 29% of their officers and 35% and 38% of their men respectively in the fighting on the 19th. Brown's Brigade of Stewart's Division had lost 28% of its line officers and 40% of its men, and Bate's Brigade, also in Stewart's Division, lost 28% and 31% of its officers and men on the 19th. The five brigades from Virginia had not recovered from their ordeal eleven weeks earlier on the Confederate right during the second day's fight at Gettysburg. This was particularly the case with regard to the loss of line and field grade officers. In Humphreys' Brigade, for example, the 18th Mississippi was still under the command of a captain when the brigade arrived in Georgia, and the same was true of the 1st Texas of Robertson's Brigade. More significantly, however, was the fact that three of these brigades from Virginia, Law's (Sheffield's/Perry's), Robertson's, and Benning's, had been heavily engaged the day before and had taken significant casualties. Henry Benning reported that in the 20th Georgia, 17 out of 23 officers were either killed or wounded in the fighting on Saturday. Conversely, of the fourteen regiments and battalions of infantry that comprised Preston's Divsion, only three had combat experience prior to Chickamauga. The staying power of those brigades which had been heavily engaged on the 19th would not be great for the coming fight, particularly those units in which officer casualties had been significant, while Preston's command was mostly untested. In terms of equipment, the troops from Virginia had arrived rather destitute. Sergeant Major R.T. Coles of the 4th Alabama recollected: "For want of transportation from Atlanta, we remained there for twenty-four hours....everything, except the guns and cartridge boxes, was left behind. Our surgeons, surgical instruments and litters were in the rear. We were in no condition whatever to go into battle." Also, the horses of Kershaw's and Humphrey's Brigades did not arrive in time, relegating the officers of these two brigades to foot command. This would further impair an already cumbersome chain of command [19]

The command structure of the extemporaneous Left Wing was another factor that affected the course of action on the 20th. Longstreet was placed in command of an *ad hoc* wing of 23,000 troops in seventeen brigades organized into six divisions. Although the wing contained two corps, Hood's and Buckner's, the latter's two divisions were located on opposite ends of the line. Since there was no time to unite the two, Buckner remained with Longstreet most of the day functioning in the latter stages of the fight as a chief of artillery and also placing his small staff at the wing commander's disposal. Since only four members of his own staff accompanied Longstreet from Catoosa Platform the day before, these, plus the few members of Buckner's staff were all that he would have to convey the orders for an unwieldy, unfamiliar command. Hood's three division, eight brigade corps made the chain of command somewhat less cumbersome, but this still left Longstreet with the formidable task of having to oversee the operations of three divisions and one corps plus the artillery for which he had no experienced chief. The seventeen brigades which comprised his wing had come from four different armies, and seven of these brigades had been in the Army of Tennessee a week or less. It bears reiteration that the last two brigades from Virginia (Kershaw's and Humphrey's) arrived without their horses. This was particularly serious in Kershaw's case as that officer commanded one the best and largest brigades in Longstreet's Wing. He was also placed in command of the small division consisting of his own and Humphreys' Brigade and would have to exercise command on foot.[20]

The loss of field grade officers in the fighting on the 19th would also affect command control in the Left Wing for the next day's offensive. Three of the four regiments in Robertson's Brigade would be commanded by captains. Benning had lost two of his four regimental commanders. In Fulton's Brigade, the commander of the 44th Tennessee had been wounded, and in Gregg's Brigade two of the regimental commanders had been wounded. Of the fourteen regiments and battalions that comprised Stewart's Division, half had lost commanders in the first day's fight. Finally, two of the brigade commanders (John Gregg and James Sheffield) were incapacitated and would be unable to command on Sunday.[21]

The Federal units opposite Longstreet's wing were from the *XIV*, *XX*, and the *XXI Army Corps*, with roughly equal numbers from each. Although the numbers would change rapidly as would the composition of the defenders, the total number opposing Longstreet at the start of the assault was just under 18,000 (excluding the Federal cavalry further to the south).

First light on the 20th came just before 5:00 a.m., and by 7:00 a.m., Bushrod Johnson reported that his lines were formed. The Left Wing's front line was approximately 400 yards east of the Lafayette Road and ran roughly parallel to it. Longstreet established his headquarters just north and east of the intersection of the Brotherton and Lafayette roads and Old Pete and his troops waited for the sound of battle to open on their right as did Bragg. The awkward command arrangement and poor staff work caused a breakdown in communications and coordination that delayed the attack on the right by some three and a half hours. It was not until around 9:30 a.m. that firing could be heard as Breckinridge's Division went forward. This delay on the right, while affording Longstreet an opportunity to perfect his dispositions, fairly unhinged Bragg, who, after riding to the right and directly ordering Hill to advance, sent Major Pollock Lee of his staff to Stewart with orders to advance and attack. This was done without informing Longstreet.[22]

Cleburne received the order from Hill to advance and, due to the overlap of the two wings, found his left and center brigades entangled with Stewart's division. Cleburne shifted his left flank brigade (Deshler) to the north leaving Wood's Brigade to connect with Stewart. Stewart had, by this time, received Bragg's order to advance, and ordered his division forward, Brown advancing in the front line with Wood, who moved his brigade up through a part of Bate's. Clayton and Bate followed in the second rank. Stewart's attack was directed against a section of the Federal works that angled (in a SW-NE direction) across the Lafayette Road before straightening and running south parallel to the road. This exposed the right of Stewart's lines to an enfilading fire from the defenders who were behind breastworks of logs and rails. The left and center regiments of Brown's Brigade managed to cross Lafayette Road and briefly drove back the Federals in their front. Wood's Brigade, on the right of Brown, was subjected to a heavy enfilade and frontal fire and gave way. Brown's Brigade, its right flank support gone, in turn retreated. Bate's and Clayton's Brigades formed the second line of attack and their assault suffered a similar fate. Thus, before Longstreet had ordered Hood's column forward, Stewart's Division had spent its attack and was in retreat back to its starting point east of the Lafayette Road. This attack, while it failed to carry any of the Federal works, riveted the attention of the defenders to their front.[23]

About the same time that Bragg dispatched Major Lee to Hill, Longstreet sent word to Bragg that he thought his wing ought to attack. Before this messenger returned, Longstreet was informed of Bragg's order to Stewart. Longstreet ordered Hood to attack and then rode south and gave Hindman the order to move forward. Preston's Division on the extreme southern part of the line was kept in place as the pivot and reserve. Hood's column advanced at 11:10 a.m., and Hindman moved forward a little past 11:20. Although Bragg's plan called for the advance to turn to the south, the lack of success by the Right Wing coupled with an event that occurred just before Longstreet gave Hood the order to attack, caused Longstreet's advance to change direction.[24]

About ten minutes before Hood's column advanced, at a point some 800 yards west of where James Longstreet, Simon Buckner and their staffs stood, Brigadier General Thomas J. Wood commanding the *1st Division, XXI Army Corps* was handed an order by Lieutenant Colonel Lyne Starling, Chief of Staff of the *XXI Corps*. This controversial order, dictated shortly before by an exhausted Rosecrans, ordered Wood to move to the left and support Major General Joseph J. Reynolds' *4th Division* of *XIV Corps*. This was done in the belief that Brigadier General John M. Brannan, whose division (the *3rd* of the *XIV Corps*) was between Wood and Reynolds, had moved north in response to a request for reinforcements from Thomas. The order was perplexing to Wood, but it was preemptory. After consulting with McCook, who had ridden to Wood's position just before the order arrived, Wood executed the order. Brannan, however, was still in place. Wood complied in the only manner that was possible given that Brannan's Division was on his left between his position and that of Reynolds. He pulled his brigades, under Colonel George P. Buell (*1/1/XXI*) and Colonel Charles G. Harker (*3/1/XXI*), plus an attached brigade under Colonel Sidney M. Barnes (*3/3/XXI*) out of their positions west of the Brotherton house and moved north behind Brannan's position.[25]

Just as Wood vacated his position, Longstreet gave Hood the order to advance. Johnson's Division, leading the column of assault, cleared the Federal skirmishers east of the Lafayette Road, crossed it, and moved across the Brotherton farm into the one-third of a mile gap in the Federal line. As Hood's column moved into the gap, Benning's Brigade, which was in the fourth line of the column of assault, veered north and struck Colonel John M. Connell's Brigade (*1/3/XIV*) of Brannan's Division and Brigadier General Samuel Beatty's Brigade (*1/3/XXI*) of Brigadier General Horatio Van Cleve's

Division and routed them. To the south, McNair's Brigade (on the right front of the column) struck Buell's Brigade (*1/1/XXI*) in flank as it was moving north, and he later reported, "My own little brigade seemed as if it were swept from the field."[26]

To the immediate south of the gap and opposite a part of Hindman's front was the *XX Corps' 1st Division*, under Brigadier General Jefferson C. Davis. He reported, "The sudden withdrawal of troops from my left and the absence of any support on my right, just as the attack was being made, made my position little better than an outpost and perfectly untenable against the overwhelming force coming against it." Fulton's Brigade (on McNair's left) struck the left flank of Colonel John A. Martin's Brigade (*3/1/XX*) of Davis' Division and routed it as it tried to get into the position vacated by Buell. Davis' other brigade, that of Brigadier General William P. Carlin (*2/1/XX*), was deployed on Martin's right and was in turn swept back when Martin's retreat exposed its left and its right (which was not covered to begin with) was overlapped by Deas' and Manigault's Brigades of Hindman's Division. As Martin and Carlin retreated in disorder, *XX Corps* commander McCook ordered Colonel Bernard Laiboldt's Brigade (*2/3/XX*), which was deployed on a hill to Carlin's rear, to charge. Laiboldt moved his brigade to the attack, but the regiments were disordered by Davis' fleeing troops and then gave way before Deas' advance. Laiboldt's Brigade belonged to Major General Philip H. Sheridan's *3rd Division, XX Corps*. Sheridan was moving with the other two brigades of his command from the vicinity of the Widow Glenn's House to the left to support Thomas when the Confederate assault hit. As Laiboldt was forced back, Sheridan was ordered to commit his remaining brigades, under Brigadier General William H. Lytle (*1/3/XX*) and Colonel Nathan H. Walworth (*3/3/XX*). Lytle moved his

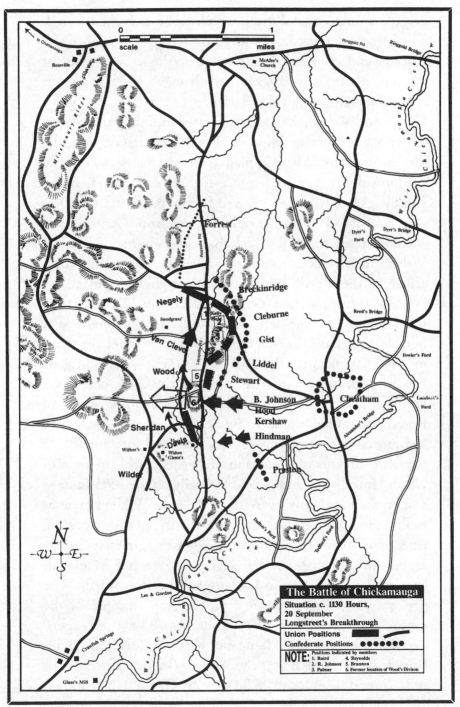

The Battle of Chickamauga
Situation c. 1130 Hours,
20 September
Longstreet's Breakthrough

Union Positions
Confederate Positions

NOTE: Positions indicated by numbers
1. Baird   4. Reynolds
2. R. Johnson   5. Brannon
3. Palmer   6. Former location of Wood's Divison

brigade up onto the hill from which Laiboldt had advanced. The brigade deployed, supported on its right by Walworth's Brigade, and stopped Deas' advance on the forward slope of the hill. Manigault's Brigade had diverged from Deas' left and advanced through the field east of the Widow Glenn's House, and Walworth's Brigade fronted into the gap between the two Confederate Brigades. Hindman's reserve brigade, Patton Anderson's Mississippians, moved up into the interval and provided the coup de grace to Sheridan's stand. Lytle's Brigade gave way under renewed frontal pressure from Deas and flank assault from the right of Anderson. General Lytle was killed on the hill which has since borne his name. Walworth's Brigade likewise gave way under frontal and flank assault by the left of Anderson and the right of Manigault.[27]

It was at this juncture, between 12:00 and 12:30, that the Confederates on the left of the advance encountered a notable adversary: the "Lightning Brigade" under the command of Colonel John T. Wilder (*1/4/XIV*). Wilder's brigade had been posted on the morning of the 20th near Cave Springs on the Dry Valley Road, one-half mile south of Rosecrans' earlier headquarters at the Widow Glenn's and had moved up in response to McCook's call for support. As the left regiments of Manigault's Brigade gained the crest of Glenn Hill, they were attacked frontally by the *39th Indiana* and on their left flank by Wilder's Brigade. Wilder's men, as well as the *39th Indiana* were armed with Spencer repeating rifles, and their tremendous fire power, directed mostly against the Confederate left, eventually forced Manigault back to the Lafayette Road. Manigault later recorded, "The fire we got under when first we became engaged in the morning exceeded anything I ever before or after experienced." After forcing Manigault back, Wilder moved his brigade back to the hill at the Widow Glenn's house. It was now around 12:30 and Wilder from Glenn Hill contemplated an attack on the southern flank of Longstreet's main column near the Dyer Farm. Wilder was dissuaded by the near-hysterical Assistant Secretary of War, Charles A. Dana and by a terse rejoinder from Sheridan "'to get out of there' as the army was 'routed'" Wilder collected his command and around 3:00 P.M. reluctantly began retiring over Missionary Ridge.[28]

After ordering Hindman forward, Longstreet rode back north to the vicinity of the intersection of the Brotherton and the Lafayette Roads and then moved to the west of the Lafayette Road in the rear of Hood's column. There he waited for reports to filter back to him. After crossing the Lafayette Road, Longstreet saw both Humphreys and Kershaw whose brigades formed the last rank in the assault column, and to Kershaw he gave some caution about about watching out for his right. The reports that Longstreet began to receive back from the van of Hood's column were encouraging indeed. The depth of the assault column and the gap through which it moved, coupled with the crippling flank attacks delivered against the Federal units on either side of the breach, had opened up the front quickly. Johnson's Division moved west toward the Dyer House, followed by Law's and Kershaw's Divisions, with the brigades beginning to bear to the right in response to the Federal retreat. Hindman's Division, to the south, had been somewhat disordered by its initial assaults and Wilder's counterattack and was in the process of regrouping and reorienting its advance toward the north. Despite the initial success, Confederate strength was diminished by the initial fighting, and their momentum decreased as the troops became fatigued and more resistance was encountered.[29]

After the breakthrough, Federal units from the right retreated west and north because their base (Chattanooga) was in that direction, and the eminences protruding from

Missionary Ridge offered practical rallying points. The Confederates advanced and conformed to the general movement of the Union right. This, coupled with the fact that the Confederate right had made no impression on the Federal salient around the Kelly farm, transformed Bragg's planned wheel left into a wheel right.

Further to the north, as Bushrod Johnson's Division advanced past the Dyer House and through the southern part of the Dyer Field, Perry's and Robertson's brigades of Law's division angled to the northwest and advanced through the northern section of the field. Federal artillery had repositioned on a ridge northwest of the field, and Johnson and Law now directed their attention against this Federal presence. Benning's depleted brigade, which had started in the fourth line on the right of Robertson, advanced due north just west of and parallel to the Lafayette Road toward Poe House.[30]

The rapid advance of his line was gratifying to Longstreet, who remarked to Brigadier General Humphreys, "Drive them General, these Western men can't stand it any better than the Yankees we left in Virginia, drive 'em." Not knowing about the gap, this was a logical deduction to account for such a rapid advance. Typical of tactical offensive operations in the Civil War, however, the Confederate momentum was diminished by fatigue, casualties, confusion, and the diminution of command control. Colonel Van H. Manning, commanding the 3rd Arkansas of Robertson's Brigade, wrote six days later, "The distance and speed with which we were required to move before engaging the enemy, together with the annoyance and confusion consequent upon our moving so close in rear of other troops, threw us into battle under severe disadvantages. The fatigue of the men and the deranged condition of the line are some of the prominent evils invariably and unavoidably experienced under the above circumstances." Lieutenant James Fraser of the 50th Alabama, Deas' Brigade wrote, "We pursued the flying enemy for more than a mile and a half, and when at last we were ordered to halt by our generals, we were tired, scattered and exhausted." [31]

The other factor which compounded all of the aforementioned was the terrain. The battle area west of the Lafayette Road was partially wooded with stands of hickory, oak, and pine that limited visibility in the forests to between 150 to 200 yards. Fields and cultivated areas opened the terrain particularly on the southern part of the field. Although Longstreet's Wing initially operated on the most open part of the battlefield (two-thirds of the 320 acre Dyer Farm was open), as it wheeled right and advanced to the north, it moved into more heavily wooded terrain and also encountered the increasing size and steepness of the hills that projected down from Missionary Ridge.[32]

It was against Federal artillery positioned on one of these spurs northwest of the Dyer Field that Sugg's and McNair's brigades of Johnson's Division and Perry's brigade of Law's Division advanced. Robertson's brigade on the right of Perry angled almost due north against a battery posted on an eminence northwest of a small field which abutted the northern end of the Dyer Field. While the brigades of McNair, Sugg, and Perry captured most of the artillery in their front, it was in this small northern field that Harker's brigade, which had been the center brigade that Wood pulled out at 11:00 a.m., faced about and counter attacked. The adjutant of the *125th Ohio* recorded that, "We fixed bayonets and charged on the double quick, breaking the rebel line and causing them to fall back in confusion." The counterattack routed first Robertson and then Perry. It was while trying to rally and reform their lines in the woods east of the Dyer Field, and also trying to get Kershaw into position, that

Major General John B. Hood was shot in the right thigh, incapacitating him from further command. This was a serious loss as Hood had command of three of Longstreet's six divisions and eight of the seventeen brigades in the Left Wing. General McNair was incapacitated by a wound just before his brigade charged the Federal artillery, and to the south, around noon, General Hindman received a painful contusion. Although he remained in command of the division until that night, his effectiveness most certainly was reduced. In the meantime, to the east of the Dyer Field, Benning's shakey brigade had been counterattacked and routed in the vicinity of the Poe House by the *105th Ohio*.[33]

Kershaw arrived in the northern Dyer Field about 12:30 p.m. and went into action against Harker who had fallen back to a position at the northwest corner of the field below the commanding eminence that Robertson had briefly occupied. This eminence is sometimes referred to as "Kershaw's Hill." Kershaw managed to get around Harker's right flank, whereupon Harker retreated to the next defensible spot; a concave of three hills, called Horseshoe Ridge, bordered on the west by a spur of Missionary Ridge and to the east by an open ridge near the Snodgrass house. Harker fell back to Snodgrass Ridge and as Kershaw pursued, the wooded arc of Horseshoe Ridge loomed up with enough Federals formed to defend it. Harker's counterattack had given Brigadier General John M. Brannan, commander of the *3rd Division, XIV Corps*, enough time to patch together a line on Horseshoe Ridge, collecting and deploying parts of the brigades of Colonel John M. Connell *(1/3/XIV)* and Colonel John T. Croxton *(2/3/XIV)*, the *21st Ohio* from Colonel William Sirwell's Brigade *(3/2/XIV)* of Major General James S. Negley's *2nd Division, XIV Corps*, plus six guns of *Battery I, 4th U.S. Artillery*, and fragments of other units. Kershaw reported that his brigade "...pursued them rapidly over the first

line of hills to the foot of the second, when I halted under
a heavy fire...." Kershaw sheltered his brigade, reformed, and
waited for support on his right from General Humphreys
Brigade. As Kershaw waited, a stray regiment from Perry's
Brigade, the 15th Alabama under the command of an
overbearing colonel, William C. Oates, came up on line in
the right center of Kershaw's Brigade. The imperious Alabama colonel commandeered two of Kershaw's regiments and
made an attack on the eastern hill (Hill Number One) of the
Horseshoe. Hearing the firing, and believing that Humphreys had arrived in support on his right, Kershaw advanced
the left of his brigade against the center hill (Hill Number
Two) and up the draw between the center and western hill
(Hill Number Three). Just after the Kershaw-Oates attack
commenced, between 1:00 and 1:30, the Federal Colonel
Timothy R. Stanley's Brigade (2/3/XIV), reinforced the
defenders on the ridge and was instrumental in repulsing the
attack on Hill number one. The left of Kershaw's Brigade,
"After one of the most gallant struggles I have ever witnessed...was compelled to fall back to a point about 250 yards
back where I determined to hold the enemy until reinforcements arrived."[34]

Shortly after Kershaw fell back, Brigadier General Benjamin Humphreys' Brigade arrived on Kershaw's right and
moved into the southern edge of the Snodgrass cornfield.
Humphreys recalled, "...I was suddenly brought to a halt by
a terrific fire of artillery and musketry from Crawfish Spring
Hill on the west of the Lafayette Road. My brave boys wanted
to charge on, but I had seen too many lines repulsed from
just such looking places....A very slight reconnaissance satisfied me that to attempt to attack would be the loss of one
half of my brigade...." The memory of Gettysburg was likely
still in the inexperienced brigade commander's mind, and he
pulled his brigade back. Humphreys then sent one of his staff

to Longstreet, "...to inform him that I was too weak to carry the hill without artillery. He soon sent me orders not to attempt it...." To his left, Kershaw's Brigade was now pinned down after its abortive assaults on Hills One and Two. The time was now about 1:30 p.m. After Kershaw's initial attacks, Patton Anderson's brigade of Hindman's Division arrived on Kershaw's left, attacked and was repulsed, largely by the fire of the Colt revolving rifles used by the *21st Ohio* who had been responsible for the earlier repulse of the left of Kershaw's Brigade. Johnson was, at this time, moving the brigades of Fulton and Sugg into position for an attack on the right of the Federal stronghold.[35]

Meanwhile, Longstreet had moved his headquarters to the vicinity of the Dyer House which stood on the east-west Dyer road near the southern end of that family's field. Shortly after 1:00 p.m., Longstreet, accompanied by Buckner and the staffs, rode north to view the front. He recalled, " I could see but little of the enemy's line and only knew of it by the occasional exchange of fire between the lines of skirmishers...." It was while on this ride that Longstreet was informed by Humphreys of the strength of the Federal position on Snodgrass Ridge. The wing commander told Humphreys, whose weak brigade represented the right of Longstreet's line west of the Lafayette Road, to hold his position while reinforcements were brought up. As Longstreet and Buckner rode back to the east, they passed the ground line of the Federal field-works that fronted the southern part of Polk's Wing, and Longstreet instructed Buckner to move up the reserve artillery and enfilade the enemy's line.[36]

At 2:00 p.m., Longstreet ordered Buckner to move up Preston's Division, leaving one regiment and a battery to watch the left. Both Longstreet and Buckner were concerned about their left flank which, given the forested terrain and the potent counterattack by Wilder against Manigault from that direction, is understandable. Preston moved Gracie's and Kelly's brigades north of the Brotherton house and Trigg's brigade just to the south of it, supporting Williams' Artillery Battalion. Longstreet wrote in his memoirs that "Calls were repeated for the cavalry to ride in pursuit of the retreating foe...", but Wheeler, who had engaged Federal troopers some eight to ten miles by road to the south at Glass's Mill around noon, did not make an appearance until around 5:00 p.m..[37]

To the northwest, the Federal position on the Horseshoe Ridge-Snodgrass line had been strengthened by the arrival of Major General George H. Thomas. When he arrived on Snodgrass Ridge after 1:00 p.m., Thomas was the senior Federal officer remaining on the field; Rosecrans, McCook, and Crittenden having all gone back to Chattanooga separately, each with his own responsibilities and reasons for doing so. Thomas had ridden back from his position in the Kelly field and discovered that the firing that he had heard from his right rear was bad news indeed. Thomas established his headquarters on the reverse slope of Snodgrass Ridge in the rear of Harker's position, and his presence gave a boost to the morale of the tired, battle-weary defenders. The Federal strength along this line prior to Granger's arrival was about 2,800.[38]

About 2:00 p.m., Major General Gordon Granger, commander of the *Reserve Corps*, arrived at Thomas' headquarters with about 3,900 troops of Brigadier General James B. Steedman's *1st Division, Reserve Corps,* comprising the brigades of Brigadier General Walter C. Whitaker (*1/1/Res*) and Colonel John G. Mitchell (*2/1/Res*). Steedman's command brought an additional supply of ammunition, which was badly needed by the defenders of the ridge line. Thomas ordered Steedman to proceed to the right of Brannan's (*3/XIV*) position on the Horseshoe as reports of Anderson's attack and Johnson's movement against that flank were

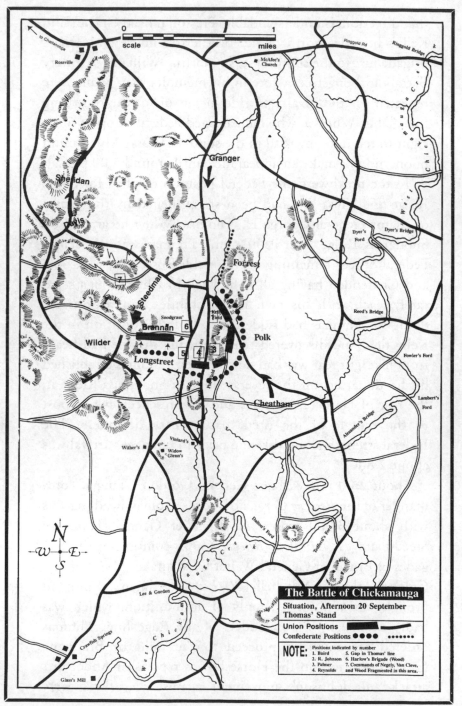

The Battle of Chickamauga

Situation, Afternoon 20 September
Thomas' Stand

Union Positions ■■■■
Confederate Positions ●●●● ••••••

NOTE: Positions indicated by number
1. Baird   5. Gap in Thomas' line
2. R. Johnson   6. Harker's Brigade (Wood)
3. Palmer   7. Commands of Negley, Van Cleve,
4. Reynolds   and Wood Fragmented in this area.

coming in. Mitchell and Whitaker marched behind the Federal position on the three hills of Horseshoe Ridge and over to ridge that connects to the Horseshoe on the west. They went up the reverse slope and engaged Fulton's and Sugg's brigades of Johnson's division who were advancing up the other side of the ridge. Fulton's Brigade advanced on the left of Sugg, but Granger's two brigades outnumbered them, and Fulton's left was overlapped. Captain William H. Harder of the 23d Tennessee of Fulton's Brigade recorded in his diary: "We advanced and when near the foot of the aclivity came to our skirmish line. They thought there was no one in front, we advance a short distance up the slope, when an overwhelming volley poured on us from the top in a semicircle completely enfilading our line. The men halted, returned the fire for a few minutes, and then fled over the turn of the hill to the rear." Harder also recorded seeing Longstreet in the rear of Fulton's Brigade conferring with Bushrod Johnson. This would have been shortly past 2:30 p.m. after Johnson's first assault was repulsed.[39]

The fight for the crest of this spur of the ridge west of the Horseshoe was critical for the Federal maintenance of their position, and the Federals had prevailed. By 2:30 p.m., they had established a solid front extending from the western ridge eastward down to the eastern end of Snodgrass Ridge, augmented by the arrival of approximately 1,200 men of the *3rd Brigade, 3rd Division, XIV Corps*, under Colonel Ferdinand Van Derveer. These relatively fresh men relieved Brannan's tired troops on the front line. The Federal line was further strengthened around 5:00 p.m. by the arrival of William B. Hazen's Brigade (*2/2/XXI*) of about 1,100 men from the Kelly salient.[40]

After his first ride to the front, Longstreet returned to his headquarters near the Dyer House. While taking a moment to eat, he saw Major William M. Owen, chief of artillery on

Preston's staff, whom Longstreet knew from Owen's Virginia days with the Washington Artillery. Longstreet hailed him, and he rode over to visit. Owen recalled that during the course of their conversation he asked Longstreet if the enemy was beaten or not? "Yes," Longstreet replied, "all along his line; a few are holding out upon the ridge yonder, not many though." The few on the ridge, however, were proving to be an obstinate band.[41]

About 3:00 p.m., Longstreet was summoned by Bragg to report on the situation. Old Pete recollected riding "...some little distance in rear of our new position," reporting his success, and asking Bragg to shift some units over from Polk's wing so that he [Longstreet] might have enough strength to finish driving the Federals and possibly cut them off. Bragg, disgusted with Polk and the failure on the right, was out of humor. In a letter to D.H. Hill written in July, 1884, Longstreet wrote:

> It is my opinion that Bragg thought at 3 p.m. that the battle was lost, though he did not say so positively. I asked him at the time to reenforce me with a few troops that had not been so severely engaged as mine, and to allow me to go down the Dry Valley road, so as to interpose behind Thomas and cut off his retreat to Chattanooga, at the same time pursuing the troops that I had beaten back from my front. His reply was that he had no troops except my own that had any fight left in them, and that I should remain in the position in which I then was. After telling me this, he left me saying, 'General, if anything happens, communicate with me at Reed's Bridge.'

Longstreet wrote in his memoirs that "There was nothing for the left wing to do but work along as best it could." There were, however, potential reinforcements from Polk's Wing readily at hand. Up until 2:00 p.m., Cheatham's four brigades (Jackson's brigade left for the right at 11:00 a.m.) of Polk's Wing remained east of the Brock field about 1,000 yards in rear of the position from which Hood's column had begun its advance. They were moved to right at 2:00 p.m. and only became lightly engaged around 6:00 p.m.[42]

After his 3:00 p.m. meeting with Bragg had made it clear that no help was coming from the right, Longstreet at 3:30 p.m. ordered Preston to move north to support the attacks on the Horseshoe Ridge line. About this time, Bushrod Johnson managed to coordinate another assault on the Federal center and right with the tired forces under his command, but the Federal line held firm At 4:30 p.m., the brigade under Brigadier General Archibald Gracie, with the brigade of Colonel John H. Kelly on its left, assaulted the eastern hill of the Horseshoe Ridge and after taking severe casualties managed to gain a foothold at 5:00 p.m. which it retained for a hour or so before falling back to replinish its ammunition. Gracie's brigade, out of 2,003 officers and men taken into action, lost 725. Thirty-six out 134 officers became casualties. Many of the Confederate and Federal units were by this time simply fought out. Most of the Left Wing had been on the offensive for six hours and it had taken its toll. A member of the 17th Tennessee of Fulton's Brigade recollected that late on the afternoon of the 20th the brigade was "well-nigh worn-out...." Johnson reported that after his division fought Steedman for possession of Missionary Ridge and fell back, none of his three brigades had over 500 rank and file remaining. Johnson further reported that one of his aides had reported the presence of 200 of Benning's Georgians in their rear and "...upon going to it the officer in command reported it utterly unserviceable on account of its having been cut up and demoralized." Along with Johnson's report was filed the following report of Lieutenant George Marchbanks, Assistant Inspector-General of Johnson's (formerly Fulton's) Brigade:

After our command had driven the enemy from and occupied the hill below the Vidito house, Deas' and Manigault's brigades were ordered up to re-enforce us. You ordered them to sweep the hills to our left, and coming up to connect with our left. They filed up the hill to the left of Crawfish [Spring] road and halted. This was some 800 yards below the Vidito House. While they were thus halted, the enemy attacked our front and you ordered me to hasten these troops forward. According to the best of my recollection, I delivered the order to General Deas. I do not recollect his reply; but the troops were not advanced immediately. I was sent back with the same instructions two or three times; but they did not come up to the field of action until our division had been engaged for some little time. They had scarcely gotten under fire until they began running back—one, two, and three together—until finally both brigades gave back in utter confusion, going principally on the road toward Crawfish Spring. Myself and other officers, however, succeeded in stopping them some 500 or 600 yards below the Vidito house, and forming them up a little ravine to their right. When formed I reported to you the fact. You told me to order them forward again. I delivered the orders to General Deas. He replied that he and General Manigault had a consultation, and that he or they thought that it would not be best to put these troops in the same place; "that they would not stand," or words to that effect. I reported this to you. You ordered me to bring them to the hill which our division formerly occupied. When they arrived at this hill, the sun was nearly down and the firing had entirely or almost ceased. I do not think these two brigades were under fire over twenty minutes.[43]

Marchbanks' report gives a fair picture of the state of the two brigades that represented the support on Johnson's left. Longstreet echoed this concern about the condition of Hindman's command in a dispatch to Bragg sent at 6:15 p.m. While Granger's timely arrival certainly prevented the

Federal right from being flanked by Johnson, any attempt to have used either Deas or Manigault for a later movement to the left would have been futile. The Federal right was vulnerable, however, and Longstreet could have moved Preston's Division to the west for a short enveloping move. Longstreet, however, did not know where the Federal right ended and knew only that Federal troops atop the spur west of the Horseshoe had overlapped Johnson's line to the west during his first assault and had repulsed the later effort when two of Hindman's Brigades had joined Johnson on his left.[44]

At approximately 4:15 p.m., Rosecrans, from Chattanooga, sent orders for Thomas to retire the army from the field and proceed to Rossville. Thomas left his Snodgrass headquarters and rode to the Kelly field to supervise the withdrawal of the troops from the salient there, leaving Granger on the Snodgrass-Horseshoe line to oversee the withdrawal on that sector. Granger left the Snodgrass headquarters shortly after Thomas departed, and before night, most Federal units had withdrawn from the Horseshoe Ridge-Snodgrass line. Steedman began pulling the two brigades of the *Reserve Corps* out around 6:00 p.m. and the units to the east under Brannan began to pull back at about the same time. In the confusion and gathering darkness, three Federal regiments, *22nd Michigan*, and the *21st* and *89th Ohio*, never received the withdrawal order and were left on the westernmost hill of the Horseshoe. Most were captured by Trigg's brigade of Preston's Division. The close of the fight saw Longstreet and Buckner at the base of Hill Number One, and Buckner recalled, "At the end of the battle, at the hour of sunset the enemy were retreating hastily from every part of the field....Here, I was joined very soon by General Longstreet."[45]

The Federal units that withdrew from the Horseshoe line, as did most of the left, proceeded to Rossville via McFarland's

Gap, located some three miles northwest of the Snodgrass house. Sheridan retreated up the Lafayette Road through the Rossville Gap after having returned to the northern sector of the battlefield with a remnant of his division. The withdrawal on both fronts by the Federal infantry was neither a panic stricken flight nor an orderly retreat. Any retrograde movement begun in gathering darkness in the face of an enemy is a confusing and debilitating endeavor. The extrication of the *Army of the Cumberland* from Chickamauga was attended by straggling and a great deal of bewilderment as this tired army made its way to Rossville. Some units fared better than others, depending on their officer casualties and the quality and energy of the survivors. Brigadier James G. Spears, whose brigade of the *Reserve Corps* arrived in Chattanooga around noon on the 20th, was ordered by Rosecrans that evening to proceed toward Rossville "...and to halt all officers and soldiers coming into Chattanooga below the rank of Major-General...and by next morning I had halted and encamped, of different corps and divisions, between 8,000 and 12,000 officers and soldiers who were...all thrown to the front again." Ambrose Bierce remembered that night.

> At last it grew too dark to fight. Then away to our left and rear some of Bragg's people set up "the rebel yell." It was taken up successively and passed round to our front, along our right and in behind us again, until it seemed almost to have got to the point whence it started. It was the ugliest sound that any mortal ever heard-even a mortal exhausted and unnerved by two days of hard fighting, without sleep, without rest, without food and without hope. There was, however, a space somewhere at the back of us across which that horrible din did not prolong itself; and through that we finally retired in profound silence and dejection, unmolested.

Thomas formed a line stretching from the Rossville Gap westward over to the Chattanooga Creek, a distance of some two miles, and a position of considerable strength.[46]

At 6:15 p.m. James Longstreet sent a dispatch to Bragg informing the commanding general "that we have been entirely successful in my command today and hope to be ready to renew the conflict at an early hour tomorrow." In this dispatch, Longstreet asked for a division to replace Hindman's in line, "...so that he may retire a little and collect his men," and rather sarcastically added "I suppose that several of General Polk's Divisions might position towards my front without inconvenience."[47]

Longstreet's wing lost about 8,000 killed, wounded, and missing out of a total 23,000 engaged. Although Longstreet was apparently willing to try a move the next morning, the practicability of renewing another attack on the *Army of Cumberland* on the 21st is doubtful, given the horrific casualties that had been sustained by the Army of Tennessee in the two day fight, (18,454 out of 66,000 engaged). The casualties suffered by the *Army of the Cumberland* were equally high, (16,100 out of about 60,000). Longstreet's wing, while virtually crippled for any further offensive action, could congratulate itself on its achievements. After driving the Federals from the field, it could count among its spoils: 40 pieces of artillery, over 3,000 prisoners, 10 regimental standards, almost 18,000 small arms, various accouterments and over 390,000 rounds of small-arms ammunitions. The success was due to the bravery and endurance of the rank and file, the hard work and experience of Longstreet and the officers under him, and partly due to good luck, which any successful army occasionally needs.[48]

It is necessary here to review Longstreet's handling of the left wing after it began its attack, especially in light of the criticisms leveled against his decisions, or lack of them as some have stated, during the course of the fight on the afternoon of the 20th. Peter Cozzens, in his battle study, *This Terrible Sound: The Battle of Chickmauga*; Archibald Gracie's *The Truth About Chickamauga*, a study of the second day's fight for the Horseshoe-Snodgrass line; Thomas Connelly's second volume of his history of the Army of Tennessee, *The Autumn of Glory*; Glenn Tucker's popular history, *Chickamauga: Bloody Battle in the West*; and Volume II of *Braxton Bragg and Confederate Defeat* by Judith Hallock as well as her *James Longstreet in the West: A Monumental Failure*, all accuse Longstreet of various command lapses and professional sins.

Tucker wrote that "Longstreet was directing the battle much after the fashion he had learned from General Lee—making careful preparations and entrusting the detail of the assaults to his subordinates. Never having acted before in concert, they became confused at times about who was in command on the firing line." Cozzens, citing these observations, elaborated and wrote that "Such a style might serve in an army in which generals were accustomed to working with one another...," but, "...was bound to fail when applied to the schismatic command structure of the Army of Tennessee...." Cozzens charged that Longstreet adopted the role of a bystander from 1:00 to 2:30 and "issued no orders of consequence to his generals who were left to muddle through as best they could," which resulted in "a good deal of confusion and a decided lack of coordination." These critics claim that this inactivity on Longstreet's part allowed the Federal line on the Horseshoe and Snodgrass ridges to coalesce. Archibald Gracie, the son of the Confederate general of the same name, in his elaborate and tedious study of the second day's fight for the Horseshoe Ridge position, *The Truth About Chickamauga*, had said pretty much the same thing. Gracie wrote that the initial assaults on the heights were attended by a "distinctly noticeable lack of unity of action on the part of these Confederate Generals" (Hindman, Johnson, and Kershaw), "due to the absence of any orders whatever from their wing commander...."[49]

Both Gracie and Cozzens criticized Longstreet for the failure to exploit the gap that developed between the two wings of the Federal Army. This gap, approximately 600 yards wide, stretched from roughly the end of Reynolds' right, which was recessed back to the Lafayette road, westward over to the Snodgrass cornfield. They cited Longstreet's account of his ride to the front with Buckner as evidence that Longstreet should have been aware of the gap that had developed after the Federal right had retreated to the Snodgrass-Horseshoe line. Cozzens also accused Longstreet of failing to summon Joe Wheeler from Glass's Mill so that the latter could have arrived in time to pursue the retreating Federals.[50]

Connelly, in his history of the Army of Tennessee, maintained that "Longstreet could have controlled McFarland's Gap even if he had not carried the Snodgrass Hill position.", and later blamed the failure to follow-up the victory with a pursuit on the 21st, partly on Longstreet for not keeping Bragg adequately informed as to the state of affairs on the Confederate left, particularly that the Federal Army had left the field. Connelly likewise lamented the failure to have gotten more out of Joe Wheeler.[51]

Judith Hallock, in her biography of Bragg, accused Longstreet, among other things, of originating the myth that Bragg rode off of the battlefield during the crisis of the fight, and she credited Bragg, not Longstreet, with giving the order for Hood's column to attack. She also criticized Longstreet for asking for reinforcements when Preston's Division "had not yet fought." These criticisms were repeated in her more recent offering about Longstreet in the west.[52]

These criticisms are ill-founded and unrealistic. James Longstreet had been on the field about twelve hours when his attack went in, just after 11:00 a.m.. on the 20th. With a staff of four, he was charged with preparing an unfamiliar command of six divisions of infantry totaling some 23,000 officers and men for an attack which was to have begun earlier than its eventual attack time of 11:00 o'clock. Any assertion that Longstreet became a bystander, or that he failed to supervise his subordinates to insure their cooperation and coordination, must be qualified by putting Longstreet's position in perspective.

Tucker wrote that "Longstreet was directing the battle much after the fashion he had learned from General Lee-making careful preparations and entrusting the detail of the assaults to his subordinates." That is much too broad a statement and is misleading in regard to Lee. Lee certainly viewed the optimum role of an army commander as bringing his army to the field and "entrusting the details to his subordinates," and giving his subordinates freedom to operate at their command level. Nonetheless, he did not hesitate to become involved with lower level operations if he felt the circumstances so dictated. Chancellorsville, Sharpsburg, and the Wilderness all offer good examples of this. While Longstreet was certainly aware of Lee's command style, his position as a wing commander at Chickamauga presented him with a different and uniquely complex command problem. Some of these circumstances, which were pointed out earlier, bear reiteration. He was placed in command of a hastily assembled admixture of 23,000 troops in six divisions, which is about the same number of troops he had under his command in three divisions at the start of the Gettysburg campaign (eleven brigades at Gettysburg versus seventeen at Chickamauga). While the eight-brigade corps under John B. Hood made the chain of command somewhat less cumbersome, this still left Longstreet with having to oversee the operations of three divisions and one corps plus the artillery for which he had no chief. Only four members of his own staff accompanied him to the field and these officers along with Buckner's small staff were all that Longstreet had at headquarters. The seventeen brigades under his command had come from four different commands (Tennessee, East Tennessee, Mississippi, and Northern Virginia) and seven of these brigades had been with the Army of Tennessee a week or less. The wounding of Hood and Hindman seriously disrupted the chain of command early in the fight (particularly the loss of Hood). Kershaw and Johnson were both inexperienced division commanders (although the latter performed admirably), and Kershaw reported "that being on foot during the engagement, I could only assume a very general command." Given the aforementioned circumstances, the terrain, the unexpectedly rapid advance of the wing, and the depleted condition of some of the units, a tighter command control would have been almost impossible to effect. The style of "making careful preparations and entrusting the details of the assaults to his subordinates" is, in effect, the proper role of any higher echelon commander. Longstreet's immediate presence in the vicinity of Hill Number One around 1:00 p.m. might have effected a more coordinated attack which might have resulted in the capture of that strongpoint. This "what if business" must be balanced with the consideration of Longstreet's position as Wing Commander and his need to keep sight of the larger scope of his responsibilities. Commanders have often immersed themselves in the minutiae of lower level operations and lost control of the larger command for which they were charged.[53]

Commanders oversee their operations and become involved in details when necessary and practicable, but to blame Longstreet because the aforementioned command style "...was bound to fail when applied to the schismatic command structure of the Army of Tennessee...", as Cozzens asserted, unfairly required Longstreet to know about command conditions in the Army of Tennessee about which he could not have been aware. Longstreet had heard something of Bragg's reputation, but he could not have known how deeply confidence in the army commander had been eroded. Longstreet did not know about the state of command deterioration in the Army or about incidents such as McLemore's Cove that had brought a cloud over one of his division commanders, Hindman. A little past 3:00 p.m. on the afternoon of the 20th, however, he would learn a good deal more about the moody and erratic commander of the army. The non-involvement with some of the brigade level operations of his wing (even if he had deemed it proper to do so) had more to with his very small staff and the large number of separate units to command than any failure to appreciate command deterioration. The lack of an adequate staff was a critical deficiency which plagued all Confederate commands. The wounding of John B. Hood in the woods east of the Dyer field, more than any other single factor on the Confederate side, prevented the seizure of at least a part of the Horseshoe-Snodgrass line early in the afternoon. Command cooperation was to some degree later effected between Johnson, Hindman and Kershaw as evidenced by their afteraction reports. While Longstreet's immediate presence early in the afternoon might have provided the cohesion necessary to have taken Horseshoe Ridge, the debilitated state of many of the Confederate units, as witnessed by reports such as Manning's and Robertson's, renders this questionable. In fact, the rapid advance had practically worn out the units before they had even reached the Horseshoe line. Corps, wing, and army commanders did, in fact, become bystanders for periods of time while events developed; that simply was how command had evolved and adapted to the technology and the nature of battle by 1863.[54]

Parallel to the discussion of command control is the question regarding the Federals' open right flank on the ridge west of Horseshoe Ridge and the possibility of Longstreet's having used Preston's Division for an envelopment of that flank. Certainly from a tactical point of view a short envelopment of the Federal right was practicable. After the deployment of Whitaker's (*1/1/Res*) and Mitchell's (*2/1/Res*) Brigades on that flank, the Federals would have been very hard pressed to extend their line much further to the west. Thus a deployment of Preston's Division against the area to the west of Mitchell's Brigade and a simultaneous assault by the units fronting the Horseshoe-Snodgrass line could have seriously endangered not only the position but most of the defenders as well. Against the absence of any exploitation of this tactical opportunity must be weighed the circumstances and the situation as was presented to Longstreet. Although in his 1884 letter to Hill he mentioned moving down the Dry Valley Road and interposing behind Thomas, it must be borne in mind that the letter was written 21 years after the event when the positions of the antagonists were known. At the time, he did not know where the Federal right ended. The terrain on this part of the field was much more obstructed than on that part from which his wing had begun its advance. Sending Preston off toward the west through the rough terrain would have compounded the command control problems and would have attenuated the Confederate line severely. Longstreet did not know what the Federals had in reserve and was aware that Johnson's attacks on the Federal line had been beaten back. As Preston's Division represented Longstreet's only creditable reserve (Law's Division was of questionable reliability at this juncture), Old Pete obviously believed that its employment against the Horseshoe section of the Federal line represented its best employment to maintain mass and concentration. Longstreet's wing had rapidly moved the Federals earlier in the day and it is reasonable to assume that Longstreet, not knowing about the gap which facilitated so rapid an advance, believed that an attack against their line with a fresh divsion would complete the work. Although there was a tendency in the Civil War for commanders to "attack them where they were" and to employ a force on force strategy, it would appear that Longstreet's employment of this tactic with regard to Preston's Division on the Snodgrass-Horseshoe Line was due more to the circumstances than to any clearly defined choice of a frontal assault versus a flanking maneuvre.[55]

Longstreet has been criticized for the failure to appreciate the gap that existed between the left of the Federal units on Snodgrass ridge and the right of Reynolds, which was recessed back from the Kelly field to the Lafayette Road. This gap developed after the Federal right center was pierced and existed throughout the day, making both wings vulnerable to flanking maneuvers and enfilade. Longstreet wrote in his memoirs:

> ...I rode with General Buckner and the staffs to view the changed conditions of the battle. I could see but little of the enemy's line, and only knew of it by the occasional exchange of fire between the lines of skirmishers, until we approached the angle of the lines. I passed the right of our skirmishers, and, thinking I had passed the enemy's, rode forward to be accurately assured, when I suddenly found myself under near fire of his sharpshooters concealed behind the trees and under the brush. I saw enough to mark the ground line of his fieldworks as they were spread along the front of the right wing, and found that I was very fortunate in having the forest to cover the ride back until out of reach of their fire.

Cozzens cited the passage above as evidence that Longstreet should have known that between the right of Colonel
Edward A. King's Brigade (*2/4/XIV*) and the left of Colonel
Charles G. Harker's (the *3/1/XXI*) in the Snodgrass cornfield,
there existed at least a 600 yard gap to the right of Humphreys' Mississippians. Cozzens, however, went on to state
that "Unquestionably, the heavy woods between the black-
smith shop and the Lafayette Road limited visibility." Heavy
woods, indeed, were the overriding terrain factor in this
battle. On a field where the forests limited vision to 150 to
200 yards and as "...on the most open parts of the Confederate side of the field one's vision could not reach farther
than the length of a brigade," the ability to ascertain the
positions of recessed or reserve enemy units was impossible.
Benjamin Humphreys, whose brigade fronted just to the west
of the wooded area of the gap, wrote that he had been shifted
to the right of Kershaw (who was in front of the eastern hill
of the Horseshoe and Snodgrass ridge) to fill up a gap
between Kershaw and Buckner. Humphreys recalled that
Longstreet approved the order with the caution "...to advance
slowly as the enemy was in great force in the woods...."
Longstreet did not know what the Federals might have in
such places. An advance by infantry for the purpose of
reconnaissance on such a wooded battlefield would have been
a dangerous undertaking for any of the limited infantry force
that Longstreet could have called on including Humphreys'
small brigade of about 1,100 men. It must be noted that this
gap was occupied by the Federal brigade of Brigadier General
August Willich (*1/2/XX*) who had been deployed behind
Reynolds. Willich's brigade numbered less than 1,000 men
and covered this space more or less like a skirmish line, but
Longstreet had no way of knowing what force was in place
in the woods. Additionally, August Willich was one of the
best brigade commanders in the *Army of the Cumberland.*

Longstreet had Law's Division near the Poe House, but these three brigades (especially Benning's) were depleted and of doubtful use for a move into such an unknown area. Robertson, whose brigade was not engaged after it retreated from the Dyer Field, reported that his casualties had been "heavy." Preston's green division, which had been moved up to the vicinity of the Brotherton farm by 3:00 p.m., represented Longstreet's only reserve, and it was evident that the situation to the west on the Snodgrass-Horseshoe Ridge line would require re-enforcement. Longstreet could count on no cooperation or re-enforcement from Polk's Wing, and he had to deal with the Federals by re-enforcing his tired and depleted forces with his only reserve, which was Preston.[56]

Archibald Gracie in his *The Truth About Chickamauga*, published in 1911, accused Longstreet of failing to use Preston to exploit this gap. Judith Hallock, in her biography of Bragg, could not understand why Longstreet asked Bragg for reinforcements from Polk's wing when Preston's Division was at hand. After the wheel to the right had begun, Preston's three brigades had been maintained in their position on Longstreet's left as a reserve and a guard against possible Federal activity from that sector. The division had moved up to Brotherton's an hour before Longstreet met with Bragg and asked the commanding general for some support from the stalled right wing. After Bragg's refusal, Longstreet's wing was on its own, and needing Preston to re-enforce his own line, Longstreet felt that he lacked the infantry to do more. He had to rely on the artillery that he had instructed Buckner to establish to enfilade the Federal line on the Lafayette Road. Longstreet's request for support from Polk's wing was entirely reasonable and sound. Polk's wing was in the same position that it had occupied at 9:00 a.m. The left wing had pierced the enemy's line and had advanced a condiderable distance before fatigue and stiffening resistance had stopped it. When

Longstreet met with Bragg, he (Longstreet) knew that Johnson's first attack on the Horseshoe line had been repulsed and that Preston's Division was all he had left as a reserve and to guard the left flank. Longstreet simply asked Bragg to apply the maximum strength where the enemy appeared to be the weakest. After the meeting with Bragg, Longstreet commited his last infantry to the Snodgrass-Horseshoe line. He could not command the infantry in Polk's wing, and he had to rely on the troops he had left in his command.[57]

The question regarding Major General Joseph Wheeler and the cavalry can essentially be reduced to an examination of time and distance. Longstreet wrote in his memoirs that "Calls were repeated for the cavalry to ride in pursuit of the retreating forces, and guard the gaps of the ridge behind the enemy standing in front of our right wing." Cozzens accused Longstreet of not summoning Wheeler and cited a letter written by Thomas Claiborne in 1891 as evidence that Longstreet did not summon the mounted arm on the left until it was too late. In this letter written to Park Commissioner Henry Boynton, Claiborne, who was a Lieutenant Colonel on Buckner's staff wrote "...that Longstreet did not believe he had the authority to send for Wheeler...." Cozzens went on to state that "he gave the matter no thought until later in the day, after the chance for a meaningful pursuit had all but vanished." Longstreet did not have the authority (given the command set-up) to order Joe Wheeler up from Glass's Mill. He could have indeed sent calls for Wheeler without actually ordering him to do anything, and he recollected as much in his memoirs. Wheeler wrote in his after action report that in the early afternoon, "...I received orders to move my available force to Lee and Gordon's Mills and attack the enemy." Although Wheeler did not specify from whom this order originated, it was probably one of the earlier requests from Longstreet delivered by a courier. If indeed, the order that Wheeler responded to was a request from Longstreet, the stipulation to attack the enemy at Lee and Gordon's Mills represented the best knowledge that Longstreet possessed as to where the Federal right was located. After his 3:00 p.m. meeting with Bragg, and given Longstreet's temperament as evidenced by his 6:15 note to the commanding general, Longstreet asserted an authority that was ill-defined regarding Wheeler's command. At 5:09, he dispatched a written order to General Wheeler that read: "Lieutenant General Longstreet orders you to proceed down the road toward the enemy's right, and with your artillery endeavor to enfilade his line with celerity." This order bore the name of Thomas Claiborne, Lieutenant Colonel, Cavalry at the bottom. Even if Wheeler had recieved definite orders to move north early in the afternoon, he was too far away, and there were too many obstacles.[58]

Major General Wheeler, who had crossed the Chickamauga at Glass's Mill about noon with his four brigades of cavalry, dismounted his command and engaged in a fight with Long's Federal cavalry brigade that lasted some two hours. It is difficult to see how Wheeler could have then reformed and completely avoided the other Federal units in the area so as to have made a coherent appearance on the battlefield. One of Wheeler's veterans wrote years later that "Had General Wheeler been promptly informed of the Confederate success, we could have been immeasurably more useful by going from Glass's Mill straight to Crawfish Spring, and on by the direct road into the immediate rear of the flying Union infantry...." If Wheeler, after his fight with Long, had proceeded directly to Crawfish Spring, he would have encountered the *1st* and *2nd Brigades* of Colonel Edward M. McCook's *1st Cavalry Division* and also an infantry brigade which had arrived there at one o'clock. Only if Wheeler could have bypassed Crawfish Spring without any attack by the cavalry force there, and gained the main roads north of the Spring, could he have had any chance of reaching the battlefield or interfering with the Federal withdrawal through McFarland's Gap. There were two good roads that led north off of the east-west road from Lee and Gordon's Mills: the Dry Valley Road which led past the Widow Glenn's and a parallel road to the west next to Missionary Ridge. If Wheeler had been able to reach the Dry Valley Road and had taken it, he would have run into Wilder's "*Lightning Brigade*" in the vicinity of the Widow Glenn's at any time before Wilder began his withdrawal at 3:00 p.m. The road west of the Dry Valley Road would have afforded the only other avenue to the north. After his fight with Long, in order to effectively interdict the Federal retreat, Wheeler would have had to have eluded the Federal Cavalry at Crawfish Spring by riding a little over two miles north by northwest cross country to gain access to the western road north. The distance then would have been approximately five miles to McFarland's Gap. Since Sheridan and Davis had managed to get most of their commands through McFarland's Gap by 3:00 o'clock, Wheeler would have been hard pressed to reform after his fight with Long and have made the difficult ride (assuming the Federal cavalry would have remained quiescent) required in order to have attacked the retreating Federal infantry. Since Wheeler did not disengage from his fight with Long until after 2:00 o'clock, it is difficult to ascertain how Joe Wheeler could have made a coherent appearance farther to the north any earlier and what difference it would have made if he had. As it was, Wheeler moved back across the Chickamauga and moved up to Lee and Gordon's Mill, recrossed and engaged Federal cavalry again around 3:00 p.m. before the latter began withdrawing. Wheeler then captured the Crawfish Springs hospital and eventually moved up the Dry Valley Road at dusk where he rounded up about 1,000 Federal stragglers.[59]

Judith Hallock, in her biography of Bragg, wrote: "When Longstreet wrote his memoirs in 1896, he claimed that Bragg had left the field during the crisis of battle. Bragg, Longstreet contended, refused to send reinforcements from Polk's command....and then rode off the field to his headquarters at Reed's Bridge." She went on to write, "Longstreet made no mention in the report of Bragg's leaving the field. Furthermore, Bragg's headquarters were not located at Reed's Bridge, but at Thedford's Ford, although dispatches throughout the afternoon were headed 'in the field'. It appears that Bragg's alleged absence from the field is, in fact, a myth, originated by Longstreet...." Unfortunately, Ms. Hallock's history is spurious. In the first place, Bragg moved his headquarters early on the morning of the 20th from Thedford's Ford to a point just south of the Brotherton Road about three quarters of a mile west of Reed's Bridge. Furthermore, James Longstreet never wrote in his memoirs that Bragg "rode off the field" as Hallock contended. Longstreet wrote, "He did not wait, nor did he express approval or disapproval of the operations of the left wing, but rode for his headquarters at Reed's Bridge." The commanding general did not ride off the field, nor did Longstreet write that he did. Bragg rode back to his headquarters, the location of which was in a small clearing just to the west of Reed's Bridge—not at Thedford's Ford.

Hallock also came up with the strange contention that Bragg, not Longstreet, should be credited with the order that started the left wing on its successful assault. She wrote, "By the time Longstreet felt prepared, Bragg had ordered units of the left wing to attack, thus setting in motion the advance that broke the Federal line, long credited to Longstreet." The facts do not support this notion.

In his report, Longstreet wrote, "The battle seemed to rage with considerable fury, but did not progress as anticipated. As soon as I was prepared I sent to the commanding general to suggest that I had probably better make my attack. Before the messanger returnedI heard that the commanding general had sent orders for the division commanders to move forward and attack. I had no time to find the officer who brought the order, as some of the troops were in motion...." Bragg's order, carried by Major Lee, reached only A.P. Stewart, whose division occupied the far right position of Longstreet's wing. Stewart went forward, and the attack had spent itself and the division in retreat when Longstreet gave Hood the order to go forward. It was Hood's column of assault that struck the gap in the Federal line.[60]

The late Thomas L. Connelly's history of the Army of Tennessee, while a necessary and useful source, abounds in hyperbole. His statement that, "Obviously, Longstreet could have controlled McFarland's Gap even if he had not carried the Snodgrass Hill position," ignored many of the realities that have been discussed. Longstreet did not know the position of all the Federal forces and could not have easily left the sizable Federal force that he knew existed on the Horseshoe line, while he marched off into the woods towards McFarland's Gap. His forces were nearing the point of exhaustion and the situation was muddled and dangerous as Federal units rallied and faced about and others appeared. Connelly likewise lamented the failure to use Wheeler's cavalry to seize McFarland's Gap, and wrote that Longstreet's 5:09 order "...mentioned nothing of seizing McFarland's Gap, but was merely a vague note relative to enfilading the Federal right." Besides all of the problems previously mentioned attendant with such a move by Joe Wheeler to seize McFarland's Gap, the presence of Wilder's *"Lightning Brigade"* bears reiteration. Wilder began withdrawing his brigade toward Missionary Ridge at 3:00 p.m. and, due to the presence of wagons in his column, was moving rather slowly, hence would have been in position to contest any move by Wheeler up either the Dry Valley Road or the western road between 3:00 and 4:00 p.m. The window of opportunity to have earlier struck the retreating Federal infantry and artillery was a small one given that Wheeler did not disengage from his fight with Long until after 2:00 p.m. and Sheridan and Davis had completed their movement through McFarland's Gap by 3:00 p.m. Between 3:00 and 4:00 p.m., Wheeler would probably have run into Wilder, and that would have done the Confederacy no good. Longstreet knew about the gaps in Missionary Ridge behind the Federals; to have gotten a substantial force there, given the circumstances, was not practicable.[61]

Connelly also partially blamed Longstreet for the failure to pursue. Connelly wrote:

> Though Bragg had ordered Longstreet to keep him informed of any new developments, the Virginia officer did not do so. He did not send news to Bragg that night that the entire Federal right wing had collapsed, nor apparently, did he dispatch later the news that Rosecrans' army had retreated.

Connelly acknowledged the 6:15 note referred to earlier in which Longstreet, among other things, said "...we have been entirely successful in my command today...," and that he hoped to renew the conflict at an early hour tomorrow. Connelly wrote that this 6:15 note left the impression that the Federals still held the field and was not explicit in its reporting. In fact there *were* Federals still present on or very near the heights, although the withdrawal had most likely begun when Longstreet wrote his dispatch. Longstreet's dispatch succinctly stated the facts as well as the wing commander appreciated them. Braxton Bragg was the commanding general of the Army of Tennessee who, if he had any doubts about the situation at 6:30 p.m., could have ridden himself or sent a staff officer to James Longstreet. Old Pete would have gladly elaborated. Any pursuit by the Army of Tennesse after the two days of horrific slaughter along the Chickamauga would have been a doubtful proposition, but that is not here pertinent. An ill and fatigued Braxton Bragg was going to listen to very little that anybody told him that Sunday night.[62]

James Longstreet's actions at Chickamauga showed this able tactician at his best. His preparations were careful and showed his appreciation of the state of the art as it had evolved by 1863. At Gettysburg, Longstreet had seen the attenuated Confederate line move the enemy, but lack the depth to break through. There, on July 2, eight brigades of his corps pressed the attack for three hours. At Chckamauga, he carefully arranged the seventeen brigades of his wing, and it sustained the offensive for almost six hours. His dispositions at Chickamauga reflected his growth as a battlefield tactician. That the column of assault struck a part of the Federal line just as units had mistakenly pulled out, does not detract from Longstreet's accomplishment nor does it detract from the bravery and endurance of the soldiers that fought under him that Sunday in the forests bordering the West Chickamauga Creek. After the fight, the Tennessee soldiers gave Longstreet a nickname—the Bull of the Woods. Dr. William Garrett Piston, in his biography of Longstreet, wrote that "Chickamauga was the greatest achievement of his career." Indeed it was. James Longstreet will forever be associated with Chickamauga, which is a combination of two Creek Indian words and means "the dwelling place of the war chief."[63]

Notes to Chapter 4

1. General G. Moxley Sorrel, *Recollections of a Confederate Staff Officer*, p. 192; *The War of the Rebellion: A Compilation of the Official Records of the Union and Confederate Armies* , Volume 30, part 2, p. 290.(hereafter cited as *OR*); Thomas Lawrence Connelly and Archer Jones, *The Politics of Command; Factions and Ideas in Confederate Strategy*, pp. 130-136; William Garrett Piston, *Lee's Tarnished Lieutenant: James Longstreet and His Place in Southern History*, pp. 64-68; Richard M. McMurry, *Two Great Rebel Armies: An Essay in Confederate Military History*, pp. 55, 146-147, 152-155. Dr. McMurry provides an excellent treatment of the South's two principle armies.

2. Thomas L. Connelly, *Autumn of Glory; The Army of Tennessee, 1862-1865*, p. 164; Dr. William Glenn Robertson, Lieutenant Colonel Edward P. Shanahan, Lieutenant Colonely John I. Boxburger, and Major George E. Knapp, *Staff Ride Handbook for the Battle of Chickamauga,18-20 September 1863*, p. 50.

3. *OR* Vol. 30, part 4, pp. 529, 540, 554, 583-84, & 607; George W. Brent Diary, Bragg Papers, Western Reserve Historical Society. Buckner gave his strength as 8,000.

4. *OR* Vol. 30, pt. 4, pp. 515-518,608, & 643; Thomas L. Livermore, *Numbers and Losses in the Civil War in America: 1861-1865*, p. 106.

5. Travis Hudson, "The Charleston and Knoxville Campaigns: History of the 59th Georgia Infantry Regiment", Part II, *The Atlanta Historical Journal*, Vol. XXV, number 3, Fall 1981. Douglas Southall Freeman, *Lee's Lieutenants: A Study in Command*, Vol. III, *Gettysburg to Appomattox*, pp. 223-224. Anderson's Brigade rejoined Longstreet in Tennessee on October 18th and participated in the attack on Knoxville.

6. James Longstreet, *From Manassas to Appomattox* , p. 437; Donald B. Sanger and Thomas R. Hay, *James Longstreet: I, The*

Soldier, II *The Politician, Officeholder, and Writer*, p.8. The exchange between Lee and Longstreet probably took place on September 10 (Freeman, *Lee's Lieutenants* III, note 43, 224). Also in the USMA Class of 1842 along with Rosecrans and Longstreet were D.H. Hill and A.P. Stewart.

7. *OR*, Vol. 30, pt.1, pp. 52-3; consultation of the author with Mr. James Ogden III, Historian, Chickamauga-Chattanooga National Military Park, Ft. Oglethorpe, Georgia, April 1, 1994.

8. The West Chickamauga will hereafter be referred to as the Chickamauga.

9. Robert C. Black III, *The Railroads of the Confederacy*, p. 185; *OR*, 30, pt. 4, p. 652; R.T. Coles, *History of the Fourth Regiment Alabama Volunteer Infantry*, Chapter 14, p. 2. These three brigades arrived at Catoosa Platform (which lies about 8 miles east-southeast of the battle area) on the 17th. Law's Brigade was the last to arrive, its members detraining on the night of the 17th.

10. Bragg's Chickamauga Report, Claiborne Papers, Southern Historical Collection, University of North Carolina; *OR* 30, pt. 2, pp. 451 & 453; Ambrose Bierce, *Ambrose Bierce's Civil War*, p. 32. Hood's Corps on the 19th comprised two divisions of three brigades each. The three brigades from Virginia formed one division under Evander Law. Colonel James Sheffield of the 48th Alabama took command of Law's Brigade. The other division was a temporary one commanded by Bushrod Johnson. It consisted of Johnson's Brigade, commanded now by Colonel John S. Fulton of the 44th Tennessee, and the two brigades from Mississippi under McNair and Gregg.

11. St. John Richardson Liddell, *Liddell's Record*, pp. 113-114; Freeman, *Lee's Lieutenants* III, p. 449; James Wylie Ratchford, *Some Reminiscences of Persons and Incidents of the Civil War*, p. 35. Lee's comment was to A.P. Hill in May of 1864.

12. Liddell, *Liddell's Record*, p. 137; Freeman, *Lee's Lieutenants* II, pp. 469-470, & 721. Freeman used the term "temperamental peculiarities" in a pointed reference to D.H. Hill.

13. *OR*, 30, pt.2, p. 33; Thomas L. Connelly, *The Autumn of Glory: The Army of Tennesee, 1862-1865*; Ezrz J. Warner, *Generals in*

Gray: The Lives of the Confederate Commanders, pp. 137, 192, & 243. Longstreet, whose date of rank was Octoer 9, 1862, became the senior lieutenant general on the field. Polk's date of rank was October 10, 1862, while Hill's was dated July 11, 1863. The command breakdown in the right wing was not Hill's fault. Bragg and Polk share the blame.

14. Peter Cozzens, *This Terible Sound: The Battle of Chickamauga*, p. 294; Telegram of H.M. Drane to F.W. Sims 14 September, 1863, Longstreet File, Chickamauga-Chattanooga National Military Park (CCNMP) Library; John W. Busey and David G. Martin, *Regimental Strengths at Gettysburg*, p. 139; O.R 27, pt. 2, p. 363; *OR* 30, pt. 1, pp. 856 & 858; *OR* 30, pt. 2, p. 245. These reinforcements were: the Confederate brigades of Brigadier Generals Joseph B. Kershaw and Benjamin G. Humphreys, both from Virginia; and States R. Gist's Brigade which came up from Rome, Ga. The *Reserve Corps* of Rosecrans' Army consisted of the brigades of Brigadier General Walter C. Whitaker and Colonels John G. Mitchell and Daniel McCook.

15. Sorrel, *Recollections of a Confederate Staff Officer*, p. 193; *OR* 30, pt. 2, p. 288.

16. William C. Oates, *The War Between the Union and the Confederacy and Its Lost Opportunities*, pp. 254-255. Colonel James L. Sheffield of the 48th Alabama commanded Law's Brigade during most of the fighting on the 19th until his horse through him injuring his back. Colonel William Flank Perry of the 44th Alabama assumed command of the brigade and led it on the 20th.

17. *OR* 30, pt. 2, p.288; Robertson, *Staff Ride Handbook*, p. 116; Longstreet, *From Manassas to Appomattox*, pp. 440 & 447; William F. Perry, "A Forgotten Account of Chickamauga", *Civil War Times Illustrated*, Sept-Oct., 1993, pp. 53-56. Longstreet evidently intended for Hood to place the five brigades from Virginia in the front rank between Johnson and Stewart, but circumstances dictated its position behind Johnson. This provided an even deeper "column of attack" than was originally planned. In both his afteraction report and his memoirs, Longstreet wrote as though Hood had occupied a position in

the front rank. Perry, who commanded Law's Brigade on the 20th, recollected that the distance between the lines in this column was "thirty or forty yards."

18. *OR* 30, pt. 2, pp. 288, 291, & 363; Robertson, *Staff Ride*, p. 31.

19. *OR* 27, pt. 2, p. 363; *OR* 30, pt. 2, pp. 373, 388, 414, 467, 495, 502, 503, 509, 513, 514, & 518; Henry L. Benning Papers, Southern Historical Collection, University of North Carolina, Chapel Hill, N.C.; Joseph H. Crute, Jr., *Units of the Confederate States Army*, pp. 28, 34, 76-77, 116-117, 132, 240, 313, 389, & 392; Lewellyn A. Shaver, *A History of the Sixtieth Alabama Regiment, Gracie's Alabama Brigade*, pp. 10-12; *Tennesseans in the Civil War*, Part One, p. 306; R.T. Coles, *History of the 4th Alabama*, ch. 14, p. 2, Cozzens, *This Terrible Sound*, p. 316.

20. *OR* 30, pt. 2, p. 290. Gregg's and McNair's Brigades came from Johnston's command in Mississippi; Trigg's, Kelly's, and Gracie's Brigades from East Tennessee; Law's, Robertson's, Benning's, Kershaw's, and Humphrey's from Virginia; and Fulton's, Bate's, Brown's, Clayton's, Anderson's, Manigault's, and Deas' were in the Army of Tennessee.

21. *OR* 30, pt. 2, pp. 371, 387, 405, 456, 473, 511, 514, 515, & 519; John B. Lindsley, *The Military Annals of Tennessee* I, p. 451. When John Gregg was wounded late on the 19th, Colonel Cyrus Sugg of the 50th Tennessee assumed command of the brigade. Lt. Col. Thomas Beaumont was killed on the 19th, which left the regiment under the command of Major C.W. Robertson. The 1st Tennessee Battalion of Gregg's Brigade lost its commander on the 19th. It was consolidated with the 50th Tennessee for the fight on the 20th.

22. *OR* 30, pt. 2, pp. 288, 363-364, & 456.

23. *OR* 30, pt. 1, pp. 409 & 420; pt. 2, pp. 155, 161, 364, & 372. Stewart's attack was opposed by the Second and part of the Third Brigades of the Third Division, Fourteenth Army Corps; Wood's Brigade took frontal and enfilade fire from the Second and Third Brigades of the Fourth Division, Fourteenth Army Corps.

24. *OR* 30, pt. 2, pp. 288 & 330; *Longstreet, Manassas to Appomattox*, p. 447.. LT James Fraser of the 50th Alabama, in Deas Brigade, wrote six days leter, "Presently Generals Buckner and Longstreet rode down the line. Longstreet is the boldest and bravest looking man I ever saw. I don't think he would dodge if a shell burst under his chin. General Deas said 'Gen. Longstreet, I presume.' 'Yes Sir,' said General L." James Fraser to his father, September 26, 1863. CCMP Library, Ft. Oglethorpe, Ga

25. *OR* 30, pt. 1, pp. 635 and 944; Robertson, *Staff Ride Handbook*, p. 54; Cozzens, *This Terrible Sound*, p. 361. Wood was aware of increased Confederate activity in his immediate front, but, supported by McCook, he obeyed the order. The order read: "The general commanding directs that you close up on Reynolds as fast as possible, and support him." The time written on the order was 10.45 a.m..

26. *OR* 30, pt. 1, pp. 656 & 809; pt. 2, p.518; Robertson, *Staff Ride Handbook*, p. 115. Beatty was deployed very closely behind Connell. Beatty reported, "The lines of my brigade were at this time but a few yards in rear of those of the troops in my front, and the four lines resembled more a column in mass than supporting lines, the rear line being exposed to the heavy fire directed on the front line."

27. *OR* 30, pt. 1, pp. 500, 580, 583, 590, & 595; pt. 2, pp. 303, 317, & 318. Colonel Martin, of the *8th Kansas* had taken command of the *3rd Brigade, 1st Division,* on the afternoon of the 19th when its commander, Colonel Hans C. Heg was mortally wounded. Colonel Walworth of the *42nd Illinois* took command of the *3rd Brigade, 3rd Division,* on the afternoon of the 19th when its commander, Colonel Luther P. Bradley, was wounded.

28. *OR* 30, pt. 1, p. 448; pt. 2, pp. 342, 346, 352, & 355; Arthur M. Manigault, *A Carolinian Goes to War*, p. 103; Samuel C. Williams, *General John T. Wilder, Commander of the Lightning Brigade*, p. 34; John T. Wilder, "Statement of the Operations of My Brigade During the Battle of Chickamauga", *17th Indiana* File, CCNMP Library. The *39th Indiana*, commanded

by Colonel Thomas J. Harrison, belonged to the *1st Brigade, 2nd Division, XX Army Corps.* It was mounted and operated independently. Wilder later wrote that he, "prepared to move my whole command in column of five regiments towards the heavy firing thinking to strike the enemy in left and rear, believing that my five lines of Spencer rifles could break any line on earth." Years after the event, Wilder, along with many others, believed that the *Lightning Brigade* could have turned the tide against Longstreet that Sunday afternoon.

29. *OR* 30, pt. 2, p. 503.

30. *OR* 30, pt. 2, pp. 458, 511, & 518.

31. *OR* 30, pt. 2, p. 513; Benjamin G. Humphreys, "History of the Sun Flower Guards", John F.H. Claiborne Papers, Southern Historical Collection, University of North Carolina; James H. Fraser to his father, Sept. 26, 1863, in 50th Alabama File, CCNMP Library.

32. James Ogden III, Park Historian, CCNMP, interview by the author, Ft. Oglethorpe, Georgia, March 9, 1993; James Ogden III, Park Historian, CCNMP, consultation with the author, April 1, 1994.

33. *OR* 30, pt. 1, pp. 441 & 470; pt. 2, pp. 305, 319, 500, & 513-515; Longstreet, *Manassas to Appomatox,* p. 448; Cozzens, *This Terrible Sound,* pp. 410-411; Diary of Edward G. Whitesides, Adjutant, *125th Ohio,* Civil War Times Illustrated Collection, United States Army Military History Institute, Carlisle Barracks, Pa. The 1st and 4th Texas gained the hill but had to fall back under Harker's counterattack. The command of McNair's Brigade passed to Colonel David Colemn of the 39th North Carolina. The *105th Ohio* (900 men) outnumbered Benning's entire brigade.

34. *OR* 30, pt. 1, pp. 379-81, 394, 438, & 695; pt. 2, pp. 503-504; Archibald Gracie, *The Truth About Chickamauga,* p. 404; Judson Bishop, *Van Derveer's Brigade at Chickamauga,* p. 65; Cozzens, *This Terrible Sound,* p. 418; Franklin Gaillard to Maria Porcher, 5 October, 1863, Franklin Gaillard Papers, Southern Historical Collection, University of North Carolina; James M. Whallon to J.S. Fullerton, May 26, 1894, in *19th*

Illinois File, CCNMP Library; John Ramage to Chickamauga-Chattanooga National Battlefield Park Commission, 17 March, 1896, *121st Ohio* File, CCNMP Library. Kershaw's Hill is now the site of the South Carolina Monument. Stanley was wounded shortly after he arrived on the Horseshoe Line, and the command of the brigade devolved upon Colonel William L. Stoughton of the *11th Michigan.* The brigade numbered less than 500 men. Horseshoe Ridge was thickly wooded with visibility ranging from a few feet to about 100 yards.

35. *OR* 30, pt. 1, p. 389; pt. 2, pp. 461-462; Cozzens, *This Terrible Sound*, pp. 435-436; Gracie, *The Truth About Chickamauga*, p. 245; Humphreys, "History of the Sun Flower Guards", Claiborne Papers, SHC, UNC. The Crawfish Spring Hill that Humphreys mentioned is Snodgrass Ridge upon which Harker's Brigade was deployed. The Colt rifle was a potent weapon, and the *21st Ohio* had over 500 men.

36. *OR* 30, pt. 2, pp. 358 & 509; Longstreet, *Manassas to Appomatox*, p. 450.

37. *OR* 30, pt. 2, pp. 357-358; Longstreet, *Manassas to Appomattox*, p. 450.

38. *OR* 3o, pt. 1, p.252; Gracie, *The Truth About Chickamauga*, p. 54.

39. *OR* 30, pt. 1, pp. 858 & 860; pt. 2, p. 483; William Henry Harder, Diary and Memoirs, Harder Papers, Tennessee State Library and Archives (TSLA), Nashville, TN.

40. *OR* 30, pt. 1, p. 767; Gracie, *The Truth About Chickamauga*, p. 55.

41. William M. Owen, *In Camp and Battle with the Washington Artillery*, p. 281.

42. *OR* 30, pt. 2, pp. 79-80; Longstreet, *Manassas to Appomattox*, pp. 451-452; Daniel Harvey Hill, "Chickamauga-The Great Battle of the West" in *Battles and Leaders of the Civil War* III, p. 659. Longstreet rode about two miles to see Bragg whose headquarters was located in a small clearing a short distance to the south of the Brotherton-Reed's Bridge Road.

43. *OR* 30, pt. 2, pp. 415, 420-421, 462-464, & 470; Cozzens, *This Terrible Sound,* pp. 456-457; Reverend P.T. Martin, "Recollections of a Confederate," *Confederate Veteran* 15, p.231. From the Confederate left to right (west to east), the brigades of Deas, Manigault, Fulton, Sugg, and Anderson, with McNair's Brigade under Col. Coleman supporting, made the attack.

44. Longstreet to Bragg, 20 September, 6:15 p.m., William P. Palmer Collection of Braxton Bragg Papers, Western Reserve Historical Society, Cleveland, Ohio.

45. Cozzens, *This Terrible Sound,* p. 485; Gracie, *The Truth About Chickamauga,* pp. 37, 393-394. The information regarding the location and the time was obtained by Gracie from Buckner in a letter of September 20, 1905. Sunset was at 6:06 p.m.

46. *OR* 30, pt. 1, p. 884; Ambrose Bierce, *Ambrose Bierce's Civil War,* p. 37.

47. Longstreet to Bragg, 20 September, 6:15 p.m., Bragg Papers, Western Reserve Historical Society. The question has arisen as to whether this dispatch was written while there were still Federal units on Horseshoe Ridge or after the Federals had completely withdrawn. Steedman pulled the two brigades of the *Reserve Corps* out about six p.m., and various other reports cite "sunset" as the time that the withdrawal commenced. Longstreet wrote the 6:15 dispatch to Bragg after the Federal withdrawal had begun, but most certainly there were still Federal troops in the immediate vicinity.

48. *OR* 30, pt. 2, pp. 290 & 291; Thomas Livermore, *Numbers and Losses in the Civil War,* pp. 105 & 106.

49. Glenn Tucker, *Chickamauga: Bloody Battle in the West,* p. 337; Cozzens, *This Terrible Sound,* p. 454; Gracie, *The Truth About Chckamauga,* p. 56.

50. Gracie, *The Truth About Chickamauga,* pp. 57-59; Cozzens, *This Terrible Sound,* pp. 454-455.

51. Thomas Connelly, *Autumn of Glory: The Army of Tennessee 1862-1865,* pp. 224-228.

52. Judith Hallock, *Braxton Bragg and Confederate Defeat* II, pp. 75, 79, & 80.

53. Glenn Tucker, *Chickamauga*, p. 337; *OR* 30, pt. 2, pp. 290 & 502; Consultation of the author with Mr. James Ogden III, Ft. Oglethorpe, Ga., April 1, 1994; Correspondence between the author and Dr. William Garrett Piston. Dr. Piston noted: "...Longstreet did pay attention to the brigade level when conditions warranted and terrain made it possible— Antietam and Gettysburg provide examples of his checking with briga- diers and even leading a charge. Second...note the danger of a commander forgetting the level at which he should operate. In the thick woods at Pea Ridge, Price, McCulloch, & Van Dorn ceased to be wing and army commanders respectively, and began placing brigades into position. They lost sight of the big picture and contributed to Southern defeat. Longstreet, like every commander, had to decide where he was needed most. Given the terrain and the circumstance of his taking command, he did well not to be distracted by brigade level events."

54. Cozzens, *This Terrible Sound*, p. 454; Longstreet, *From Manssas to Appomattox*, p. 452; *OR* 30, pt. 2, pp. 304, & 512-513. Hood's Corps contained just about half of the infantry in the wing.

55. Consultation of the author with Mr. James Ogden III, Chickamauga-Chattanooga National Military Park, April 1, 1994. The whole discussion of the vulnerability of the Federal right to enfilade was undertaken at the suggestion of Mr. Ogden. The quote is his as well as the observation regarding the force on force application.

56. Longstreet, *Manassas to Appomattox*, pp. 449-451; Cozzens, *This Terrible Sound*, p. 455; Benjamin G. Humphreys, "History of the Sun Flower Guards," SHC, UNC; *OR* 30, pt. 2, p. 512; James Ogden III, interview with the author, March 9, 1993, Ft. Oglethorpe, Ga. The Prussian born Willich was a master tactician who wrote a manual regarding advancing and firing.

57. Gracie, *The Truth About Chickamauga*, pp. 57-58; Hallock, *Braxton Bragg and Confederate Defeat* II, p. 80.

58. Longstreet, *Manassas to Appomattox*, pp. 450 & 453; Cozzens, *This Terrible Sound*, pp. 454-455, & 608; *OR* 30, pt. 2, p. 521; pt. 4, p. 675. Longstreet wrote in his memoirs, "Day was on the wane...when Lt. Col. Claiborne reported that the cavalry was not riding in response to my calls. He was asked to repeat the order *in writing*" (my italics).

59. Report of Committee and W.L. Curry, 30 September, 1892, Eli Long Papers, United States Military History Institute, Carlisle Barracks, Pa.; John A. Wyeth, *With Sabre and Scalpel*, pp. 247 & 249; *OR* 30, pt. 1, p. 507; pt. 2, p. 521.

60. Judith Lee Hallock, *Braxton Bragg and Confederate Defeat* II, pp. 75, & 79-80; John B. Hood, *Advance and Retreat: Personal Experiences in the United States and Confederate Armies*, p. 63; Longstreet, Manassas to Appomattox, p. 452; *OR* 30, pt. 2, pp. 33, 303, 457, & 503. As Longstreet was with Hood, it is reasonable to assume that Longstreet gave Hood the order to go forward.

61. Connelly, *Autumn of Glory*, pp. 224-226; Wyeth, *With Sabre and Scalpel*, p. 247; Cozzens, *This Terrible Sound*, p. 466. The post-war writings about seizing the gaps behind the Federal line all enjoy twenty-twenty hindsight. This includes Longstreet's memoir. After the passage of time, and all of the troop positions were known, it became easy to suggest what should have been done. At the time, Longstreet was simply trying to get Wheeler to move up and reinforce the left wing.

62. Connelly, *Autumn of Glory*, pp. 227-228; Longstreet to Bragg, 20 September, 6:15 p.m., Bragg Papers, Western Reserve Historical Society; *OR* 23, pt. 2, pp. 924-925; Kate Cumming, *Kate: The Journal of a Confederate Nurse*, p. 129; Benedict J. Semmes to his wife, 24 September, 1863, Benedict J. Semmes Papers, SHC, UNC. Bragg was suffering from, among other things, chronic diarrhea. As darkness fell, no Confederate commander knew the true situation. Longstreet did not report that Rosecrans' Army had retreated because he did not definitely know this until the next morning.

63. William G. Piston, *Lee's Tarnished Lieutenant*, pp. 71-72; Jeffry D. Wert, *General James Longstreet, The Confederacy's Most*

Controversial General, p. 321; Gilbert E. Govan and James W. Livingood, *The Chattanooga Country, 1540-1976,* pp. 20-21; Busey and Martin, *Regimental Strengths at Gettysburg,* p. 130. Hood's and McLaw's Divisions attacked with just over 14,000 infantry on a front of approximately one mile at Gettysburg on the second day. At Chickamauga, Longstreet's wing initially occupied a frontage of approximately one and one-quarter miles. The southern-most brigades advanced a total of two and one-half miles.

CHAPTER 5

Longstreet and Jackson Compared

Corps Staffs and the Exercise of Command in the Army of Northern Virginia

by

R.L. DiNardo

*N*o event in American History has been written about in more extraordinary detail than the American Civil War. Campaigns, battles and individual personalities have been covered in what would seem to be exhaustive detail. Despite this wholesale consumption of wood pulp, however, there are some crucial issues that remain unexplored. One of these is how the Union and Confederate commanders and their staffs functioned during campaigns and battles. When one reads descriptions of Civil War battles, it all seems a little too cut and dried. One reads lines such as "Lee ordered, Jackson commanded, Longstreet attacked...," and so on. All this, however, invites an important question. How did Civil War generals exercise command? In earlier times, commanders such as Marlborough and Napoleon could survey battlefields such as Blenheim and Austerlitz in their entirety from a commanding position. Civil War generals such as Robert E. Lee, George G. Meade, Braxton Bragg, and William S. Rosecrans did not have any such luxury. Owing to the tactical dispersion created by rifled small arms and improved artillery, not even corps commanders such as James Longstreet, Stonewall Jackson, and John Sedgwick could observe all of the divisions under their command in a battle. How does one exercise command when the new element of tactical dispersion is added to the chaos of battle?

The crucial element here is the role of the staff. One often reads of staff officers, but little is written about their activities. Douglas Southall Freeman, for example, in his classic work *Lee's Lieutenants*, devoted an entire chapter in volume two to staff officers, "The Developing Staff."[1] Although Freeman, with his usual literary skill and flair, paints charming biographical portraits of the staff officers of the Army of Northern Virginia, he does not tell us a great deal about what they did. Longstreet's biographers, Hamilton J. Eckenrode and Bryan Conrad, described the principal officer of Longstreet's staff, G. Moxley Sorrel, as the best staff officer in the Confederate Army.[2] They do not explain, however, why Sorrel was such a good staff officer. The purpose of this article is to explore how Jackson and Longstreet employed their respective staffs, and what this tells us about "Stonewall" and "Old Pete" as commanders. Before continuing, however, one must ask why this work focuses on corps staffs, and on those of Jackson and Longstreet in particular? The answer to the first part of the question lays in the manner in which Robert E. Lee conducted his campaigns and fought his battles. Lee would give rather general directives, and then leave their execution to his able subordinates, most notably Longstreet and Jackson. Since it was then up to the two corps commanders to translate Lee's wishes into reality, it would be well worth examining the nuts and bolts of how they did it. The answer to the second part of the question is based on the sources available to us in pursuing our examination. Of all of Lee's major commanders, only Jackson and Longstreet were relatively explicit as to what their staffs did during operations. By contrast A.P. Hill, in his reports on the Third Corps' operations in the Gettysburg and Bristoe Station campaigns, did not even mention the names of his staff officers, let alone what they did.[3] Among the staff officers who served under Jackson and Longstreet, there are a large number of collections of wartime papers and diaries, as well as post-war correspondence.[4] Several officers from these staffs have left post-war memoirs of varying degrees of accuracy.[5] The same certainly cannot be said for A.P. Hill and J.E.B. Stuart.[6]

When the war began in 1861, staff practice in both the Union and Confederate armies was non-existent. The only staff regulations in the United States Army (which applied to the Confederate Army as well, since it was modeled on its Federal counterpart) dated back to the Revolutionary War.[7] In the words of Russell Weigley, "there was no staff school, no adequate theory of staff work, upon which to found adequate assistance to army, corps and division commanders in the complex work of caring for and moving thousands of men."[8] Thus, commanders were really left to their own devices when it came to the selection and employment of their staffs. This was clearly indicated in the Confederate War Department's regulations.[9]

In looking at how Jackson and Longstreet ran their operations through their staffs, a number of significant differences can be seen. These begin with the very criteria by which staff officers were selected. The major factor in Jackson's selection of staff officers was the connection they had to Jackson from his pre-war days in Lexington, Virginia. Among the officers who served on Jackson's staff, Alexander

S. "Sandie" Pendleton, Robert L. Dabney, George Junkin, and James Power Smith were acquainted with Jackson before the war.[10] Hunter McGuire, although not a pre-war acquaintance of Jackson's, had clearly established a personal relationship with him before Jackson appointed him medical director of the Army of the Valley in early 1862.[11]

This manner of selecting staff officers led Jackson to make some poor choices for his staff. The most notable of these was Robert L. Dabney, who was chosen by Jackson to be chief of staff largely on the basis of the fact that he was a preacher, and thus a moral man.[12] Fortunately for Jackson, Dabney resigned soon after the Seven Days campaign.

Jackson's relationship with his staff, while not strained, was not always as cordial as some post-war memoirs or biographies would have people believe. Part of this was due to the presence of a new member of the staff, who joined the staff at the onset of the Fredericksburg campaign. With the apparent lull in operations following Antietam, the Confederate War Department began to press Jackson for the submission of his battle reports, which he had not done since First Kernstown.[13] Instead of using his staff to prepare them, Jackson contacted a noted lawyer and diplomat, Charles J. Faulkner, and invited him to join his staff as his "senior adjutant general," in other words, his principal staff officer.[14] Faulkner's job was to prepare Jackson's reports, some of which Jackson dictated personally, all of which would naturally be subject to his approval.[15] Faulkner was indeed appointed to Jackson's staff with the rank of lieutenant colonel, with his commission being dated November 15, 1862.[16]

The addition of Faulkner to the staff was a tactless move on Jackson's part for several reasons, not to mention being militarily unsound. Faulkner, being about 56 years old at the time, was poorly suited to undergo the rigors of active military service. In the actual event, Faulkner played no part in the Fredericksburg campaign, and was not even mentioned in Jackson's report on the campaign.[17] The appointment was certainly not a popular one with some members of the staff. Jedediah Hotchkiss referred to Faulkner as the "...'chief of staff'..." in a post-war letter.[18] The quotation marks certainly seem to indicate that Hotchkiss did not take Faulkner seriously as a staff officer. Henry Kyd Douglas was much more direct about this matter. He considered Faulkner's appointment "manifestly wrong."[19]

It was also unnecessary in that there were others available for the task. The most logical choice was Sandie Pendleton. By that time he was, for all practical purposes, Jackson's chief of staff. He had been involved in all of Jackson's campaigns, with the exception of Second Manassas, and by the standards of the day, was certainly well-educated, having been a graduate of Washington College and a student at the University of Virginia.[20]

The appointment of Faulkner at so high a rank might have also surprised Jackson's staff in another way. Normally, Jackson was rather cheap with rank. This certainly grated with Pendleton. Although Jackson had been promoted to Lieutenant General on October 11, 1862, Pendleton was still a captain. The ambitious Sandie, who had in effect been Jackson's chief of staff since Dabney's resignation, felt his position entailed a commensurate rank. On November 15, 1862, he raised the issue in a letter to his mother:[21]

> Now I want your advice. The Genl. has received his as Lieutenant General and is thereby entitled to a staff of higher grade—I think I have fairly earned my right to a majority—but fear he does not agree with me. I know full well that he ought to have for his Chief of Staff an older and more experienced person, and one better fitted to make a good impression and take the position in society which the General's bashfulness renders unpleasant to him. He wants a companion also, and desires naturally to get a man

who can in some measure share his confidence. Feeling all this as I do, I feel also that it is due to myself not to let Gen. Jackson think I am beholden to him, willing to stay with him do all of the work, and be continually passed over. I want your opinion as to whether I am not shortly promoted, I had not better offer my resignation. I rather think my very doubt on this subject shows that I ought not. But I am decidedly in a quandary.

Eventually, Pendleton did receive his promotion, in January of 1863.

Jackson's slowness in promoting officers on his staff is perhaps understandable if we look at how he employed his staff on campaign and in battle. Edward Hagerman, in his book *The American Civil War and the Origins of Modern Warfare*, stated that Jackson's[22] concept of staff was more in the German than in the American tradition. He saw to it that officers or couriers from his efficient and well-organized staff were always present to give divisional commanders guidance with respect to orders or the plan of battle should they waver or be in doubt.

Nothing could be further from the truth. In fact, Jackson used his staff officers as nothing more than ciphers. Frank Vandiver commented that when Jackson created his staff as a brigadier general, he selected men such as Pendleton and Junkin because they were men who could be relied on to do promptly what Jackson told them to do.[23]

Hagerman's argument rests on an important but ultimately erroneous supposition. For staff officers to provide tactical coordination to Jackson's corps, Jackson would have to give them a reasonably clear idea of what his plans were. This flies in the face of Stonewall's well-known uncommunicativeness regarding his subordinate commanders. The same applied to his staff as well. During the Shenandoah Valley campaign, Jackson's secretiveness drove his badly harassed quartermaster, Major John Harman, to refer to Jackson as "crack-brained," and ultimately offer his resignation to Jackson, who refused it.[24] Henry Kyd Douglas wrote to Helen Macomb Boteler that Jackson had evidently not informed his staff of the impending move from the Shenandoah Valley to the Richmond area.[25]

The Fredericksburg campaign, however, provided perhaps the best example which illustrates the state of ignorance Jackson's staff was kept in. On December 5, 1862, Sandie Pendleton wrote to one of his sisters about the military prospects for the near future. "We, by we I mean the members of the staff, who judge from appearance and know nothing, do not consider a battle imminent."[26] Certainly, all the available evidence indicates that Jackson was not exactly a fountain of information to his staff.

The lack of information provided by Jackson to his staff was consistent with the manner in which Jackson employed them on campaign and in battle. For Jackson, the staff officer was basically a glorified courier, whose principal mission was to carry messages. This may well have been done in part because Jackson's headquarters suffered from a lack of enlisted men detailed for such duty. In a post-war memo to Jackson's British biographer G.F.R. Henderson, Dabney explained some of the problems involved in staff work:[27]

> What did I have for orderlies and couriers? A detail from some cavalry company which happened to bivouac near. Perfect stupes, even then demanded back by their Captain after three or four days service. They were sent to me without reference to their local knowledge of the roads, intelligence or bravery: most probably they were selected for me by their Captain for their lack of. Occasionally I got hold of a very good man, but could not keep him.

In this connection it is important to note that before the Second Manassas campaign, Lee assigned some 25 men from the Black Horse Cavalry to run a courier service between his headquarters and Jackson's while Stonewall conducted his march around John Pope's right flank.[28] Lee's action in this regard may have indicated a lack of confidence in Jackson's ability to keep him informed of his movements.

The reports dictated to or prepared by Faulkner and approved by Jackson give the clearest indication as to what his staff did during operations. The activities of his staff in the Fredericksburg campaign, for example, are covered in the following statement:[29]

> During the action I received valuable assistance in trans-mitting orders and discharging other duties from the following members of my staff: Col. S. Crutchfield, chief of artillery; Col. A. Smead, inspector-general; Capt. A.S. Pendleton, assistant adjutant-general; Capt. J.K. Boswell, chief engineer; First Lieuts. J.G. Morrison and J.P. Smith, aides-de-camp, and Second Lieut. W.G. Williams, engineer department.

A literal interpretation of this means that what these officers did was to physically carry messages, a task which Douglas, Smith and even Hotchkiss, who in some ways was the most important asset on the Second Corps staff, all performed.30

This interpretation is also supported by the circumstances of Sandie Pendleton's wounding at Fredericksburg. Pendleton outlined them in a letter to his mother the day after the battle. Pendleton was wounded in the afternoon while taking a message to General William Taliaferro, the commander of one of Jackson's reserve divisions.[31] Freeman claimed that the disabling of Pendleton "threw the staff work of the Second Corps entirely out of gear that afternoon," but did not explain how.[32] This statement, however, begs a question: if Pendleton was so vital to the Second Corps' staff work, why did Jackson send him off on an errand that any courier could have performed? The question becomes even more curious when one remembers that Taliaferro's Division was being called in to relieve A.P. Hill's Division after the major fighting was over, suffering only 190 casualties in the course of the day.[33]

There is also no indication at all that Jackson ever gave his staff officers any discretionary authority, with perhaps the singular exceptions of Stapleton Crutchfield, John Harman, and Wells J. Hawks, whose positions would necessarily require them to have some degree of authority. On the whole, however, Jackson demanded of his staff officers the same unquestioning obedience he demanded of his subordinate commanders.

The staff of Lee's second-in-command, James Longstreet, was quite different from Jackson's, beginning with the manner by which "Old Pete" selected his staff officers. Of all the officers on Longstreet's staff, only two of them, Thomas Walton and Peyton Manning, were either related to or acquainted with him from before the war.[34] If there was any quality Longstreet sought above all from his staff officers, it was intelligence. All of Longstreet's staff officers who left papers or memoirs show themselves to be men of high intelligence. Longstreet generally picked up his staff officers from anywhere he could. Thomas Goree, for example, met Longstreet on a train going from Galveston to Richmond.[35] Sorrel impressed Longstreet sufficiently as a volunteer aide-de-camp at First Manassas that Longstreet secured a permanent place on his staff for him.[36] Commissary officer Raphael J. Moses came to Longstreet's staff after proving his abilities in that position for Robert Toombs' Brigade and then D.R. Jones' Division, as did Osmun Latrobe, who also became a valued staff officer.[37]

The relationship between Longstreet and his staff was definitely cordial. The staff certainly understood their general, as the following letter from Goree to his mother indicates:[38]

At home with his staff, he is some days very sociable and agreeable, then again for a few days he will confine himself mostly to his room, or tent, without having very much to say to anyone, and is as grim as you please, though, when this is the case, he is either not very well or something has not gone to suit him. When anything has gone wrong, he does not say much, but merely looks grim. We all know now how to take him, and do not now talk much to him without we find out he is in a talkative mood.

Even Francis Dawson, certainly not one of Longstreet's most ardent post-war defenders from among his staff, welcomed him back with open arms when Longstreet returned to duty in October of 1864.[39] Perhaps the best measure of the wartime relationship between Longstreet and his staff is this; aside from Dawson, who did not get along with a number of members of the staff, Sorrel, who was promoted to brigadier general, and Raphael Moses, who wound up with a permanent position in Georgia by accident, all of Longstreet's staff remained with him throughout the war.[40] The close relationship of Longstreet and his staff lasted into the post-war period as well. After the war, Longstreet wrote to his staff officers, asking them for their photographs.[41] They also stood by Longstreet, even though some disagreed with him politically, long after Longstreet had been made a pariah in the South.[42]

Unlike Jackson, service on Longstreet's staff was rewarded lavishly with promotion. When it came to dispensing rank, as Moxley Sorrel put it, "there was no illiberality about him."[43] Goree, for example, rose to the rank of captain in less than a year.[44] Sorrel also enjoyed rapid promotion. In fact, if one compares the staffs of Jackson and Longstreet during the period before Jackson's death, on average Longstreet's staff officers were at ranks generally one grade higher than those of Jackson.[45]

The higher ranks accorded Longstreet's staff by "Old Pete" was consistent with the responsibility he placed upon them, and the manner in which his staff was organized and operated. In this regard, the difference between Jackson and Longstreet as commanders was literally like night and day. This began with the staff's organization. The biggest difference was the number of men permanently detailed to carry messages. Whereas Jackson had perhaps only a few men detailed to carry messages, in his Second Manassas/Sharpsburg report, Longstreet mentions his "party of couriers."[46] The couriers were drawn from a South Carolinian cavalry company, the Kirkwood Rangers, which provided "escort and courier service" for the First Corps headquarters.[47] This company had evidently been providing these services for Longstreet's headquarters since the corps was organized prior to the Second Manassas campaign, and continued to do so well into 1864.[48] Thus, while Jackson had normally only a detail (generally an officer and five men) to carry messages, one can reasonably assume that Longstreet had several times that number of men assigned to that duty.

Equally different from Jackson was Longstreet's habit of keeping his staff and subordinate commanders "in the know." We have a fine example of this from the Fredericksburg campaign. On November 22, 1862, Sorrel sent the following message to Longstreet's de facto chief of artillery, E. Porter Alexander:[49]

> Gen. Longstreet wishes you to ride on a-head and select positions at once for all of our batteries including the Washington Artillery and the Brigade Batteries. Please use dispatch. Gen. Longstreet will probably be at Gen. Lee's H.Q. which are on the Telegraph Road 2 1/2 miles from town.

This order is of great interest to us for two reasons. First, the precision of the order is noteworthy for an age when imprecision was often the rule and not the exception. Second, Longstreet has informed both Alexander and his staff officers where he can be found if needed. This is also in striking contrast to Jackson.[50]

Another remarkable aspect of Longstreet's staff was the degree of latitude they were allowed in making decisions. In his fine study of the Second Manassas campaign, John J. Hennessy noted that when Longstreet launched his decisive attack on August 30, 1862, with four divisions on a front a mile long, no more than forty-five minutes elapsed from the time the attack was conceived to the time it actually began.[51] How Longstreet was able to accomplish this and his staff's part in this was outlined in his report on the campaign: [52]

> To my staff officers—Maj. G.M. Sorrel, assistant adjutant general, who was wounded at Sharpsburg; Lieut.Col. P.T. Manning, chief of ordnance, Maj. J.W. Fairfax; Maj. Thomas Walton, who was also wounded at Sharpsburg; Capt. Thomas Goree and Lieut. R.W. Blackwell—I am under renewed and lasting obligations. The officers, full of courage, intelligence, patience and experience, were able to give directions to the commands such as they saw proper, which were at once approved and commanded my admiration.

In his report on Fredericksburg, Longstreet once again emphasized the "intelligent" nature of the service rendered by his staff.[53]

In this respect Moxley Sorrel, in his capacity as Longstreet's effective chief of staff, was certainly Longstreet's alter ego. Sorrel himself gave an excellent description of his role on the staff in his memoir. It is quoted here at length: [54]

> With the growth of Longstreet's command my duties had become doubly important, and with weighty responsibilites. The General left much to me, both in camp and on the field. As chief of staff it was my part to respond to calls for instruction and to anticipate them. The General was

kept fully advised after the event, if he was not nearby at the time; but action had to be swift and sure, without waiting to hunt him up on a different part of the field.

The change of movement of a brigade or division in battle certainly carried a grave responsibility, but it has often to be faced by the chief staff officer if the general happened to be out of reach. Nearly two years of war on a grand scale had given me experience and confidence, and Longstreet was always generous with good support when things were done apparently for the best.

During the battle of Fredericksburg, for example, it would seem that, from going through the material in the E. Porter Alexander Papers at the Southern Historical Collection at Chapel Hill, North Carolina, Sorrel spent his time writing dispatches to subordinate commanders.[55] Given the kind of latitude Longstreet gave Sorrel on other occasions, one can safely assume that part of Sorrel's duties would have included clarifying and interpreting orders to suit the immediate situation.[56]

We have three well-detailed examples of the kind of latitude Longstreet gave his staff. The first concerns Osmun Latrobe, who joined the staff just after Antietam, and the battle of Fredericksburg.[57] At one point during the battle, three Union regiments were preparing to charge a position held by part of Robert Ransom's Division. The three Federal regiments were in a position in which they were safely sheltered from infantry fire as well as from the closest Confederate battery, the Donaldsonville Artillery. Latrobe, then a captain, happened to be nearby.

Reports differ slightly as to what happened next. The battery commander, Captain Victor Maurin, stated that Latrobe "suggested" that a gun be brought forward from its emplacement to shell the three Union regiments, while Ransom's report stated that Latrobe "directed" that this be done. Semantic differences notwithstanding, the important thing here is that Latrobe's suggestion/direction was acted on immediately. Lieutenant R.P. Landry ordered a gun brought out from its emplacement into the open to fire on the three Union regiments, with Latrobe assisting the crew. Although several of the crew became casualties and the gun was eventually disabled (results that were not unanticipated), enough rounds were fired to drive off the threatening Union force.[58]

The second example comes from the second day at the battle of Chickamauga. During the course of Longstreet's successful attack on September 20, 1863, Sorrel observed a column of Union troops that he believed were reinforcing Union positions in the area (in fact they were retreating). Seeing their vulnerability to an immediate attack, Sorrel rode to Major General A.P. Stewart, and told him to launch an immediate assault against the Union column he had observed. Stewart, who was more accustomed to doing things by the book in the faction-ridden Army of Tennessee, refused to do anything without a written order from Longstreet, rejecting Sorrel's explanation that as Longstreet's chief of staff, he knew as much as Longstreet did about the situation, and spoke with his full authority. Fortunately for Sorrel, he found Longstreet nearby, who let Stewart know in no uncertain terms that Sorrel's orders were to be obeyed.[59] The attack was then launched and attended with great success. Sorrel's part in this was generously attested to by Longstreet in his report.[60]

The final example here comes from the battle of the Wilderness. On May 6, 1864, Longstreet's First Corps deployed for its attack against the left flank of the *Army of the Potomac*. Overlapping the extreme Union left between the Orange Plank Road and the Brock Road were three brigades from three different divisions of two corps, Wofford's and G.T. Anderson's of the First Corps, plus Mahone's of the Third Corps. Later on Joseph Davis' Brigade of the Third Corps was also involved in the action. Since Longstreet was involved in organizing and launching the attack of the major elements of his command, he told Sorrel to go out and take command of the afore-mentioned brigades and put them into an attack on the Union flank, according to Sorrel's recollection.[61] Sorrel accomplished this mission with the greatest success, contributing enormously to the general effectiveness of Longstreet's attack, which was halted only after Longstreet was wounded in a manner eerily reminiscent of Jackson's fatal wounding at Chancellorsville one year earlier.

Freeman, in *Lee's Lieutenants,* minimized Sorrel's part in this operation, giving credit instead to Mahone, as the senior brigade commander in charge of the operation.[62] To be sure, there is some evidence to support this. Both Mahone's report and Longstreet's endorsement of Mahone's promotion to Major General, dated July 14, 1864, name Mahone as the commander responsible for the execution of the attack of the four brigades.[63] Sorrel's role in this operation, however, cannot be understated. Of the five principals involved in the attack, Sorrel, Mahone, Wofford, Anderson and Davis, only Sorrel was in a position to know precisely what Longstreet's intentions were. In his report on the action, Longstreet credited Sorrel with having "conducted" the movement.[64] Finally, Sorrel's part in the operation earned him a promotion to brigadier general, something which would not have happened if he had not shown ability in the exercise of command over troops on the battlefield.[65] The idea of Jackson sending Dabney or Pendleton on such a mission is almost unthinkable.

What can we conclude from this examination of the staffs of Jackson and Longstreet? The most basic conclusion is that the way each staff was employed reflected each general's personality and approach to command. Jackson, who as a general might best be described as an erratic genius, took an almost Napoleonic approach to command. While his staff might have functioned well in an administrative sense, Jackson was in essence his own chief staff officer. While not a factor when Jackson was enjoying his good days, it became critical on Jackson's bad days, and even during some of his better battles. His two most notable failures as a commander were his inexplicably lethargic performance during the Seven Days, and at Fredericksburg, where he and A.P. Hill managed to leave a 600 yard gap in the line, which almost resulted in a disaster on the Confederate right flank.[66] In both cases a well-informed staff with wide latitude to make decisions in Jackson's absence or incapacity could have made a major difference. This even had an impact on Jackson's finest moment at Chancellorsville. Wise, in *The Long Arm of Lee*, asserted that Jackson distributed staff officers along the line to ensure that the troops were properly deployed and the attack properly conducted.[67] There is no direct evidence to support this, but if Wise's claim is true, Jackson's staff performed their tasks very poorly. In the deployment, Colquitt's Brigade overlapped that of Ramseur in the second line. Nicholls' Brigade, which was supposed to be in the second line, formed in the third by mistake.[68] When the attack was delivered, it quickly swept away the Union *XI Corps*, but then became very disjointed and rapidly lost its edge.[69] Thus, regardless of how well or poorly Jackson fought his battles, his staff did not play a major part in them.

Longstreet, by contrast, seemed to have a much better grasp of the elements of modern command. While it would be silly to claim that Longstreet was influenced by the developing staff practices in Prussia, (indeed, there is not one scintilla of evidence to support such an assertion), one can instead look to an element of Longstreet's character. Longstreet, like his friend and commander Robert E. Lee, was endowed with a healthy dose of common sense. Just as Longstreet's common sense would call to his attention the defensive power of the combination of field fortifications and the rifled musket, so it would also suggest to him the system of command he ultimately developed. In fact, one would do well to compare the way Longstreet ran the First Corps to the way Lee exercised command over the Army of Northern Virginia when it was at its height in the summer and fall of 1862. As Lee explained to Prussian observer Captain Justus Scheibert, his job was to get the troops to the right place at the right time. Once the battle began, matters were to be left largely in the hands of his subordinate officers.[70] Lee took a common sense approach to the exercise of command at the operational and tactical level. Realizing that close control would not be possible under the prevailing conditions of operational and tactical dispersion, Lee wisely chose to leave matters at those levels to his able subordinates. It can be plausibly argued that Longstreet, while wanting to maintain control over his command, realized he could not be everywhere. For him, the common sense approach would be to give his staff, and Sorrel in particular, the knowledge of his plans and the authority required to make decisions in his absence. This system of command served Longstreet well throughout the war.

Longstreet's most recent biographer, Jeffry D. Wert, asserted, correctly in my opinion, that Longstreet was the best corps commander in the Army of Northern Virginia, and arguably on either side in the war.[71] This was due in no small part to Longstreet's staff, as valuable an asset any possessed by a commander during the war.

Notes to Chapter 5

1. Douglas Southall Freeman, *Lee's Lieutenants* (New York, 1942-1944), Vol. 2, pp. 428-443.

2. Hamilton J. Eckenrode and Bryan Conrad, *James Longstreet: Lee's War Horse* (Chapel Hill, 1936), p. 364.

3. United States War Department, *Official Records of the War of the Rebellion* (Washington, 1880-1902), Series I, Vol. XXVII, Part 2, pp. 606-609 and Vol. XXIX, Part 1, pp. 426-427. (Hereafter cited as *OR*. All references to *OR* are from Series I, unless otherwise noted.)

4. For Jackson's staff, Alexander Pendleton, Jedediah Hotchkiss, John Harman, and Henry Kyd Douglas have left collections of papers or diaries. On Longstreet's side, the list includes Raphael Moses, E. Porter Alexander, Thomas Goree, and Francis Dawson.

5. Some examples include Gen. G. Moxley Sorrel, *Recollections of a Confederate Staff Officer* (New York, 1905), E. Porter Alexander, *Military Memoirs of a Confederate: A Critical Narrative* (New York, 1907), and *Fighting For the Confederacy* (Gary W. Gallagher ed.) (Chapel Hill, 1989), and Hotchkiss' diary, *Make Me a Map of the Valley* (Archie P. McDonald ed.) (Dallas, 1973). Much less reliable is Henry Kyd Douglas, *I Rode With Stonewall* (Chapel Hill, 1940).

6. For Hill's staff, there are only a few scattered letters. Professor James I. Robertson described the lack of information on Hill's staff as one of the real frustrations he encountered in doing the research for his biography of A.P. Hill. For Stuart's staff, the two most notable memoirs are H.B. McClellan, *I Rode With Jeb Stuart* (Bloomington, 1958) and the highly suspect Heros von Borcke, *Memoirs of the Confederate War For Independence* (New York, 1938), 2 Vols.

7. J.D. Hittle, *The Military Staff: Its History and Development* (Harrisburg, 1944), p. 165.

8. Russell F. Weigley, *History of the United States Army* (New York, 1967), p. 241.

9. Confederate States of America, War Department, *Regulation For the Army of the Confederate* States (New Orleans, 1861), pp. 73-74.

10. See for example W.G. Bean, *Stonewall's Man: Sandie Pendleton* (Chapel Hill, 1959), p. 8 and Frank Vandiver, *Mighty Stonewall*, p. 218. James Power Smith claimed to have met Jackson in 1859. Whether or not the meeting made any impression on Jackson is unclear, but when Smith was appointed to Jackson's staff just before Antietam, Smith claimed that Jackson asked specifically for him. James Power Smith, "With Stonewall Jackson," *Southern Historical Society Papers,* Vol. XLIII (1920): pp. 2, 17. (Hereafter cited as SHSP.)

11. Thomas J. Jackson to Dr. W.F. Carrington, January 28, 1862, Jedediah Hotchkiss Papers, Library of Congress, Washington, D.C. (Hereafter cited as Hotchkiss Papers, LOC.)

12. Vandiver, *Mighty Stonewall*, p. 218. Certainly one of the most confusing aspects of Civil War history is reconciling the inconsistencies in wartime terminology. For us, this principally concerns the term "chief of staff." Officially, the position did not exist in the Confederate Army. In the Army of Northern Virginia, officers such as Pendleton and Sorrel had the title of Assistant Adjutant General, although Pendleton did refer to himself in a letter to his mother as Chief of Staff. Alexander S. Pendleton to Mother, November 15, 1862, William N. Pendleton Papers, Southern Historical Collection, Library of the University of North Carolina at Chapel Hill, North Carolina. (Hereafter cited as Pendleton Papers, SHC.) In the Army of Tennessee, however, the term chief of staff was used all the way down to division level. *OR*, Vol. XX, Part 1, pp. 671, 692, 779, 850 and 915. See also June I. Gow, "Chiefs of Staff in the Army of Tennessee Under Braxton Bragg," *Tennessee Historical Quarterly*, Vol. XXVII, No. 4 (Winter 1968): pp. 341-360.

13. Vandiver, *Mighty Stonewall,* p. 442.

14. Thomas J. Jackson to Charles J. Faulkner, November 14, 1862, Thomas J. Jackson Papers, LOC.

15. Vandiver, *Mighty Stonewall,* pp. 442-443, and *SHSP,* Vol. XLIII, p. 40.

16. Service Record of Lieutenant Colonel Charles J. Faulkner, National Archives Records Section, Microcopy 331, Roll 91. (Hereafter cited as NARS M-331/91.)

17. *OR,* Vol. XXI, p. 635. Faulkner completed his reports on April 17, 1863. Hotchkiss, *Make Me a Map of the Valley,* p. 131. He then went on twenty days' leave and resigned on May 14, 1863. Service Record of Lieutenant Colonel Charles J. Faulkner, NARS M-331/91.

18. Jedediah Hotchkiss to William Chase, March 28, 1892, Hotchkiss Papers, LOC.

19. Douglas, *I Rode With Stonewall,* p. 210.

20. Bean, *Stonewall's Man: Sandie Pendleton,* pp. 11, 18-27.

21. Alexander S. Pendleton to Mother, November 15, 1862, Pendleton Papers, SHC.

22. Edward Hagerman, *The American Civil War and the Origins of Modern Warfare* (Bloomington, 1988), p. 112.

23. Vandiver, *Mighty Stonewall,* p. 149.

24. For Jackson's secretiveness, see John Harman to Col. A.W. Harman, April 23, 1862, Hotchkiss Papers, LOC. For his resignation, see John Harman to Col. A.W. Harman, May 15, 1862, Hotchkiss Papers, LOC.

25. Henry Kyd Douglas to Helen Macomb Boteler, July 24, 1862, Henry Kyd Douglas Papers, Special Collections Library, Duke University, Durham, North Carolina. (Hereafter cited as DU.)

26. Alexander S. Pendleton to Sister, December 5, 1862, Pendleton Papers, SHC.

27. Memo from R.L. Dabney to G.F.R. Henderson, part of R.L. Dabney to Jedediah Hotchkiss, March 31, 1896, Hotchkiss Papers, LOC.

28. John J. Hennessy, *Return to Bull Run* (New York, 1993), p. 94.

29. *OR*, Vol. XXI, p. 635.

30. Douglas, *I Rode With Stonewall*, p. 86, *SHSP*, Vol. XLIII, p. 28, and Hotchkiss, *Make Me a Map of the Valley*, p. 50.

31. Alexander S. Pendleton to Mother, December 14, 1862, Pendleton Papers, SHC.

32. Freeman, *Lee's Lieutenants*, Vol. 2, p. 437.

33. *OR*, Vol. XXI, pp. 675-677.

34. Francis M. Dawson, *Reminiscences of Confederate Service 1861-1865* (Baton Rouge, 1980), p. 87. Manning may have been acquainted with Longstreet from before the war, while Walton was an in-law of Longstreet's. Jeffry D. Wert, *General James Longstreet* (New York, 1993), pp. 63, 225.

35. T.J. Goree to Sarah Williams Kittrell Goree (Mother), Richmond, Va., June 23, 1861, in Thomas Jewett Goree, *The Thomas Jewett Goree Letters*, Vol. 1, *The Civil War Correspondence* (Langston James Goree ed.) (Bryan, Tex., 1981), p. 46. (Hereafter cited as Goree Letters.)

36. Sorrel, *Recollections of a Confederate Staff Officer*, pp. 25-26.

37. Raphael J. Moses Manuscript, p. 66, SHC. See also Wert, *General James Longstreet*, p. 211.

38. T.J. Goree to Mother, Near Centreville, Va., December 14, 1861, Goree Letters, p. 111.

39. Francis W. Dawson to Mother, October 13, 1864, Francis Warrington Dawson I and II Papers, DU. (Hereafter cited as Dawson Papers.)

40. Dawson thought Sorrel "bad-tempered and overbearing," quartermaster John Fairfax "clownish and silly," and Walton "supercilious." Dawson, *Reminiscences of Confederate Service 1861-1865*, pp. 128-129. Dawson went to Fitz Lee's staff in November 1864, although he boasted to his mother that Longstreet gave him up only reluctantly. Francis W. Dawson to Mother, December 17, 1864, Dawson Papers, DU. Moses became Chief Commissary for Georgia because the previous

Commissary, Major Locke, died while Moses was on a trip there to secure supplies in May 1864. Moses Manuscript, pp. 66-69, SHC. Sorrel left the staff in October 1864 at the request of A.P. Hill, who wanted him to take command of Ambrose R. Wright's old brigade. Sorrel, *Recollections of a Confederate Staff Officer*, pp. 263-266, Freeman, *Lee's Lieutenants*, Vol. 3, p. 633.

41. James Longstreet to T.J. Goree, New Orleans, February 25, 1866, Goree Letters, p. 265. Whether this had anything to do with the projected history of the First Corps or not is unclear. There is correspondence about that project between Goree and Alexander, who was to write it, but that correspondence took place during the 1870s.

42. See for example T.J. Goree to James Longstreet, May 17, 1875, James Longstreet Papers, SHC. See also Wert, *General James Longstreet*, p. 424.

43. Sorrel, *Recollections of a Confederate Staff Officer*, p. 106.

44. T.J. Goree to Mother, Near Centreville, January 18, 1862 and T.J. Goree to Mary Frances Goree Kittrell (Sister), Near Richmond, June 17, 1862, Goree Letters, pp. 125-126, 155.

45. This imbalance continued after Fredericksburg. Pendleton was promoted to major on January 3, 1863, but Sorrel was promoted to lieutenant colonel on June 23, 1863, a rank Pendleton did not attain until August 26, 1863. Service Records of Alexander Pendleton and G. Moxley Sorrel, NARS M-331/196 and NARS M-331/233.

46. *OR*, Vol. XII, Part 2, p. 567.

47. Sorrel, *Recollections of a Confederate Staff Officer*, p. 118.

48. Although Longstreet did not mention the unit by name, he stated in his Second Manassas/Sharpsburg report that the cavalry escort was commanded by a Captain Doby. *OR*, Vol. XII, Part 2, p. 568. Sorrel specifically mentioned the Kirkwood Rangers providing escort and courier service at the time of the Fredericksburg campaign, although he turned Captain Doby into Captain Tobey. Sorrel, *Recollections of a Confederate Staff Officer*, p. 118. The Kirkwood Rangers was organized in

November 1861 as part of Holcombe's Legion. In June 1862 it was assigned to the 6th Virginia Cavalry. From 1862 to 1864 it was commanded by Captain Alfred E. Doby. Its strength was probably anywhere from 75 to 100 officers and men. It is worth noting that Doby was killed in the same volley that brought Longstreet down at the Wilderness. General James Longstreet, *From Manassas to Appomattox* (Reprinted, New York, 1991), p. 564. Dawson also mentioned the circumstances of Doby's death, although he spelled Doby's name as Dobie. Francis W. Dawson to Mother, June 1, 1864, Dawson Papers, DU. For the information on the Kirkwood Rangers, I am indebted to Dr. J. Tracy Power of the South Carolina State Library and Archives, Columbia, South Carolina.

49. G.M. Sorrel to E.P. Alexander, 9 AM, November 22, 1862, Edward Porter Alexander Papers, SHC. (Hereafter cited as Alexander Papers.)

50. To be absolutely fair, Jackson could also give very clear orders, but in this area, like others, Stonewall was erratic. Some of his orders to Richard Ewell during the Shenadoah Valley campaign were models of clarity. See for example *OR*, Vol. XII, Part 3, pp. 889-891. On the other hand, consider the following message from Jackson to Harman: "A.S. Pendleton says to Major Harman at McDowell: 'The Gen'l says send a courier at once to Capt. Mason to bring on his working party at once. Let him start bright and early Monday morning and join us as soon as possible, wherever we are.'" John Harman to Col. A.W. Harman, May 10, 1862, Hotchkiss Papers, LOC.

51. Hennessy, *Return to Bull Run*, p. 459.

52. *OR*, Vol. XII, Part 2, p. 567.

53. *OR*, Vol. XXI, p. 571.

54. Sorrel, *Recollections of a Confederate Staff Officer*, p. 121.

55. See for example Sorrel to R.H. Anderson, December 13, 1862, Alexander Papers, SHC.

56. It is difficult to determine Sorrel's precise location during the battle. While Sorrel provided corroboration with other accounts that place Longstreet and Lee together during the battle,

Sorrel himself gave no indication of his own location. Sorrel, *Recollections of a Confederate Staff Officer*, p. 131. All of the orders emanating from Longstreet during the battle that have been preserved in the Alexander Papers, however, are in Sorrel's holograph.

57. Sorrel, *Recollections of a Confederate Staff Officer*, p. 118. See also Wert, *General James Longstreet*, p. 210.

58. For Maurin's report, see *OR*, Vol. XXI, pp. 620-621. For Ransom's report, see *OR*, Vol. XXI, pp. 625-628. Jennings Wise, claimed that Latrobe was sent by Longstreet to redeploy the gun, but there is no evidence to support such an assertion: Jennings C. Wise, *The Long Arm of Lee* (New York, 1959), p. 389. All available information indicates that Latrobe acted on his own initiative.

59. Sorrel, *Recollections of a Confederate Staff Officer*, p. 201.

60. *OR*, Vol. XXX, Part 2, p. 290. Unfortunately, we do not have Stewart's side of the incident. He certainly made no mention of it in his report. *OR*, Vol. XXX, Part 2, pp. 360-367.

61. Sorrel, *Recollections of a Confederate Staff Officer*, pp. 231-232.

62. Freeman, *Lee's Lieutenants*, Vol. 3, p. 361.

63. *OR*, Vol. XXXVI, Part 1, p. 1090, and Vol. XL, Part 3, p. 775.

64. *OR*, Vol. XXXVI, Part 1, p. 1055.

65. After Sorrel's departure, Osmun Latrobe took over as chief of staff. Wert, *General James Longstreet*, p. 394.

66. In Hill's case, he may well have been distracted by the fact that his eldest daughter, Netty, had died in the second week of December. James I. Robertson, *General A.P. Hill* (New York, 1987), p. 291.

67. Wise, *The Long Arm of Lee*, p. 471.

68. John Bigelow, Jr., *The Campaign of Chancellorsville* (New Haven, 1910), p. 291.

69. Robertson, *General A.P. Hill*, p. 184.

70. "General Robert E. Lee, Ober-Commandeur der ehemaligen Sudstaatlichen Armee im Nord Amerika," *Jahrbucher für die*

Deutsche Armee und Marine, Vol. XVI (September 1875): pp. 208-209.

71. Wert, *General James Longstreet,* p. 405.

CHAPTER 6

Marked In Bronze
James Longstreet and Southern History

by

William Garrett Piston

A man's place in history can be marked in bronze. Since the dawn of civilization, great men have been captured in effigy, their visage frozen in stone or metal for passage to future generations. Statues reflect cultural values, for they reveal to us what sort of man a particular society chooses to honor. The American South is rich in bronze, particularly Confederate bronze. Yet nowhere in the South, or in the whole nation for that matter, could you find prior to 1998 a statue commemorating Lieutenant General James Longstreet. Although he played a crucial role in the Civil War, Longstreet's reputation became tarnished in a manner which kept his image off of pedestals, and his name out of the pantheon of Confederate heroes.

Longstreet is the victim of a double standard in American history, for actions and characteristics which in others would be interpreted in a positive light have in Longstreet's case been interpreted negatively. Longstreet fought for a cause in which he believed, sacrificing his own fortune, welfare, and physical health, but when defeated he preached compromise and reconciliation with his enemies. In other men, such as Robert E. Lee, this is nobility of character, but Longstreet has been labeled a traitor for his actions. As a soldier, Longstreet sought every possible way to defeat his enemies, and he corresponded with those both higher and lower in rank than himself in an attempt to prosecute the war more effectively. In others, such as "Stonewall" Jackson, this is called drive and initiative, but in Longstreet it is interpreted as presumption and interference. Longstreet possessed a healthy ego, one neither larger nor smaller than those of his contemporaries. He enjoyed command and sought opportunities to exercise it. In Patrick Cleburne and Joshua Chamberlain this is called self-confidence, but in Longstreet it is labeled not merely egotism, but corrupting self-promotion. Longstreet sought alternatives to operations which promised to shed lives without reasonable hope of success. In William S. Rosecrans and Joseph E. Johnston, these traits have led historians to label them masters of maneuver and defensive warfare, but their display by Longstreet has led him to be described as obstinate and obstructionist.

The application of the double standard has not been limited to Longstreet's military record. He attended one of the best engineering schools of the nineteenth century, the United States Military Academy at West Point. Fifty percent of Longstreet's class washed out, and his graduation made him better educated than ninety percent of the American and European white males of his generation. But historians remember only that Longstreet graduated near the bottom of the fifty percent who survived, presenting his impressive educational achievement as if it were a shortcoming. Although he had no previous experience in politics, Longstreet became passionately involved in party activities following the war. So did P.G.T. Beauregard, Fitzhugh Lee, Winfield Scott Hancock, and a host of other West Pointers. Only in Longstreet's case is a fascination with politics seen as a personal weakness and a presumptuous entry into a field in which he had no business.

Longstreet did not routinely have a high portion of his command strung out as stragglers. He informed his subordinates thoroughly about his intended operations rather than keeping his plans obsessively secret. He did not habitually arrest his subordinates, suck on lemons, or attribute the outcome of battle to Divine Providence. He did not hire a banjo player, wear feathers, or flatter newspaper correspondents in order to get himself written up as a hero. Longstreet was a professional soldier, not a hypochondriac, an eccentric, or a fop. But like Omar Bradley of World War II, Longstreet's lack of flamboyance or idiosyncracies allowed hack writers to puff up men of lesser talent and present them as superior to Longstreet.

How does one account for the manner in which Longstreet has been misrepresented? His place in Southern history has actually been shaped by many factors. Of particular importance, however, was his membership in the Republican party during Reconstruction. In addition, there was the long-running controversy over the Battle of Gettysburg, in which he was blamed not only for losing the battle, but also for losing the war itself. As a result, Longstreet has the image not of a hero, but of a villain, even a Judas. He stands as a dark brooding presence behind the saber-wielding Cavaliers, explaining how a superior people could have lost the war—for surely the Yankees never beat the South in a fair fight!

As scapegoat of the Confederate defeat, Longstreet has affected our perceptions of the Civil War down to the present day. His negative image is all the more fascinating by being completely divorced from reality. It was artificially created by the General's postwar enemies, and by his own ineptitude as a politician and writer after the war. By joining the "enemy" during Reconstruction, Longstreet lost his status as a Confederate hero at a time when the Southern people, responding to the shock of defeat, were transforming their heroes from ordinary human beings into veritable saints. Robert E. Lee became the dominant Confederate hero only after his own death in 1870, when a group of Virginia officers launched an intensive campaign to make Longstreet publicly bear the blame for Lee's defeat at Gettysburg and for the loss of the war. This deification of Lee, analyzed in Thomas L. Connelly's 1977 book *The Marble Man; Robert E. Lee and His Image in American Society*, was actually first described in detail by Virginia-born author Marshall Fishwick in *Virginians on Olympus*, published in 1951.[1]

When Longstreet attempted to defend his reputation, his writings served to confirm rather than disprove his guilt in the eyes of many of his contemporaries, for in his prose Longstreet displayed, particularly in old age, vanity and jealousy which had not been evident during his wartime service. The deeply religious people of the South viewed Longstreet's alleged guilt as accounting for the failure of a righteous, God-fearing populace in its bid for nationhood. A plethora of novels, poems, and plays published in the nineteenth century reinforced Longstreet's infamy in the public eye by presenting his guilt as established fact rather than a matter open to debate.

This article concentrates on only one portion of Longstreet's complex story: the manner in which his military reputation came under attack, and his response to that attack. It reveals strengths and weaknesses in Longstreet which are a fascinating commentary on the human condition, providing insights not only into the manner in which history is made, but also into the complicated process by which history becomes a part of memory and written record.[2]

It is important to remember just how laudable Longstreet's reputation was in 1865. He served with the Army of Northern Virginia longer than any other high-ranking officer, including Lee. He was present at First Manassas and all the major battles from 1861 through 1863, except for Chancellorsville, when he was on detached service. Sent west to aid the Army of Tennessee, he performed brilliantly at Chickamauga, but his brief independent command in East Tennessee during the winter of 1863-1864 raised questions concerning his leadership. He returned to Virginia the following spring, only to be gravely wounded at the Wilderness, in an accident eerily parallel to the one that cost "Stonewall" Jackson's life. By the time he resumed active service in October 1864, Lee was pinned down to the trenches at Petersburg. When the end finally came the following April at Appomattox, Longstreet's proud First Corps was appropriately the last portion of the Army of Northern Virginia to lay down its arms.

Longstreet not only served widely, he served well. "Old Pete," as he was known to his comrades, was a tower of strength for the Confederate cause. Although he made his share of mistakes, his skill at directing troops in battle was without peer, and his strategic insights were remarkably sophisticated. His most recent biographer, Jeffry D. Wert, proclaims Longstreet "arguably the best corps commander in the conflict on either side."[3] It is not surprising, then, that four army commanders—Beauregard, Joseph E. Johnston, Lee, and Hood—sought Longstreet as their second-in-command. Longstreet, not Jackson, was Lee's most talented and most trusted subordinate.

Longstreet was also one of the most "modern" military thinkers of his time. This is apparent from his emphasis on field fortifications, and his identification of Northern civilian morale, rather than the Federal armies, as the proper target of Confederate strategy. It is also seen in the way Longstreet utilized his staff officers to direct his forces in battle. All too many Civil War commanders used their staff as glorified clerks and messengers. Jackson, for example, was notoriously secretive about his plans. Longstreet, however, thoroughly briefed his staff (which was headed for most of the war by the incomparable G. Moxley Sorrel). He used his trusted aides to issue orders upon his authority, allowing them interpret his stated intentions to meet the immediate circumstances at any given point on the battlefield. In an era before electronic communications, this was the most effective means of coordinating troops over a large geographic area, and it paid off for Longstreet at Second Manassas, Sharpsburg, Chickamauga, the Wilderness, and elsewhere.[4]

Longstreet thus ended the war with a highly laudable reputation. When Lee and Longstreet parted amid tears and hugs following Appomattox, any veteran of the Army of Northern Virginia would have felt safe in predicting that Southern history would honor both of these gallant men as long as anyone remembered the War Between the States. How then can one explain that a decade later Longstreet was a figure of scorn and derision? That one hundred years later, during the Centennial of the Civil War, Longstreet filled a villain's role? A consideration of these question can focus on three things. First, Longstreet's Republican affiliation and the significance of race relations. Second, the workings of the group I label the Anti-Longstreet Faction. Third, Longstreet's attempts to defend his military record. All are closely intertwined.

Longstreet's postwar affiliation with the Republican party was the greatest single factor in shaping his place in Southern history, as his actions during Reconstruction made him appear to be nothing less than a traitor to the white race. Following Appomattox, Longstreet settled in New Orleans, where he became a cotton broker in partnership with former general John Bell Hood. When Congress passed the Reconstruction Acts in 1867 that divided the defeated South into military districts, Longstreet was one of many former leaders who counseled peaceful submission as the quickest means of getting through the difficult period until the South's traditional conservative white leaders could return to power. But he went beyond others. In a series of letters, printed in the New Orleans press and widely copied by other newspapers, he urged Southerners to work within the Republican party rather than against it. While some Southerners lauded this Machiavellian scheme, most opposed it vehemently. Debate over Longstreet's suggestions raged from Massachusetts to Texas in newspaper articles, letters, and editorials. When Southern white Republicans (most of whom were former Whigs or Unionists) began to speak of Longstreet as one of their own, the ire of their Democratic opponents increased accordingly.[5]

To understand the severity with which Southerners reacted to Longstreet, one must remember that most blamed the recent devastating war directly on the aggression of the "Black Republicans." For Longstreet to advocate cooperation with the Federal occupation troops was acceptable, as the valor shown by Union soldiers during the war had been acknowledged and the soldiers were only doing their duty. But the slightest hint that Southerners themselves might join the abolition party was another matter entirely. The Republicans were seen as nothing less than a threat to Southern civilization. As one historian has noted, "In every ex-Confederate state a new Republican party—biracial in makeup, nationally rather than sectionally oriented—constituted a presence as unsettling to traditional southern life as the Union army or the Freedmen's Bureau."[6]

Longstreet's former comrades never seemed to appreciate that his interest in reconciliation with the North was matched by a determination to preserve much of the old order in the South. One reason for this misunderstanding was his failure in public letters to express his commitment to white supremacy as strongly as he did in private ones. For example, he wrote a colleague on July 4, 1867:[7]

> Congress requires reconstruction on the Republican [Party] basis. If the whites won't do this, the thing will be done by the blacks, and we shall be set aside, if not expatriated. It then seems plain to me that we should do the work ourselves, & have it white instead of black & have our best men in public office.

The permanent forced exile of former Confederate leaders did not seem an unlikely prospect when Longstreet wrote those words, thanks to the triumph of the Radical Republicans over President Andrew Johnson. Although Longstreet's concerns about expatriation were exaggerated, they were not unreasonable given the circumstances.

Race relations, not expatriation, however, were at the center of Longstreet's proposals for working with the Republicans. But the fact that Longstreet sought to control the black vote was largely lost on his fellow white Southerners, who saw only that he dared to collaborate with the party that had freed the slaves. For Longstreet exercised the courage of his convictions and eventually became a full-fledged Republican himself. This was a gradual decision, made over the course of two years, as he formed acquaintances in New Orleans with James F. Casey, John G. Parker, J. G. Taliaferro, and Henry C. Warmoth—men destined to play crucial roles in governing Louisiana over the next decade.

Why Longstreet found these men attractive is not clear. Like many former soldiers, he apparently found politics the sole activity which could approach military service in terms of excitement and power. In this respect he differed from his fellow Southerners only in his choice of political party—but that made all the difference. After wining a federal pardon, Longstreet endorsed his prewar friend Ulysses S. Grant during the presidential election of 1868. In addition, he accepted a number of lucrative political offices from the Grant administration and the carpet bag Louisiana state government over the next several years. These included the positions of surveyor of the port of New Orleans; levee board commissioner; adjutant general of the state of Louisiana; and commander of the Louisiana state militia.[8]

If Longstreet's contemporaries had been able to judge him in a vacuum, his pragmatic approach to Reconstruction might have been appreciated, if not endorsed. But Longstreet's actions occurred at a time of immense emotional turmoil throughout the South. To explain how a righteous cause, blessed of God, could fail, former Confederates devoted themselves to the memory of their own acts, cultivating an intensely nostalgic form of self-worship historians usually call the Lost Cause Myth. They exaggerated the characteristics of the antebellum South until it resembled a lost Eden. By focusing on Southern prowess on the battlefield, in terms of both the common soldiers and famous leaders, they made their very participation in the war a badge of honor which outshone defeat. The principles of total sacrifice and undying devotion which made Turner Ashby, "Stonewall" Jackson, and "Jeb" Stuart suitable wartime heroes made them also the first symbols of the Lost Cause. Lee joined this group of pristine heroes when he died in 1870 without writing any memoirs to alienate his former comrades in arms.

The defeated Confederates had only their pride, their honor, and their memories with which to face the formidable task of rebuilding the South. Given the Southern emphasis on masculinity and honor revealed in the studies of historian Bertram Wyatt-Brown, it should not surprise us that these defeated white males fixated on a pantheon of heroes, exaggerating the abilities of admittedly talented men until they assumed the status of demigods.[9] For with such men to emulate, it was easy following Appomattox for Confederate veterans to conclude that they had been overwhelmed, not really beaten, and that Reconstruction was a continuation of the same struggle in a different manner. When the South faced the supposed threat of "Negro Rule" rather than Northern bayonets, the loyalty given to Lee, Jackson, and others easily transferred to the Democratic party during Reconstruction. When Longstreet joined the Republicans instead of rallying to the Lost Cause, he exposed not only his present motives but also his Confederate past to attack. For unlike the other veterans who returned home to face Federal occupation, Longstreet's loyalty appeared to be quite limited and conditional. When self-advancement appeared to the Longstreet's motive, his wartime sacrifices were easily obscured by his image as a "scalawag."

By making defeat seem honorable, the Lost Cause heightened the South's already high concept of honor. Consequently, no group of men ever incurred greater dishonor in the eyes of their peers than the minority of white Southerners who supported the Republicans. "Scalawag" was a contemporary term for shabby, verminous cattle. "Therefore," wrote a Southern news article, "there is a manifest fitness in calling the native southerner, of white complexion, who adopts the politics of the Radical party, a Scalawag." Such men were seen as traitors not only to their region, but to the white race as well. A popular definition ran: "A scalawag is a white man who thinks that he is no better than a Negro and in so thinking makes a correct appraisal of himself."[10]

It is in this emotionally charged context that one must view the lasting consequences of Longstreet's actions in 1874. In that fateful year the Crescent City White League, a white supremacist organization led by former Confederate officers and manned largely by former Confederate veterans, attempted to overthrow the carpetbag government of Louisiana by force of arms. Longstreet commanded the state's militia and the metropolitan police force, which were composed almost entirely of former slaves. He led these black men into battle against the whites in the streets of New Orleans on September 14—and was both defeated and captured. Longstreet was released almost immediately by his captors, but his humiliation must have been acute. Although Federal troops eventually restored order, nothing could undo the damage to Longstreet's reputation.[11] The man whose attack at Chickamauga shattered the *Army of the Cumberland* had assisted former slaves in shedding the blood of some of the very men who had bought him his greatest victory! The New Orleans debacle received the widest possible newspaper coverage, and when Longstreet's heretical action became known, most Southerners were forever thereafter willing to believe anything negative about him, past or present. This was crucial to the success of the Anti-Longstreet Faction.

"Anti-Longstreet Faction" is an accurate label for the group of men within the Lee Cult who cooperated with each other over a period of more than a decade to erase Longstreet's name from Confederate history by attacking his military record and character, and also by refuting everything that he wrote, in self-defense or otherwise. The Anti-Longstreet Faction consisted primarily of Jubal Anderson Early, one-time commander of Lee's Second Corps; William Nelson Pendleton, Lee's chief of artillery; Charles S. Venable, A. L.

Long, Walter H. Taylor, and Charles Marshall, all officers on Lee's staff; Fitzhugh Lee (General Lee's nephew); and J. William Jones, a former chaplain in the 13th Virginia Infantry. They drew support from Confederate officers such as Braxton Bragg, John B. Gordon, Wade Hampton, William Preston Johnston, and Cadmus M. Wilcox, and also from the former Confederate president, Jefferson Davis. Their long-term campaign against Longstreet is amply documented in their surviving correspondences, located in archives across the nation.[12]

Motives within this diverse group varied. Early, Pendleton, and Jones, the triumvirate at the core of the Anti-Longstreet Faction, were weak, insecure individuals whose postwar manipulation of Lee's memory gave meaning to otherwise empty lives. For a while following Lee's death in 1870, Early's Lee Monument Association in Richmond squabbled with Pendleton's Lee Memorial Association in Lexington over the possession of Lee's remains and the erection of a suitable monument. But they began cooperating together in 1872, along with Jones, who became editor of the *Southern Historical Society Papers* the most popular postwar historical journal in the South. Connelly's book *The Marble Man* amply chronicles their Lee Cult, the manner in which these three men dominated Confederate veterans affairs, radically influencing Lee's image in history and the writing of Confederate history in general.[13] The focus here will be on their relations with Longstreet.

Early began the attack on January 19, 1872, when he delivered an address to commemorate Lee's birthday at Washington and Lee College, where Lee had been president until his death. (The school, located in Lexington, Virginia, was originally Washington College, but it was renamed following Lee's death.) Early asserted that during the night of July 1 at Gettysburg, in a conference with division commanders Ewell, Rodes, and Early, Lee had expressed his intention of attacking at dawn on July 2 with Longstreet's Corps. Had Longstreet attacked at the hour Lee intended, Early claimed, Lee would have won the battle and the South its independence.[14]

Early's motives deserve consideration, as he, more than any other man, convinced nineteenth century Americans and twentieth century historians that Longstreet's military career deserved censure. Profane and bad-tempered by nature, Early was a formidable soldier who conducted many skillful and daring operations. But his military career also included controversy and failure. His hesitation on July 1, when Cemetery and Culp's hills were still vulnerable, is considered by some to be one of the major blunders of the Gettysburg campaign. Late in the war he was so badly defeated while leading the Second Corps in the Shenandoah Valley that Lee relived him of command. Further humiliation followed, as Early fled the country after Appomattox, fearing retaliation for his having ordered the burning of Chambersburg, Pennsylvania, during a raid. Living in Canada in acute poverty, he wrote a caustic defense of his last campaign, only to have Lee politely but firmly withhold approval of either the book or his expatriation.[15]

Yet with this book Early found himself. Writing Confederate history became his passion, as it gave him the chance to achieve with the pen the reputation he had failed to win with the sword. Returning the Virginia in 1867, he filled Southern newspapers with such vitriolic attacks on Reconstruction that men who had previously considered Early a failure began to solicit his opinions with respect.[16] When Early attacked Longstreet in his 1872 speech, he could have felt confident that most Southerners would automatically support him against Longstreet, a man whose name was linked in the popular mind with disloyalty and betrayal.

Already seen as a Judas figure, Longstreet made a perfect scapegoat for the Confederate defeat. His loyalty seemed limited and his actions an insult to the Confederate dead. And with Lee no longer alive to set the record straight, Longstreet's military record was an easy target. It was particularly vulnerable if the person casting aspersions appeared to be defending the record of a soldier such as Lee who remained "true" to the cause.

Pendleton joined Early in condemning Longstreet when he delivered the Lee birthday address the following year. In a speech which he apparently modified upon Early's specific recommendations (there are numerous alterations in the manuscript text), he accused Longstreet of "culpable disobedience" and "treachery" in failing to attack at dawn on July 2. Lee's acceptance of responsibility for the defeat therefore amounted to a magnanimous cover-up unparalleled in history. As Christ assumed the burden of humankind's sins at Golgotha, Pendleton implied, so had Lee assumed the sins of Longstreet the Judas at Gettysburg.[17]

Despite his position on Lee's staff, Pendleton did not become intimate with the great Confederate commander until the postwar period when they both lived in Lexington. For as chief of artillery Pendleton had been notoriously incompetent, and his retention was often cited as a criticism of Lee. But like Early, Pendleton discovered that attacking Longstreet and praising Lee was a formula for winning the accolades he had not achieved on the fields of Mars. There was an additional facet to Pendleton's association with the Anti-Longstreet Faction, however. Although an Episcopal minister, Pendleton was tortured by religious doubts throughout his life, and he seized upon what he called "Lee's sacred memory" as a drowning man grasps a life preserver. Indeed, he devoted his life to enshrining Lee with such overtly religious fervor that anyone who reads his unpublished private correspondence must wonder whether in his later years Pendleton could distinguish between Marse Robert and Jesus of Nazareth at all. (Charles S. Venable, of Lee's staff, questioned Pendleton's mental stability.) Not surprisingly, Longstreet became something of an Anti-Christ for Parson Pendleton.[18]

Early and Pendleton were unmitigated, willful liars who hated Longstreet because of his postwar Republican affiliation. This fact is thoroughly established by frequent comments in their postwar private correspondence (neither man's wartime letters, official or private, held anything but praise for Longstreet). Their churlish fabrications should not have been credited. At Longstreet's request, a number of Lee's staff officers stated in print that Lee never ordered a sunrise attack. Moreover, Pendleton's own wartime report in relation to Gettysburg demonstrated that no dawn attack had been contemplated. But Early and Pendleton hired agents to tour the South and deliver their speeches as a means of raising funds for memorials to Lee.[19] Once Longstreet erased his own credibility with the Southern people by his heretical actions the streets of New Orleans in 1874, the Early-Pendleton version of Gettysburg found ready listeners. By placing the blame on Longstreet, they provided an explanation for the defeat which neither conceded the loss of God's Grace, not questioned Southern manhood. Thus was Longstreet's reputation tarnished at the grass roots level.

J. William Jones completed the triangle. A Baptist minister and born sycophant, he became intimate with the Lee family following the war. In 1874, with the family's blessing, he published *Personal Reminiscences, Anecdotes, and Letters of General Robert E. Lee.* The first fifty-five pages of this widely selling book were a verbatim reprint of Early's speech slandering Longstreet. As editor of the *Southern Historical Society*

Papers, Jones deferred constantly to Early and rejoiced in making the *Papers* a vehicle for destroying Longstreet.[20]

The Anti-Longstreet Faction quickly expanded, as events assumed a pattern of action and reaction. This brings in the third factor, Longstreet's writings. In 1874, the former commander of the First Corps wrote an article for the *New Orleans Republican* which denied the allegations of Early and Pendleton. Early counterattacked, reaffirming their claims in an article for the *Lynchburg Tri-Weekly Virginian*. Longstreet replied with a second article, suggesting that Early's perform-ance in the Shenandoah Valley disqualified him as a military critic. Such sarcasm was counterproductive, however, for most Southerners could remember only that since the war Early had been an outspoken critic of Reconstruction, while Longstreet had joined the Republicans. The greatest liability of Longstreet's article, however, lay in a single long sentence, which read: "As General Lee, upon assuming command of the Army of Northern Virginia, asked General Longstreet and other superior officers of that army their counsel as to the best plans to be pursued in our protection, and did General Longstreet the honor to adopt the plan he suggested, to cross the river and turn General McClellan's right, it may seem possible that General Longstreet had greater claims for respectful consideration than most of the young officers who volunteered suggestions."[21]

Lee's staff officers (Long, Marshall, Scott, and Venable) were aghast at this passage. Longstreet seemed to be setting himself up as the brains behind Lee, taking credit for Lee's victories. They had refuted Early's sunrise attack thesis because they knew it was erroneous, but in the wake of Longstreet's apparent egotism they enthusiastically joined Early's campaign to vilify Longstreet. A. L. Long now claimed that Lee had expected Longstreet to attack earlier than he did. This conveniently vague assertion provided common ground for men who combined a desire to free their beloved former commander from responsibility for the Gettysburg disaster with an increasing hatred of Longstreet because of his politics. They worked closely with Early thereafter. Taylor confided in a letter to him, "From the course pursued by Longstreet, I now feel that he should be handed with ungloved hands."[22]

Early himself remained the key figure. He sent unsolicited copies of his criticisms of Longstreet to influential people throughout the South, and the replies he received testify to the immediate, immense popularity of his derogatory attitude toward Longstreet. How easy it was to blame Gettysburg, the failure to win independence, and by implication all the woes of Reconstruction, on a scalawag! Fitzhugh Lee, Braxton Bragg, Wade Hampton, and other less prominent Southerners praised Early lavishly.[23]

Meanwhile, Alexander K. McClure, editor of the *Philadelphia Weekly Times,* jumped on the Gettysburg controversy as a means of boosting his paper's circulation, soliciting an article from Taylor on the Pennsylvania campaign. Taylor's piece accused Longstreet of deliberately delaying his attack on July 2 from the forenoon to the afternoon, the results being fatal to Lee's plans.[24]

Not surprisingly, McClure found Longstreet anxious to reply, which he did in "Lee In Pennsylvania" (November 1877) and "The Mistakes of Gettysburg" (February 1878). At first glance Longstreet's work seemed irrefutable. His lengthy quotation from letters by Lee's staff officers, including Taylor himself, demonstrated the perjury inherent in Taylor's new claim that he had been late. Indeed, Longstreet's writings might have won considerable popular approval had he taken into account when composing them that Lee had become a veritable saint in the eyes of many Southerners. Had he expressed profound reverence for Lee's memory and recounted his own actions in humble prose, he might have gotten a fair hearing despite his scalawag notoriety.

But Longstreet was neither humble nor reverent. Stung by the abuse he had suffered for his political convictions, Lee's Old War Horse lashed out almost blindly in print, making excessive claims for himself. His portrayal of Lee as a man who was often narrow and provincial in his strategic views was historically accurate, but hardly calculated to please his readers. Worst of all, in recalling discussions with Lee prior to the invasion of Pennsylvania concerning the propriety of using defensive tactics, Longstreet left the egotistical impression that he thought he had entered the campaign on some sort of contractual basis, after negotiating with Lee as an equal. Through such needless exaggeration and a general tone of arrogance, Longstreet gave his readers reason to suspect that self-advancement, not self-defense, was the motive for his writings. And because of his Republican affiliation, not one Southerner in a thousand was likely to concede that Longstreet had the right to criticize *any* soldier who had remained loyal to the Cause, much less the saintly Lee.[25]

While Longstreet was thus engaged in damaging his own reputation, Jubal Early renewed his attack, with a strategy that surpassed anything he had displayed during the war. In 1877 Louis Philippe Albert d'Orleans, Comte de Paris, a noted historian who visited American during the Civil War, wrote the Southern Historical Society seeking information on the battle of Gettysburg. On Early's instructions, Jones (who acknowledged his disgust at the way Longstreet was helping to "oppress the white people of La.") solicited manuscripts for publication in the *Papers* as replies to the Count, taking care to contact persons who could be counted upon to blame Longstreet. A lengthy piece by Early himself in August 1877 began what became known as the "Gettysburg Series." Early not only repeated his "sunrise attack" charges against Longstreet, he now claimed that Lee had expected Longstreet to send the divisions of John Bell Hood and Lafayette McLaws forward on July 3 as part of the famous (if misnamed) "Pickett's Charge." The next issues contained attacks on Longstreet by Lee's staff, and by other former Confederates who like Early had at Gettysburg been neither in a geographic position, nor in a position within the Confederate chain of command, to pass judgement on Longstreet's account of the battle. Early then persuaded Jones to reprint Longstreet's first article from the *Weekly Times*. Appearing in the January 1878 number of the *Papers*, it stood precondemned.[26]

As each month passed, the assault continued. The April issue contained a statement by former Maryland governor John Lee Carroll, who claimed that after the war he heard Lee blame Longstreet for losing the battle. In June, the *Papers* reprinted Longstreet's second article, followed by a point-by-point refutation by Early. The September number included an article by Cadmus Wilcox, who had commanded a brigade in A. P. Hill's Third Corps, accusing Longstreet of wilfully disobeying Lee's orders on July 2. William C. Oates, commander of the 15th Alabama at Gettysburg, made similar accusations in the October issue, bringing the series to an end.[27]

Most of these men were not intimate with Lee, nor were they privy to his plans, but that fact was lost on the public (as it would be on many twentieth century historians).

Gloating over their accomplishment, Jones wrote triumphantly to Pendleton, "I suspect Longstreet is very sick of Gettysburg before this. Certainly there has not been left 'a grease spot' of him."[28] The large number of articles in the "Gettysburg Series," the variety of the authors, and the inclusion (without his permission) of Longstreet's own pieces, left the false impression that Longstreet had been convicted by his peers of losing the battle of Gettysburg, but only after a fair and objective hearing. In fact, the deck had been stacked against him, and the so-called "evidence" consisted entirely of unsubstantiated accusations and innuendo. Jubal Early was the absolute master of this. In one of his articles he cleverly forced his readers to make a direct choice between Longstreet the Judas and the Christ-like Lee, by writing: "Either General Lee or General Longstreet was responsible for the remarkable delay that took place in making the July 2 attack. I choose to believe that it was not General Lee."[29]

Longstreet, of course, had not been late at all. When preparing his biography of Longstreet in the 1930s, Colonel Donald B. Sanger actually walked the ground traversed by Longstreet's troops at Gettysburg (something Jubal Early never did). Sanger's calculations indicate that Longstreet's men did not take an excessive amount of time to get into position. To date no one has discovered any letter, diary, or document of any kind composed or dated before Longstreet joined the Republicans which indicates that Lee expected Longstreet to attack earlier than he did. Unfortunately, rational calculations of how much roadway two infantry divisions occupy (seven miles), and when the *last* man at the end of a column of march can be ready for battle, were not the formulas by which Longstreet's peers would judge him.[30]

This was largely his own fault, although he, like other Civil War generals, continued to be exploited by publishers seeking sensational articles to boost their sales. When *The Century* magazine began its "War Series" (later reprinted as the four volume *Battles and Leaders of the Civil War*), Longstreet became one of its most prolific contributors.

The editors first asked Longstreet (who had moved from Louisiana to Gainesville, Georgia) for an article on Fredericksburg. Because the wound he received accidentally at the battle of the Wilderness made writing physically painful, they provided two assistants, *Atlanta Constitution* journalists Joel Chandler Harris (later famous as author of the Uncle Remus tales) and Josiah Carter. Longstreet eventually wrote five articles, covering the Fredericksburg, Peninsula, Second Manassas, Maryland, and Pennsylvania campaigns. Harris worked with him only on Fredericksburg (written first, but published fourth), while Carter handled the rest. Although Longstreet approved and was fully responsible for the contents of each piece, he granted Carter a free hand with the prose, instructing him, for instance to "touch up" the manuscripts "with as much pathos as you may be pleased to apply."[31]

Pathos not withstanding, Longstreet's *Century* articles served only to blacken his already tarnished reputation still further. The first article printed, "The Seven Days Fighting Around Richmond," appeared in July 1885. It contained criticisms of Jackson's sluggish performance which were quite justified. But Longstreet couched these in language bound to alienate not only Confederate veterans but the whole generation of Southerners who had grown up since Jackson had been martyred. Some of Longstreet's remarks seemed childish and petty, as when he wrote: "Jackson should have done more for me than he did. When he wanted me at Second Manassas, I marched two columns by night to clear the way at Thoroughfare Gap, and joined him in due season."[32] As in his articles for the Philadelphia *Weekly Times*, Longstreet left the conceited impression that he thought he had fought the war under some sort of contractual basis and that he alone had kept the bargains struck.

Jealousy of Jackson and belittlement of Lee's strategic ability pervaded Longstreet's next two articles for *The Century*. In "Our March against Pope," published in February 1886, he accused Jackson of not supporting him during some points of the campaign. He gave Jackson scant credit for his brilliant maneuvers against Pope, and none at all for his stalwart defense during the battle of Second Manassas. In "The Invasion of Maryland," which appeared in June of that same year, Longstreet slighted Jackson's capture of Harper's Ferry, arguing that McLaws had faced the greater danger.[33]

For anyone already prejudiced against Longstreet, much of what he wrote about Lee in *The Century* must have confirmed suspicions that he was stubborn and argumentative by nature and had sought to force his will upon Lee throughout the war. Hindsight thoroughly warped his narratives. No plan of Lee's was so good that Longstreet did not claim to have offered a better one, nor did Lee's strategy ever prove weak without Longstreet's having predicted that it would. Often Longstreet's prose seemed deliberately disparaging of his commander and nothing of their warm friendship and complete mutual trust was evident. Longstreet's portrayal of their relationship was often as distorted as anything his detractors invented. Readers in the 1880s, as well as future historians, would fail to appreciate how thoroughly Longstreet's *Century* articles were a product of frustration, a reaction to the years of abuse he suffered for his political affiliation, while Lee and Jackson, in contrast, were deified by the Southern people.

Longstreet's fourth article, on Fredericksburg, was markedly different in tone, perhaps because it was actually the first one written, and the only one prepared with the assistance of Joel Chandler Harris. It did not describe Jackson's reputation as inflated, nor criticize Lee.[34] One wonders if Harris was responsible for its moderation. Conversely, did Carter deliberately shape the other articles to provoke controversy and increase sales for *The Century?* While that is possible, Longstreet nevertheless wrote the rough draft of every article and approved the final drafts as well.

Longstreet's final article, "Lee's Invasion of Pennsylvania," appeared in February 1887. He largely refrained from ascribing specific times to events in his account of Gettysburg, but as in previous writings he described the campaign as if it had been a joint project he undertook only after negotiating with Lee as an equal. When Lee attacked, Longstreet implied, he broke an agreement between them that the Confederates would remain on the defensive. His own plans "would and could have saved every man lost at Gettysburg," yet the public perversely blamed him, rather than Lee, for the defeat.[35]

The general reaction to Longstreet's articles was quite negative. *The Century* printed some direct rebuttals, and he was sharply criticized in some of the articles other Confederates wrote for the series. That he was not more thoroughly abused was not fault of the magazine's editors, who sought articles from Jubal Early, Fitzhugh Lee, and Charles Marshall as responses to Longstreet. Marshall refused and Early merely granted them permission to reprint some of his previous writings attacking Longstreet. Fitzhugh Lee, who initially contacted Early to assist him with an article, produced nothing at the time; he was too busy exploiting his late uncle's famous name to win political office in Virginia.[36]

Jefferson Davis did reply, although in the pages of a different journal. Flattered by a long series of sycophantic letters from Early, who liked to tuck little gifts in with his communications, the former Confederate president had quoted Early's and Pendleton's accusations of tardiness against Longstreet in his tedious two-volume *The Rise and Fall of the Confederate Government* in 1881. In a piece published posthumously in January 1890 in the *North American Review*, Davis not only blamed Longstreet for the

Gettysburg debacle, he denied that Longstreet was exonerated by Lee's famous "all my fault" statement, which the Confederate commander had uttered following "Pickett's Charge."[37]

Meanwhile, Old Jube attacked Longstreet in the pages of the *State*, a Richmond newspaper, labeling him a "renegade," a "viper" and comparing him to a jackass.[38] Throughout the 1880s and 1890s members of the Anti-Longstreet Faction continued to publish books and articles making Longstreet the scapegoat for the Southern defeat and belittling his military record. Most notable were A. L. Long's *Memoirs of Robert E. Lee* and Fitzhugh Lee's *Robert E. Lee*, each of which enjoyed a wide audience.[39]

The acceptance by most late-nineteenth century Southerners of Longstreet's responsibility for Gettysburg was sharply illuminated by a lengthy series of articles in the *North American Review* by Sir Garnett Wolseley, the eminent Victorian soldier and scholar. The British author's writings provided an assessment of Longstreet's place in history as seen by a detached outsider. Wolseley accepted the *Southern Historical Society Papers'* "Gettysburg Series" and other writings by the Anti-Longstreet Faction as proof that the alleged failure by Longstreet lost the famous battle for the South. He thought Longstreet's criticisms of Lee and Jackson in *The Century* inappropriate and unseemly, concluding from them that Longstreet had fought the war in a mood of consuming jealously and with delusions of grandeur.[40]

In Wolseley's opinion, Lee's "all my fault" statement did more than testify to his Christ-like spirit; it marked Lee's superior devotion to the South and explained why Lee never charged Longstreet with any failures at Gettysburg. Wolseley wrote: "Nothing is more characteristic of [Lee] than that...he should realize how all-important it was to the cause of the Confederacy that no personal difference should arise between him and Longstreet, and that he should consequently have taken all the blame upon himself. Most soldiers will think that General Longstreet has not served his own cause well by appealing so much to the generous silence of his chief. He has, at least so far as all future histories of the war are concerned, deprived himself of the benefit of that silence by the way in which he has laid himself out to make charges against the chief who refrained, under the most dire provocation, from one word of reproach against him."[41]

With this argument the anti-Longstreet thesis in Southern history reached its fullest development. The fact that Lee never criticized Longstreet became acceptable proof of his guilt. The repeated assaults made by Early and his supporters and Longstreet's own exaggerated counterclaims were both necessary for such twisted logic to be embraced by an intelligent man such as Wolseley. Longstreet had proven to be his own worst enemy, fleshing out and lending credence to a picture of himself that the Lee partisans had created. Persons such as Wolseley, who knew neither Lee nor Longstreet, proved quite willing to believe that the postwar images of both men were historical reality, and all facts to the contrary were either consciously or unconsciously interpreted so that they would conform to these images.

Longstreet had the satisfaction of outliving many of his detractors. The Reverend Pendleton succumbed in 1883, while Jubal Early died in 1894 after falling down a set of stairs. Unfortunately, Longstreet's longevity enabled him to write more bad history. In his memoirs, published in 1896 under the title *From Manassas to Appomattox*, Lee's Old War Horse wallowed in the same mud as his detractors, using the same sorts fabrications and innuendo to attack the reputations of Early and his followers which they had used against him. His jealousy of the reputations of Lee and Jackson was more embarrassing than ever. He even wrote, in a footnote, that Jackson had temporarily absented himself from the field of battle at Sharpsburg for refreshments![42] In the final analysis, the Anti-Longstreet Faction had no greater ally than James Longstreet himself.

The above sketch is not, of course, the whole story. Many other factors shaped Longstreet's place in Southern history, among them the romantic, cavalier image of the Confederate hero that developed in postwar fiction and poetry. The establishment of Confederate veterans organizations, and the transformation of their ceremonies into a secular religion, were significant as well.[43] It is also important to note that condemnation of Longstreet was never universal. Although they disliked his politics, his staff remained loyal, as did his friends D. H. Hill and E. P. Alexander. Longstreet also received a great deal of affection from the veteran common soldiers of the First Corps, most of whom probably faulted him for Gettysburg, but saw him as a living symbol of the Cause, even though he persisted in supporting the Republicans to his dying day.[44]

When Longstreet passed away in 1904, he and those who had argued with him left behind a collection of writings calculated to mislead future historians—even brilliant ones such as Douglas Southall Freeman. Of the many twentieth century historians who have written about Longstreet, Virginia-born Freeman has been by far the most influential. As a researcher, Freeman had no peer, and the monumental multi-volume studies of Lee and his subordinates which he published in the 1930s and 1940s are rightly considered to be some of the finest historical works in the English language. But Freeman grew up in a time and place where the vilification of Longstreet was as much a part of accepted cultural norms as racial segregation.

In *R.E. Lee* Freeman often presents the Civil War in the eastern theater as much in terms of a contest of wills between

Lee and Longstreet as a struggle against the Yankees. This contest began at on August 29, 1862, at Second Manassas, when Longstreet suggested that Lee not attack. According to Freeman, the "seeds of much of the disaster at Gettysburg were sewn in that instant— when Lee yielded to Longstreet and Longstreet discovered that he would," for Longstreet concluded that "he could dominate Lee."[45] The subsequent contest at Gettysburg was actually lost not on the battlefield, but on the evening of July 1, "in the mind of Longstreet, who at his camp, a few miles away, was eating his heart away in sullen resentment that Lee had rejected his long-cherished plan of a strategic offensive and a tactical defensive."[46] In *Lee's Lieutenants; A Study in Command,* Freeman still blamed Longstreet for losing the war, although he modified his thesis somewhat. He portrayed Longstreet not so much as trying to force his will on Lee as being so stubborn by nature that he was unable to comply with Lee's orders with the speed and enthusiasm needed to ensure victory.[47]

In thirty-eight years of research Freeman never uncovered a single wartime document which reflected negatively on Longstreet's relationship with Lee; his criticism of Longstreet was based exclusively upon the postwar writings of Longstreet's avowed enemies. But his exhaustive works appeared to set the seal of professional scholarship on Jubal Early's long campaign of character assassination against Longstreet. Subsequent historians, noting Freeman's massive bibliography of primary source materials and the thousands of footnotes which meticulously documented his thousands of pages, accepted Freeman's conclusions without questioning the sources he used in relation to Longstreet.

Freeman is important not because he was a bad historian, but because he was, except when writing about Longstreet, a superb one, meticulous and painstaking in his analysis of Civil War personnel. The fact that Freeman was led astray says a great deal about the success of the Anti-Longstreet Faction. But no single person or factor created Longstreet's negative image. It resulted from a complex combination of personalities and circumstances. Contributing factors included Jubal Early's guilt for having fled the South in 1865 and his obsession with Confederate history as a means of assuaging that guilt and compensating for the disgrace in which his career had ended. They included the desire of William Nelson Pendleton and J. William Jones to bask in the reflected glory of Robert E. Lee, and win among Confederate veterans in peacetime a status they had not enjoyed as soldiers. It also involved, of course, the entire Southern reaction to defeat, Reconstruction, and race relations, which made Longstreet's Republican affiliation appear to be such an abomination and made his scapegoat role so believable. Finally, it included Longstreet's reaction to his accusers. When his own prose displayed such overt jealousy of the reputations of Lee and Jackson, and shamelessly exaggerated his own accomplishments, it is not surprising that many contemporary Southerners and later historians assumed the worst about him.

I concluded my 1987 study of Longstreet by stating that he had assumed a villain's role in Southern culture, and that scholarship alone would not change his place in Southern history. As long as Southern history remains something that is lived and felt as much as read, I argued, Longstreet will be remembered primarily as Lee's tarnished lieutenant. In terms of scholarship, both positive and negative appraisals continue. Longstreet received very favorable treatment in Jeffry D. Wert's 1993 biography *General James Longstreet; The Confederacy's Most Controversial Soldier.* But in 1995 Emory M. Thomas' *Robert E. Lee; A Biography* replicated Freeman's bias, citing the very writings by Longstreet's postwar enemies which have now been so thoroughly discredited.[48] Thus scholars continue to be divided in their assessment of Longstreet. But when one moves to the realm of public opinion, there is evidence that Longstreet's image and place in history are changing in a positive direction, thanks largely to the work of four individuals: Michael Shaara, Ted Turner, Garland Reynolds, and Robert C. Thomas.

In 1974 Michael Shaara wrote *The Killer Angels*, a novel about Gettysburg which presented Longstreet in a very positive light. Despite winning the Pulitzer Prize, it did not reach so wide an audience that it significantly modified Longstreet's popular image. Then, almost two decades later, Atlanta media mogul Ted Turner turned Shaara's novel into a marathon-length motion picture extravaganza entitled *Gettysburg*. The film leaves much to be desired, both in terms of drama and historical accuracy. The quality of the acting is extremely low and the attempts at Southern accents are laughable. The main characters look extremely uncomfortable in their cleanly pressed Hollywood costumes, and the lengths of their fake beards change from scene to scene in a most distracting manner. Some of the over-age, over-weight Civil War re-enactors who portray the soldiers look like refugees from a ZZ Top music video. But *Gettysburg* faithfully captures Shaara's laudatory portrait of Longstreet. Whether you agree with the author's portrayal of Lee as sickly and enfeebled is beside the point. Nor does it matter whether you laugh at Martin Sheen's goofy accent or Tom Beringer's ludicrous hat. For in *Gettysburg* Longstreet is freed from the vicious lies of Jubal Early and his coterie. Shaara's Longstreet is neither slow nor stubborn. He is instead competent, wise, forebearing and compassionate, Lee's friend and greatest source of strength.

Viewed by millions to date, with a prospective audience extending into the next century, Turner's movie has done, and will do, more to change Longstreet's image than either my biography or that of Wert, because despite its shortcomings *Gettysburg* is "felt" history of the most powerful type. Every time a white Southern male watches the re-enactors come out of the woods to line up for "Picket's Charge," reality is suspended and the fate of the Confederacy hangs in the balance. For in that wonderful extended sequence where the troops are getting into position, the audience is confronted with the same "everlasting if" which William Faulkner wrote about in his famous 1948 novel *Intruder in the Dust:*

> For every Southern boy fourteen years old, not once, but whenever he wants it, there is the instant when it's still not yet two o'clock on that July afternoon in 1863, the brigades are in position behind the rail fence, the guns are laid and ready in the woods and the furled flags are already loosened to break out and Pickett himself with his long oiled ringlets and his pistol in one hand probably and his sword in the other looking up the hill waiting for Longstreet to give the word...and that moment doesn't need even a fourteen-year-old boy to think *This time, Maybe this time....*[49]

Yet the contrast between readers of *Intruder in the Dust* and viewers of *Gettysburg* could hardly be sharper. The average reader of Faulkner in the 1940s, immersed in Lost Cause myths as codified by Freeman, would assume that Longstreet was the reason the South failed at Gettysburg, even though Faulkner never says so directly. Turner's audience in the 1990s, however, learns through the film that Longstreet is one of the primary reasons that the South nearly won.

It is unfortunate that projects with a goal more worthy than entertainment have not received as much attention as *Gettysburg,* for two men have all but moved mountains in their efforts to restore Longstreet's reputation. In 1994

Gainesville, Georgia, architect Garland Reynolds and other concerned citizens established the Longstreet Society in the general's hometown. The Society is working to restore a surviving portion of the Piedmont Hotel, which Longstreet owned, and establish within it a Longstreet museum, with emphasis on his postwar career. The Society's main goal, however, is patterned on Longstreet's own example of peaceful reconciliation. It sponsors and supports community projects, serving as a forum for mediation, reconciliation, and conflict resolution. Most recently, it played an important supporting role in the successful restoration of the Gainesville home of Beulah Rucker and the establishment of the Rucker Museum and Community center, thus honoring Beulah Rucker Oliver, a pioneering African American educator and champion of women's rights.

But no one has worked harder to change the general's image than Robert C. Thomas of Sanford, North Carolina. On his initiative, but with the support of many hard working men and women, the North Carolina Division of the Sons of Confederate Veterans established the Longstreet Memorial Fund on June 1, 1991, with the goal of placing an equestrian monument of Longstreet at the Gettysburg National Battlefield Park. Under Thomas's leadership, the Memorial Fund secured permission for the monument from the National Park Service, and the statue designed and sculpted by Gary Casteel, will be unveiled on July 3, 1998. Significantly, almost all donations have come from private sources, mostly in small amounts. Thomas and his friends have refurbished Longstreet's image at the grassroots level while establishing a permanent memorial to his valor.[50]

Longstreet's place in history can indeed be marked in bronze. His memory can be perpetuated in many ways for many reasons: by a novelist and by a broadcaster, to provide entertainment and make money; by his hometown, to foster a spirit of peace and reconciliation; and by the Sons of Confederate Veterans, to overturn more than a century of slander and achieve for a maligned hero a symbol of the status he richly deserves. For this is the human condition, simultaneously to embrace, manipulate, revere, and exploit our heroes, as we pass their memory down to succeeding generations. Like all monuments, any statue erected to honor James Longstreet must inevitably weather, its bright finish dulled by the forces of sun, wind, and rain. Ironically, such a faded visage will still be a major step in restoring Longstreet to his proper place in history, as Lee's *untarnished* lieutenant.

Notes to Chapter 6

1. Thomas Connelly, *The Marble Man; Robert E. Lee and His Image in American Society* (New York: Alfred A. Knopf, 1977); Marshall William Fishwick, *Virginians on Olympus; A Cultural Analysis of Four Great Men* (Richmond: p. pub., 1951).

2. For a fuller discussion of these issues, see William Garrett Piston, *Lee's Tarnished Lieutenant; James Longstreet and His Place in Southern History* (Athens: University of Georgia Press, 1987).

3. Jeffry D. Wert, *General James Longstreet; The Confederacy's Most Controversial Soldier* (New York: Simon and Schuster, 1993), 402.

4. Piston, *Lee's Tarnished Lieutenant*, 32, 34-35, 82-86.

5. Despite his overt hostility towards his subject, Thomas Hay remains the best source for Longstreet during Reconstruction; Wert's biography devotes scant attention to this portion of Longstreet's life. See Donald Bridgman Sanger and Thomas Robson Hay, *James Longstreet; Soldier, Politician, Officeholder, and Writer* (Baton Rouge: Louisiana State University Press, 1952), 322-75.

6. Morton Keller, *Affairs of State; Public Life in Late Nineteenth Century America* (Cambridge: Harvard University Press, 209.

7. James Longstreet to R. H. Taliaferro, July 4, 1867, collection of Edward M. Boagni, M.D., Baton Rouge, La.

8. Sanger and Hay, *James Longstreet*, 347-75.

9. See Bertram Wyatt-Brown, *Southern Honor; Ethics and Behavior in the Old South* (New York: Oxford University Press, 1982); *Honor and Violence in the Old South* (New York: Oxford University Press, 1986); *Yankee Saints and Southern Sinners* (Baton Rouge: Louisiana State University Press, 1985).

10. W. C. Elam, "A Scalawag," *Southern Magazine* 8 (April 1871), 456; Josephus Daniels, *Tar Heel Editor* (Chapel Hill: University of North Carolina Press, 1939), 129.

11. Sanger and Hay, *James Longstreet*, 370-71.

12. For the fullest analysis and most complete list of this correspondence, see William Garrett Piston, "Lee's Tarnished Lieutenant: James Longstreet and His Image in American Society," Ph.D. dissertation, University of South Carolina, 1982, 395-616.

13. Fishwick, *Virginians on Olympus*, 53-55; Connelly, *The Marble Man*, 20-30, 42-43.

14. Jubal A. Early, *The Campaigns of Robert E. Lee; An Address by Lieut. Gen. Jubal A. Early before Washington and Lee University, January 19, 1872* (Baltimore: John Murphy & Co., 1872), 29-32.

15. Millard Keesler Bushong, *Old Jube: A Biography of General Jubal A. Early* (Boyce, Va.: The Carr Publishing Company, Inc., 1955), 2, 14, 15-24, 30-34, 265, 286-87; Robert E. Lee to Jubal A. Early, Nov. 22, 1865, Jubal Anderson Early Papers, Library of Congress; Jubal Anderson Early, *A Memoir of the Last Year of the War for Independence In the Confederate States of America* (New Orleans: Blelock & Co., 1867).

16. Connelly, *The Marble Man*, 51-56.

17. For the text, with changes, see Piston, "Lee's Tarnished Lieutenant," 412-414.

18. Susan P. Lee, *Memoirs of William Nelson Pendleton* (Philadelphia: J. B. Lippincott Company, 1893), 30, 40, 50, 55-59, 67, 69-70, 138-40; Connelly, *The Marble Man*, 37-38; C. S. Venable to James Longstreet, n.d., James Longstreet Papers, Emory University.

19. Piston, *Lee's Tarnished Lieutenant*, 121-22.

20. Connelly, *The Marble Man*, 41; J. William Jones, *Personal Reminiscences, Anecdotes and Letters of Robert E. Lee* (New York: D. Appleton, 1874), 1-55; J. William Jones to Jubal A. Early, March 15, 1876, Early Papers.

21. Piston, *Lee's Tarnished Lieutenant*, 124-28.

22. A. L. Long to Jubal A. Early, March 13, 1876; C. S. Venable to Jubal A. Early, March 13, May 3, 1876; Charles Marshall to Jubal A. Early, April 10, 1876, March 24, 1877; Walter H. Taylor to Jubal A. Early, May 5, 1876, all in Early Papers.

23. For a complete discussion and list of this correspondence, see Piston, "Lee's Tarnished Lieutenant," 439-46.

24. Alexander K. McClure, *Recollections of Half a Century* (Salem, Mass.: The Salem Press, 1902), 400; Walter H. Taylor, "The Campaign in Pennsylvania," in *The Annals of the War Written by Leading Participants North and South* (Philadelphia: The Times Publishing Company, 1879), 305-318.

25. James Longstreet, "Lee in Pennsylvania," and "The Mistakes of Gettysburg," *ibid.*, 414-26; 619-33.

26. J. William Jones to Jubal A. Early, March 23, 1876; Feb. 16, March 22, 1877, Early Papers; Jubal Anderson Early, "Leading Confederates on the Battle of Gettysburg; A Review by General Early," *Southern Historical Society Papers*, IV (Dec. 1877), 241-302; "Letter from Gen. J. A. Early," *ibid.*, (Aug. 1877), 50-66; James Longstreet, "General James Longstreet's Account of the Campaign and Battle," *ibid.*, V (Jan. 1878), 54-86; Fitzhugh Lee, "Letter from General Fitz. Lee," *ibid.*, IV (Aug. 1877), 69-76; William Allan, "Letter from William Allan, of Ewell's Staff," *ibid.*, IV (Aug. 1877), 76-80; Walter H. Taylor, " Memorandum from Colonel Walter H. Taylor," *ibid.*, IV (Aug. 1877), 80-87; "Second Paper by Col. Walter H. Taylor, of Lee's Staff," *ibid.*, IV (Sept. 1877), 124-39; A. L. Long, "Letter from A. L. Long, Military Secretary to General R. E. Lee," *ibid.*, IV (Sept. 1877), 118-23.

27. John Lee Carroll to Fitzhugh Lee, April 15, 1876; Fitzhugh Lee to Jubal A. Early, April 29, 1876, Early Papers; Fitzhugh Lee, "A Review of the First Two Days' Operations at Gettysburg and a Reply to General Longstreet," *Southern Historical Society Papers*, V (April 1878), 162-94; James Longstreet, "General Longstreet's Second Paper on Gettysburg," *ibid.*, V (June 1878), 257-69; Jubal Anderson Early, "Reply to General Longstreet's Second Paper," *ibid.*, V (July 1878), 270-87; Cadmus M. Wilcox, "General C. M. Wilcox on the Battle of

Gettysburg," *ibid.*, VI (Sept. 1878), 97-124; William C. Oates, "Gettysburg—The Battle on the Right," *ibid.*, VI (Oct. 1878), 172-82.

28. J. William Jones to William Nelson Pendleton, Aug. 14, 1878, William Nelson Pendleton Papers, Southern Historical Collection, University of North Carolina-Chapel Hill.

29. Jubal A. Early, "Leading Confederates on the Battle of Gettysburg; A Review by General Early," *Southern Historical Society Papers* IV (Dec. 1877): 273-74.

30. Sanger and Hay, *James Longstreet*, 174-77.

31. Robert Underwood Johnson, *Remembered Yesterdays* (Boston: Little, Brown, and Company, 1923), 189-203; James Longstreet to Robert U. Johnson, July 31, Oct. 1, 1884; James Longstreet to Editors of *The Century*, Dec. 22, 1884; March 21, April 22, May 3, Dec. 20, 1885; Jan. 24, 1886; James Longstreet to Josiah Carter, July 10, Aug. 21, 1885, all in *The Century* Collection, New York Public Library.

32. James Longstreet, "The Seven Days Fighting Around Richmond," *The Century* XXX (July 1885): 470-74, 576.

33. James Longstreet, "Our March Against Pope," *The Century*, XXXI (Feb. 1886), 601-14; "The Invasion of Pennsylvania," *ibid.*, XXXII (June 1886), 309-15.

34. James Longstreet, "The Battle of Fredericksburg," *The Century*, XXXII (Aug. 1886): 609-626.

35. James Longstreet, "Lee's Invasion of Pennsylvania," *The Century*, XXXIII (Feb. 1887): 634-43.

36. Fitzhugh Lee to Jubal A. Early, June 29, 1883, Early Papers; Johnson, *Remembered Yesterdays*, 196.

37. Dunbar Rowland, *Jefferson Davis, Constitutionalist*, 10 vols. (New York: J.J. Little & Iver Company, 1923) 8: 5-25, 73-74, 82-105, 136-37, 300; 10: 112-13; Jefferson Davis, *The Rise and Fall of the Confederate Government* (New York: D. Appleton and Co., 1881), 441-42.

38. Jubal A. Early to Jefferson Davis, Jan. 19, 1888, enclosing clipping from *The State*, in *ibid*, 10:26-31.

39. A. L. Long, *Memoirs of Robert E. Lee: His Military and Personal History* (New York: J. M. Stoddart & Company, 1886); Fitzhugh Lee, *General Lee* (New York: D. Appleton and Company 1894).

40. Garnett Wolseley, "An English View of the Civil War," *The North American Review* CXLVIII (May 1889): 538-63; CXLIX (July 1889): 30-43; (Aug. 1889): 164-81; (Sept. 1889): 278-92; (Oct. 1889): 446-59; (Nov. 1889): 594-606; (Dec. 1889): 713-27.

42. *Ibid.*, (Sept. 1889), 289.

43. James Longstreet, *From Manassas to Appomattox* (Philadelphia: J. B. Lippincott and Co., 1896), 401n.

44. See Herman Hattaway, "Clio's Southern Soldiers: The United Confederate Veterans and History," *Louisiana History* XII (Summer 1971), 213-42; Charles Reagan Wilson, *Baptized in Blood; The Religion of the Lost Cause* (Athens: University of Georgia Press, 1980); Gaines M. Foster, *Ghosts of the Confederacy; Defeat, the Lost Cause; and the Emergence of the New South* (New York: Oxford University Press, 1987).

45. See Piston, *Lee's Tarnished Lieutenant*, 160-66.

46. Douglas Southall Freeman, *R.E. Lee; A Biography*, 4 vols. (New York: Charles Scribner's Sons, 1934-35), II, 325, 348.

47. *Ibid.*, III, 85.

48. Douglas Southall Freeman, *Lee's Lieutenants; A Study in Command*, 3 vols. (New York: Charles Scribner's Sons, 1942-44), III, 110, 113-22, 140, 143-48, 151-58, 161-67.

49. Emory M. Thomas, *Robert E. Lee; A Biography* (New York: W.W. Norton & Company, 1995), 297-303. Thomas cites A. L. Long and Charles Marshall. His account of Gettysburg is also based in part on the even greater bias and faulty analysis of historian Robert K. Krick.

50. William Faulkner, *Intruder in the Dust* (New York: Random House, Inc.), 194.

51. Bill Johnson, "Victory at Gettysburg; Longstreet Memorial Fund 'Takes the High Ground,'" *The Carolina Confederate* X (Nov./Dec. 1995), 6-7.

A Short Biographical Guide to Persons Mentioned in the Text

by

James R. Furqueron and Albert A. Nofi

NOTE: Prominent persons—Robert E. Lee, Braxton Bragg, Thomas "Stonewall" Jackson, to mention but a few—have been omitted from this guide, which concentrates on less well-known persons. Also omitted are persons mentioned only in passing.

Alexander, Edmund Brooke (c.1808-1888). A Virginia-born regular army officer (USMA, 1823), he saw extensive service on the frontier and in Mexico (2 brevets). For a time in the early 1850s, as a major, he was Longstreet's commanding officer at Fort Bliss. Colonel of the 10th Infantry from 1855, he remained loyal on the outbreak of the Civil War, but saw no active service, retiring in 1868 as a brevet brigadier general.

Alexander, Edward Porter (1835-1910). A Georgia-born regular army officer (USMA, 1857), he served on the frontier and as an instructor at West Point before the Civil War. Entering Confederate service, he was on Beauregard's staff at Bull Run. He shortly became an artilleryman, serving in the Peninsula, Second Bull Run, and Antietam campaigns, while rising to major. In November 1862 he was given command of an artillery battalion in Longstreet's First Corps, Army of Northern Virginia, which he commanded at Fredericksburg and Chancellorsville (at the latter while temporarily under Stonewall Jackson's command). At Gettysburg he directed the artillery preparation for "Pickett's Charge," despite there being two gunners superior to him in the chain of command. He went west with Longstreet in the fall of 1863, arriving too late for Chickamauga, but took part in the Knoxville campaign. In early 1864 he was commissioned a brigadier general of artillery, only one of three Confederate officers to attain that rank. He served with the Army of Northern Virginia through to the end of the war, being seriously wounded at Petersburg. Afterwards, Alexander taught, dabbled in business, and wrote *Military Memoirs of a Confederate.*

Anderson, George Thomas (1824-1901). A Georgian, Anderson served in the army as a volunteer during the Mexican War and again for several years during the mid-1850s. He was commissioned colonel of the 11th Georgia on the outbreak of the Civil War. Nicknamed "Tige," short for "Tiger," Anderson was given a brigade in what would become Longstreet's First Corps in time for the Seven Days, and commanded it for the rest of the war while rising to brigadier general in late 1862. After the war he was for a time engaged in railroading, but later served as chief of police for Atlanta and in Alabama.

Anderson, James Patton (1822-1872). Tennessee-born, before the Civil War Anderson practiced medicine in Mississippi, recruited the 1st Battalion, Mississippi Rifles, which he commanded in Mexico, dabbled in local politics in Mississippi, Washington Territory, and Florida, where he was a delegate to the state's secession convention. Commissioned colonel of the 1st Florida in March of 1861, he served under Bragg at Pensacola, and was promoted brigadier general in early 1862. Most of his wartime service was with the Army of Tennessee. He commanded a brigade at Shiloh, a division at Perryville, and a brigade at Murfreesboro, where his command was particularly honored for capturing some Federal artillery. Anderson led his brigade during the Tulla-homa and Chickamauga Campaigns, during which he was temporarily a division commander on two occasions, reverting to brigade command on 20 September, only to be given a division again that evening when Thomas C. Hindman was wounded. He commanded Hindman's division during the Chattanooga Campaign and subsequent Confederate retreat into Georgia, being promoted major general in early 1864. Anderson for a time commanded the District of Florida, but was recalled to the Army of Tennessee to once again command Hindman's division later in 1864. Severely wounded at Jonesboro (31 August 1864), he only returned to service in the closing weeks of the war, when he commanded a division under Joseph E. Johnston in North Carolina. After the war he edited an agricultural newspaper and served as a tax collector in Tennessee.

Bate, William Brimage (1826-1905). Born in Tennessee, Bate worked as a riverboatman on the Mississippi for a while, served as a volunteer in the Mexican War, edited a newspaper, read law, and later served in the Tennessee state legislature, while becoming a strong proponent of states' rights and secession. At the outbreak of the Civil War he was appointed colonel of the 2nd Tennessee, which he commanded at Shiloh, where he was severely wounded. Appointed a briga-dier general in October 1862, he was given a brigade in the Army of Tennessee, which he commanded from Murfrees-boro through Chattanooga and during the retreat into Georgia. Appointed a major general in early 1864, Bate was given a division, which he commanded during the Atlanta

Campaign and at Franklin and Nashville, and during the Carolina Campaign in the closing weeks of the war. After the war he practice law in Nashville, was elected governor of Tennessee for two terms, and served in the U.S. Senate from 1886 until his death.

Benning, Henry Lewis (1814-1875). A native Georgian, Benning graduated from the University of Georgia in 1834 and entered the practice of law, a profession in which he did well, rising to become an associate justice of the Georgia Supreme Court. Vice-President of the Democratic National Convention in Baltimore in 1860, which nominated Stephen A. Douglas for the Presidency, Benning was later a delegate to the Virginia Convention. Commissioned colonel of the 17th Georgia in August 1861, he led the regiment at Malvern Hill and Second Bull Run, and commanded Toombs' brigade at Antietam and Fredericksburg. Promoted brigadier general in April of 1863 (to date from 17 January), he commanded a brigade of Georgians at Gettysburg, Chickamauga, Knoxville, and the Wilderness, where he was severely wounded. Later returning to command, Benning fought through to Appomattox. After the war he returned to Columbus, Georgia, and resumed the practice of law. Nicknamed "Rock," Benning, who was part Cherokee, died on his way to court one morning.

Bierce, Ambrose Gwinett (1842-1914?). The tenth of thirteen children, Bierce was born in Ohio, but the family relocated to Indiana when he was a boy. At fifteen he left home and worked for a while on the *Northern Indianan*, a newspaper published at Warsaw, Indiana. He later spent a year at the Kentucky Military Institute, and then worked in a store-saloon in Warsaw until he enlisted in the *9th Indiana* on April 15, 1861. This began what one writer termed "the great educational nightmare of [Bierce's] formative years." With his regiment, Bierce saw action at Grafton, Girard Hill, and Carrick's Ford, in [West] Virginia during the spring and summer. When the regiment's initial 90-day enlistment was up, Bierce reenlisted in the regiment and was appointed sergeant-major, seeing action at Cheat Mountain. In February 1862 the regiment was ordered to Nashville, where it was incorporated in William B. Hazen's *19th Brigade, 4th Army of the Ohio* (later redesignated *2/2/Left Wing*, and still later, *2/2/XV*). Bierce served with the regiment on the second day at Shiloh and during the Corinth Campaign. He was shortly given a field commission to second lieutenant, and went on to fight at Stones River. In February 1863 he was promoted to first lieutenant and assigned as a topographical engineer on Hazen's brigade staff. Bierce idolized the tough, professional brigade commander, and served on his staff through the Tullahoma Campaign, at Chickamauga (Hazen's after action report included a commendation for Bierce), at Chattanooga, and in the Atlanta Campaign, where he was wounded at Kennesaw Mountain while directing the brigade skirmish line. Bierce shortly returned to duty and was present at Franklin and Nashville. He resigned from the army shortly before the war ended, with a brevet for major.

After the war Hazen unsuccessfully tried to secure for Bierce a captaincy in the Regular Army, and Bierce left the service over what he called the army's "ingratitude." Bierce held a variety of jobs, but by 1868 had begun a career as a writer and editor, which would make him "...America's unappeasable critic, the most unrelenting disturber of the peace until H.L. Mencken came along." His most notable works are *The Devil's Dictionary* and *Tales of Soldiers and Civilians.* He wrote some splendid horror stories, many with a Civil War theme. In October 1913 he said goodbye to all his friends, made a tour of the fields on which he had fought 50 years earlier, and went on into Mexico. He is last known to have been alive on December 26, 1913, when he posted a letter from Chihuahua, in which he indicated that he intended to travel to the city of Ojinaga. He was never heard from again.

Brannan, John Milton (1819-1892). A native of Washington, D.C., Brannan graduated from West Point in 1841 and entered the artillery. Regimental adjutant of the 4th Artillery during the Mexican War, he earned a brevet as captain for gallantry at Contreras and Churubusco. Remaining in the Regular Army, he held various assignments until appointed brigadier general of volunteers in September 1861. After coast defense duty on the Atlantic seaboard, he was assigned to divisional command in the *Army of the Cumberland*. During the Tullahoma and Chickamauga Campaigns he commanded the *3rd Division, XIV Army Corps*. On September 20 he organized the initial defense of Horseshoe Ridge. After Grant arrived in October 1863 he was made chief of artillery of the *Army of the Cumberland*, in which post he served until the end of the war. Breveted a major general in both the regular and volunteer armies, he continued on duty with the 1st Artillery until he retired in 1888.

Breckinridge, John Cabell (1821-1875). A native Kentuckian, Breckinridge studied law at Transylvania University before graduating from Center College in 1839, and practiced law in Lexington. Entering politics, he served in the Kentucky state legislature (1849-1851) and the U.S. House of Representatives (1851-1855), before being elected vice-president in 1856, the youngest (and arguably the handsomest) man ever to hold that position. Losing a bid for president in the four-way race of 1860 against Lincoln, Douglas, and Bell, Breckinridge was elected senator from Kentucky even before his term as vice-president was up, and after secession had begun to sweep the South. He served in the senate for several months in mid-1861, but came under suspicion of treasonous activities, and fled south in October of that year. Accepting a commission as a brigadier general in the Confederate army, Breckinridge commanded the Reserve Corps at Shiloh, shortly after which he was promoted major general. He served for a time in Louisiana, at Baton Rouge and Port Hudson, and at Murfreesboro commanded the 2nd Division of Hardee's corps, which made an ill-fated assault on the afternoon 2 January 1863, an incident which soured his relations with Braxton Bragg thereafter. In May 1863 he was sent with his division to Mississippi, serving in Joe Johnston's abortive attempts to relieve Vicksburg. Returning to Tennessee, he led his division at Chickamauga as part of D.H. Hill's corps, and commanded a corps at Missionary ridge. He later commanded the Department of Southwest Virginia, defeating Union Major General Franz Sigel at New Market (May 15, 1864). Transferred to the Army of Northern Virginia, Breckinridge commanded a division at Cold Harbor and accompanied Jubal Early's "Raid on Washington." For a time once again in command of the Department of Southwest Virginia, Breckinridge was appointed Secretary of War by Jefferson Davis on 4 February 1865. After Appomattox he fled south with the rest of the Confederate cabinet, and was present when Johnston negotiated the surrender of the Army of Tennessee to William T. Sherman. After the war he spent several years abroad before returning to Kentucky in 1869 to resume his law practice.

Brown, John Calvin (1827-1889). A native of Tennessee, Brown was an attorney in his home state. A Bell-Everett elector in the election of 1860, at the outbreak of the Civil War Brown enlisted in the Confederate Army as a private, but in May 1861 was made colonel of the 3rd Tennessee, which he led into Kentucky, only to be captured at Fort Donelson. Exchanged in August 1862, he was appointed brigadier general. Brown commanded a brigade at Perryville, where he was wounded, in the Tullahoma Campaign, at Chickamauga, Chattanooga, and through the Atlanta Campaign. Promoted to major general to rank from August 1864, he served in Hood's Tennessee Campaign, being so severely wounded at Franklin that he did not rejoin the army until April 1865. After the war he resumed the practice of law in his home state, was elected governor in 1870 and 1872, lost a bid for senator to former President Andrew Johnson in 1875, and went into the railroad business.

Buckner, Simon Bolivar (1823-1914). A Kentucky-born regular army officer (USMA, 1844), Buckner's early career included garrison duty and a tour as an instructor at West Point, before serving in Mexico, receiving a wound and two brevets. After the war he returned to West Point, served for a time on the frontier, and resigned from the army in 1855. Active in business and the state militia, at the outbreak of the Civil War Buckner strove to keep Kentucky neutral. However, declining a commission as brigadier general from Lincoln, in September 1861 he accepted one in the Confederate army. Sent to help relieve Fort Donelson in early 1862, Buckner ended up surrendering it to U.S. Grant when his pusillanimous superiors, John B. Floyd and Gideon J. Pillow, fled leaving him in command. Exchanged that August, he commanded a division at Perryville, and was later sent to supervise the fortification of Mobile. In May 1863 he took command of the Department of East Tennessee, until August, when he was ordered to bring his troops to Bragg's support at Chattanooga. Designated a corps commander in the Army of Tennessee, Buckner commanded Stewart's and Preston's divisions at the Battle of Chickamauga. After the battle he assumed direct command of Preston's old division, but became ill, and it was led by Bushrod Johnson during the Knoxville Campaign. In April 1864 Buckner assumed command of the resurrected Department of East Tennessee (Longstreet meanwhile having asked Jefferson Davis to give Buckner the gravely-wounded Hood's division in his corps, a request which the Confederate president refused, giving the command to the less able Charles W. Field). In May Buckner was transferred to the Trans-Mississippi Department under Lieutenant General E. Kirby Smith. He was himself promoted lieutenant general that September. From then until the end of the war, Buckner held a variety of posts under Kirby Smith in the Trans-Mississippi, at the end being appointed chief-of-staff, just seventeen days before the surrender. After the war Buckner settled in New Orleans, but returned to Kentucky in 1868. He became a newspaper editor, was elected governor in 1887, and ran for vice-president as a "Gold Democrat" in 1896 (his presidential running-mate was former Union Major General John McCauley Palmer, who had commanded *2/XXI* at Chickamauga). He was the last Confederate lieutenant general to die. His son, Lieutenant General Simon Bolivar Buckner, Jr., was killed in action on Okinawa in 1945.

Brooke, John Mercer (d.1851). Entered the Army as a first lieutenant in 1803. Brooke earned several brevets during the War of 1812, and by 1831 he was a colonel of the 5th Infantry. He held brevets in the rank of brigadier general (1828) and major general (1848).

Buell, George P. (1833-1883). A native of Indiana, Buell was a civil engineer when the war broke out. He volunteered and became colonel of the *58th Indiana*, commanding it at Stones River, where he assumed temporary command of Hascall's brigade on the night of December 31, 1862. Given command of the brigade in May 1863, he led it through the Tullahoma Campaign, the advance on Chattanooga, and at Chickamauga. After Chickamauga he was given command of the *Pioneer Brigade*. He continued in the regular army after the war, being breveted a brigadier general in 1867.

Brown, John Calvin (1827-1889). From Tennessee, Brown graduated Jackson College in 1846 and practiced law while dabbling in politics: In 1860 he was an elector for the Bell-Everett ticket. At the outbreak of the Civil War he entered Confederate service as a private, but was shortly commissioned colonel of the 3rd Tennessee, with which he was captured at Fort Donelson in early 1862. Exchanged in August, he was promoted brigadier general to rank from the end of that month. He led a brigade at Perryville, where he was wounded, through the Tullahoma Campaign, at Chickamauga, Chattanooga, and through the Atlanta Campaign. Promoted major general to rank from 4 August 1864, Brown was severely wounded at Franklin and did not rejoin the army until April of 1865, just before it surrendered. Returning to Tennessee, he resumed the practice of law, and was elected governor in 1870 and 1872. Defeated for the senate by former President Andrew Johnson, Brown engaged in the railroad business, and during the rest of his life was a railroad president.

Carlin, William Passmore (1829-1903). A native of Illinois, he graduated from USMA in 1850 and entered the infantry, seeing active service in the West. A captain in the Regular Army on the outbreak of the Civil War, he was commissioned colonel of the *38th Illinois* in August 1861. He commanded a brigade at Perryville, and was promoted brigadier general of volunteers in November 1862. He commanded a brigade at Stones River, in the Tullahoma Campaign, at Chickamauga, Missionary Ridge, and in the Atlanta Campaign, rising to division command in August 1864. By the end of the war he held brevets for major general in both the regular and volunteer service. Continuing in the Regular Army, he rose to brigadier general in 1893, and retired the same year.

Cheatham, Benjamin Franklin (1820-1886). A planter, the Tennessee-born Cheatham served as a volunteer officer in the 1st Tennessee early in the Mexican War, and was later colonel of the 3rd Tennessee. He joined the California gold rush in 1849, not returning to Tennessee until 1853. Active in local politics and the state militia, in which he rose to major general, he was made a brigadier general of the state's

"Provisional Army" on 9 May 1861, a rank confirmed when that body was absorbed into the "Provisional Army of the Confederate States." He commanded a brigade against U.S. Grant at Belmont, with whom he engaged in some friendly prisoner-of-war negotiations after the battle. Cheatham was promoted major general in March 1862 and commanded a division in the Army of Tennessee from Shiloh, through Perryville, Murfreesboro, Tullahoma, Chickamauga, Chattanooga, and Atlanta. When Hardee left the army in September of 1864, Cheatham assumed command of his corps, leading it at Franklin and Nashville. He surrendered with Joe Johnston in North Carolina in April 1865. After the war he resumed farming and served in various state and postal positions.

Clark, John Donnell (d.1848). An 1842 USMA graduate, Clark served with the 8th Infantry 1842 to his death from drowning in 1848, rising to brevet captain and regimental quartermaster during the Mexican War.

Clayton, Henry DeLamar (1827-1889). Born in Georgia, Clayton graduated from Emory and Henry College in Virginia, and went on to practice law in Clayton, Alabama. A member of the Alabama legislature from 1857, in March 1861 he was named commander of the 1st Alabama, and later organized the 39th Alabama, which he commanded at Murfreesboro, where he was severely wounded. Promoted to brigadier general to rank from 22 April 1863, he commanded a brigade in Stewart's division, Army of Tennessee, during the Tullahoma Campaign and at Chickamauga. Promoted major general to rank from 7 July 1864, he commanded Stewart's old division during the Atlanta Campaign and Hood's invasion of Tennessee. He surrendered with Johnston in North Carolina, and after the war engaged in planting and law in Alabama.

Crittenden, Thomas Leonidas (1819-1881). A native of Kentucky, he was the son of U.S. Senator John J. Crittenden, brother of Confederate Major General George B. Crittenden, and a first cousin of Union Brigadier General Thomas T. Crittenden. Admitted to the bar in 1840, during the Mexican War he served as an aide to Major General Zachary Taylor and was later colonel of the 3rd Kentucky (in which John C. Breckinridge was major). In 1849 President Taylor appointed him U.S. Consul at Liverpool, a post which he held until 1853, when he returned to the practice of law in his native state. After the Civil War broke out he held command of that portion of the state forces which remained loyal to the Union, and was commissioned a brigadier general of volunteers in October 1861. He commanded the *5th Division, Army of the Ohio*, at Shiloh, and was appointed major general of volunteers a few days later. At Perryville he commanded *II Corps* and at Stones River the *Left Wing*. The reorganization of January 9, 1863, saw his wing become the *XXI Corps*, which he led during the Tullahoma Campaign and at Chickamauga. When his corps was splintered during the second day's fighting at Chickamauga he retired to Chattanooga amidst the confusion that attended the break up of the Federal right. A subsequent court of inquiry exonerated him of any wrong doing, and found his actions fully justified, but his only subsequent command was that of a division in *IX Corps* in Virginia. He resigned his volunteer commission in December 1864 and in July 1866 entered the Regular Army as colonel of the 32nd Infantry, transferring to the 17th Infantry in 1869. He remained in command of the regiment until his retirement in 1881.

Crozet, Alfred St. Amand (d.1855). Son of Claude Crozet, a French émigré professor at West Point 1818-1823, Crozet graduated from the Academy in 1843. He served in the 8th Infantry 1845-1854, when he went on extended sick leave.

Crutchfield, Stapleton (1835-1865). A native Virginian, Crutchfield graduated from VMI in 1855 with first honors. He entered Confederate service as a major of the 9th Virginia in July 1861, from civilian life. That October he became a major in the 58th Virginia, rose to lieutenant colonel in early 1862. He shortly afterwards declined command of the 16th Virginia to accept a colonelcy in the artillery, becoming Stonewall Jackson's chief of artillery. Crutchfield served in this capacity until Chancellorsville, when he was severely wounded on 2 May 1863, losing a leg. He did not return to duty until March 1864, serving as an inspector of artillery until January 1865, when he commanded the fortress artillery in the Department of Richmond. Upon the evacuation of Richmond, he marched his brigade off to join Lee's army, became engaged in the Battle of Saylor's Creek, and was decapitated by a cannon ball on 6 April.

Dabney, Robert Lewis (1820-1898). A native of Virginia, Dabney was a Presbyterian minister. He entered Confederate service as chaplain of the 18th Virginia, but in April of 1862 reluctantly accepted appointment as Stonewall Jackson's chief-of-staff. Dabney served in this capacity during Jackson's Valley Campaign and the Seven Days, resigning in July of 1862 to resume his religious duties. In post-war years Dabney was a decidedly unreconstructed Confederate, and even proposed the emigration of Southern whites. Although apparently an able enough manager when not under pressure, Dabney appears to have lacked the temperament to serve as a staff officer during operations.

Davis, Jefferson Columbus (1828-1879). A native of Indiana, but of Kentuckian ancestry, Davis entered the army as an 18-year old volunteer in the 3rd Indiana during the Mexican War, and was commissioned in the Regular Army in 1848, as a second lieutenant in the 1st Artillery. In April of 1861, he was a captain in the garrison of Fort Sumter. Appointed colonel of the *22nd Indiana* in August 1861, he commanded a brigade at Wilson's Creek and the *4th Division* at Pea Ridge, and another during the siege of Corinth. In May 1862 he was promoted to brigadier general of volunteers to date from December 18, 1861. On September 29, 1862, he killed Major General William Nelson during a violent confrontation at a hotel in Louisville, a deed for which he was never called to account, due partially to Bragg's invasion of Kentucky, Buell's removal and then restoration to command, and the influence of Governor Morton of Indiana. He commanded the *1ˢᵗ Division, Right Wing,* at Stones River, and, after the army's reorganization, the *1st Division, XX Army Corps,* through the Tullahoma Campaign and at Chickamauga. He then took command of the *2nd Division, XIV Corps,* which he led at Chattanooga and through the Atlanta Campaign, after which he commanded *XIV Corps* during the March to the Sea and in the Carolinas Campaign. Breveted a major general in both the Regular and Volunteer Armies, after the war he served as colonel of the 23rd Infantry, taking part in the Modoc War. By some accounts he was a distant kinsman of Confederate President Jefferson Davis.

Davis, Joseph Robert (1825-1896). A nephew of Jefferson Davis, Joseph R. Davis was likewise a native of Mississippi. Educated at Miami University, Ohio, he practiced law in Madison County while dabbling in politics, entering the state senate in 1860. He entered state service as a captain in 1861, but was soon made lieutenant colonel of the 10 Mississippi. Promoted colonel, he served on the presidential military staff in Richmond for a time, before being commissioned brigadier general after an acrimonious debate over possible nepotism. He received a brigade in the Army of Northern Virginia, commanding it in all subsequent battles of the war (at Gettysburg his brigade formed one of the supports for "Pickett's Charge"). Paroled at Appomattox, he settled in Biloxi and resumed the practice of law.

Dawson, Francis M. One of Longstreet's staff officers, Dawson was the only one who had a prickly relationship with other members of the staff, being highly critical of several of his colleagues. In November 1864 he transferred to Fitzhugh Lee's staff. After the war he was the only one of the general's former staff officers who more or less sided with his critics. He wrote *Reminiscences of Confederate Services, 1861-1865*, and left some valuable letters and papers

Deas, George. A native of Pennsylvania, Deas received a direct commission in the Army in 1838. He served in the 5th Infantry, 1838-1861, rising to captain, with a brevet promotion to major for Contreras and Churubusco. On the outbreak of the Civil War he resigned from the Army and entered Confederate service, rising to lieutenant colonel and assistant adjutant general.

Deas, Zacariah Cantey (1819-1882). Born in South Carolina, Deas grew up in Alabama, where he was in the cotton business, at which he prospered. He served as a volunteer in the Mexican War, and on the outbreak of the Civil War raised and equipped the 22nd Alabama with his own funds. He led the regiment into Shiloh, assumed command of the brigade when Brigadier General Adley H. Gladden was mortally wounded, during which battle he was himself wounded. He commanded his regiment during Bragg's Kentucky Campaign and was promoted brigadier general to rank from 13 December 1862, but was not given a brigade until after Murfreesboro. He led his brigade through the Tullahoma Campaign, at Chickamauga and Chattanooga, in the Atlanta Campaign, and at Franklin and Nashville. After the war he moved to New York and resumed his business as a cotton broker, rising to a seat on the New York Stock exchange. He was a cousin of Confederate Brigadier General James Chestnut, Jr.

Douglas, Henry Kyd (1838-1903). A Virginian, Douglas was engaged in studying law when the Civil War broke out.

He enlisted as a private in the 2nd Virginia in April of 1861 and rose rapidly through the ranks, being commissioned a second lieutenant in August. In the spring of 1862 he was appointed assistant inspector general to Jackson's Valley District. His service thereafter was primarily in staff positions, mostly in Second (Jackson's) Corps, while he rose to major (May 1863). Captured at Gettysburg, he was not released until March of 1864, whereupon he resumed service as a staff officer, again mostly with Second Corps. During the last weeks of the war he was provisionally in command of a brigade. Arrested after Appomattox, being personally acquainted with several persons implicated in Lincoln's assassination, he was shortly released. After the war, during which he was wounded six times, he practiced law and managed some business interests, and wrote his memoirs, *I Rode with Stonewall.*

Faulkner, Charles J. A noted lawyer and diplomat, Faulkner became Jackson's "senior adjutant general" with the rank of lieutenant colonel (thereby senior to all of Jackson's other staff officers, including men who had been with him since first Bull Run) in November 1862, effectively his chief of staff. At 56, he was poorly suited for the task, and was often absent for reasons of health. In any case, his principal function appears to have been to prepare Jackson's reports. Not present for Chancellorsville, he resigned from the service shortly after Jackson's death. Unpopular in the army, Henry Kyd Douglas, a capable officer, termed his appointment "manifestly wrong."

Field, Charles William (1828-1892). A Kentucky-born regular army officer (USMA, 1849), before the Civil War Field served with the dragoons on the frontier and as a cavalry instructor at West Point, rising to captain. He resigned from the U.S. Army in May 1861, and was shortly commissioned a captain in the Virginia cavalry, in which he served under

J.E.B. Stuart. Appointed a brigadier general in March 1862, Field commanded an infantry brigade during the Peninsular Campaign, at Cedar Mountain, and at Second Bull Run, where he received a wound through the hips from which he never fully recovered. Returning to active service only in early 1864, Field was promoted major general in February and led Hood's old division in Longstreet's First Corps from then until Appomattox. After the war he was involved in business and civil engineering in Baltimore and Georgia until 1875, when he accepted a commission in the Egyptian Army. Returning to the United States in 1878, Field served as doorkeeper to the House of Representatives until 1881.

Fulton, John S. (1828-1864). A native of Tennessee, Fulton practiced law in his home state before the Civil War, and for almost a year after it began. Not until 27 March 1862 did he enlist, as a private in the 44th Tennessee. After Shiloh, the regiment was consolidated with the 55th Tennessee. Fulton was promoted captain on 18 April, major the next day, and elected colonel on 15 May by the company officers. He commanded the regiment in Bushrod Johnson's brigade of the Army of Tennessee at Perryville and Murfreesboro, and during the Tullahoma Campaign. Temporarily commanding Johnson's brigade in September of 1863, Fulton led it at Chickamauga, and then reverted to command of his regiment, which was shortly consolidated with the 25th Tennessee. He served under Longstreet in the Knoxville Campaign, where he once again assumed command of Johnson's brigade when Johnson assumed a divisional command. In the spring of 1864 the division, including Fulton and his brigade, was transferred to the east, serving in North Carolina and Southern Virginia. Heavily engaged in the fighting south of Richmond that spring, Fulton was mortally wounded in the trenches near Petersburg on 30 June, dying on 4 July 1864.

Garland, John (d.1861). Commissioned from civilian life in 1813, Garland saw no action during the War of 1812, but rose steadily in the post-war army, becoming lieutenant colonel of the 4th Infantry in 1839. Promoted colonel and brevet brigadier general for his services during the war with Mexico, in 1848 he became the father-in-law of James Longstreet. Thereafter, until shortly before his death in 1861, Garland exerted considerable influence in securing for Longstreet plum assignments.

Gibson, George (d.1861). A native of Pennsylvania, Gibson joined the regular army in 1808. During the War of 1812 he rose to field grade rank in the infantry, but was mustered out of service at the end of hostilities in 1815. He reentered the army in 1816 and was appointed Commissary General of Subsistence for the Southern Department, ranking as a colonel. Two years later he was made commissary general for the entire army, a post which he retained for over 40 years, meanwhile accumulating brevets to brigadier general in 1826 and major general in 1848. He died in September of 1861, by which time he had for several years been retired.

Gracie, Archibald, Jr. (1832-1864). Born into a wealthy New York family, Gracie was educated at Heidelberg before entering West Point, from which he graduated in 1854, as a brevet second lieutenant in the 4th Infantry. In March 1885 he was promoted second lieutenant in the 5th Infantry, with which he took part in the Snake River expedition. Resigning from the army in 1856, with the help of his father Gracie set himself up in the banking business in Mobile, at which he prospered. Meanwhile he entered the militia, becoming commander of the Washington Light Infantry. When Alabama seceded the company became part of the 3rd Alabama. In July 1861 Gracie was promoted major in the 11th Alabama, which he helped organize. The regiment shortly deployed to Virginia, where it joined what was to become the Army of Northern Virginia. During the opening phases of the Peninsular Campaign Gracie commanded a battalion of sharpshooters which helped cover the Confederate retreat.

Just before the Seven Days he was promoted colonel and given the newly organized 43rd Alabama, assigned to Kirby Smith's East Tennessee command. Although the regiment served during Smith's invasion of Kentucky in late 1862, it saw no significant action, but during the campaign Gracie received a brigade command, and was promoted brigadier general on 4 November. He spent the next ten months with his brigade guarding Cumberland Gap, in the Department of East Tennessee, which passed to Simon Bolivar Buckner's command, until August of 1863. When Buckner was ordered to join Bragg at Chattanooga, Gracie and his brigade went with him. At Chickamauga Gracie's brigade formed part of Preston's division, taking part in the assault on the Federal stronghold on the Horseshoe Ridge on the afternoon of 20 September. Despite tremendous casualties the brigade gained a foothold on the eastern hill of the ridge which it held for an hour. After Chickamauga, Gracie's brigade took part in the Knoxville Campaign under Bushrod Johnson. Although not engaged in the attack on Fort Sanders, it was heavily engaged in the subsequent action at Bean's Station, where Gracie was wounded. He did not return to his command until early 1864, when he accompanied it to Virginia, where the brigade became involved in the defense of Drewry's Bluff on 16 May 1864. The brigade was thereafter assigned to a portion of the trenches before Petersburg, and on 2 December 1864 Gracie was killed instantly by an exploding shell. His son, Archibald Gracie, Jr., wrote an exhaustive study of the fight for Horseshoe Ridge, *The Truth About Chickamauga*. The family's New York home is now the official residence of the mayors of the City of New York.

Granger, Gordon (1822-1876). A native of New York, he graduated from West Point in 1845 and earned two brevets in the Mexican War. Thereafter he served in the West with the Mounted Rifles (3rd Cavalry) until the outbreak of the Civil War. For gallantry at Wilson's Creek he was promoted colonel of the *2nd Michigan Cavalry*. In March 1862 he was promoted brigadier general of volunteers, and subsequently commanded the cavalry of the *Army of Mississippi* at New Madrid, Island Number Ten, and Corinth. Appointed major general of volunteers in September 1862, he commanded the *Army of Kentucky* and the *District of Central Kentucky* until June 1863, when those commands became the *Reserve Corps* of the *Army of the Cumberland*. He commanded this corps through the Tullahoma Campaign and at Chickamauga, where he distinguished himself with his timely arrival on the field with reinforcements and ammunition for Thomas' hard pressed forces on the Horseshoe-Snodgrass Ridge line. When the *XX* and *XXI Army Corps* were consolidated into the *IV Corps* in late September 1863, Granger became commander and he led the new corps at Missionary Ridge and in the relief of Knoxville. He subsequently commanded the *District of Southern Alabama, Department of the Gulf,* the *XIII Corps*, and the *Reserve Corps* at Mobile. Continuing in the Regular Army after the war, he died on active duty as colonel of the 15th Infantry. A hard-drinking, hot-tempered, out-spoken (he referred to Assistant Secretary of War Charles Dana as "a loathsome pimp.") disciplinarian, Granger appears to have run afoul of Grant after the latter came to Chattanooga in October of 1863, hence his relegation to peripheral commands after Missionary Ridge.

Gregg, John (1828-1864). A native of Alabama and an attorney, in 1861 he was resident in Texas, and served in that state's "secession convention" and as a delegate to the provisional Confederate Congress. In the Fall of 1861 he recruited the 7th Texas and commanded it until its surrender with the garrison of Fort Donelson in early 1862. Exchanged, he was promoted brigadier general. He commanded a brigade under Joseph Johnston during the Vicksburg Campaign, and in Bushrod Johnson's division at Chickamauga, where he was wounded. Upon returning to duty he assumed command of the Texas Brigade in the First Corps, and commanded it during Grant's Overland Campaign in 1864, until killed in action on the Darbytown Road on 7 October of that year.

Harker, Charles Garrison (1835-1864). A native of New Jersey, Harker graduated from West Point in 1858 and entered the infantry. Promoted to captain in the Regular Army in October 1861, he drilled Ohio volunteers and was shortly commissioned colonel of the *65th Ohio*. He led his regiment at Shiloh, and later was given command of the *20th Brigade,* which he led at Perryville. He distinguished himself in brigade command at Stones River and during the Tulla-homa Campaign. At Chickamauga, Harker's brigade (*3/1/XXI*) that delivered the timely counterattack which bought time for Brannan to organize the defense of the Horseshoe-Snodgrass Line, then defended Snodgrass Ridge until the Federal forces withdrew from the field. Harker continued in brigade command at Missionary Ridge and during the Atlanta Campaign, until mortally wounded at the head of his brigade in the attack on Kennesaw Mountain.

Harman, John For most of the war he served as a major and quartermaster general to Thomas J. Jackson, a singularly trying assignment, given the latter's lack of interest in the subject and his reluctance to impart his intentions to anyone. So frustrated was Harman that at one point he offered his resignation, which Jackson refused.

Harney, William Selby (1800-1889). Commissioned into the Regular Army in 1818, Harney served with distinction in the Florida War, and by 1836 was lieutenant colonel of the 2nd Dragoons, a rapid rise for the day. Promoted colonel of the regiment on the eve of the Mexican War, Harney was relieved of his command by Winfield Scott during the Mexico City Campaign, but was restored to duty by President James K. Polk, a life-long acquaintance. Harney distinguished himself at Cerro Gordo, earning a brevet promotion to brigadier general. He thereafter served against Indians in the West, rising to substantive brigadier general in 1858. On the outbreak of the Civil War he was commander of the *Department of the West*, at St. Louis. When he concluded an agreement with Confederate-sympathizers to permit the formation of a secessionist "State Guard" so long as it made no immediate overt moves against Federal authority, Harney was relieved of command. He retired in 1863, with a brevet for major general.

Harrison, Henry T. (c. 1832-1900). Apparently originally from Mississippi, a very hazy character known to his contemporaries only as "Harrison." One of the most effective intelligence operatives of the Civil War, and James Longstreet's most reliable intelligence operative. He began his espionage career as a scout for the Army of Northern Virginia, in late 1861. The following year he served as an agent for Confederate Secretary of War James A. Seddon. Early in 1863 he passed into Longstreet's service. During the Gettysburg Campaign, he was the first Confederate agent to report that George Meade had replaced Joseph Hooker in command of the *Army of the Potomac*, and the first to bring word that that army had crossed the river which was its namesake. He appears to have remained behind with the Army of Northern Virginia when Longstreet went to the west, and he was shortly discharged for drunkenness. He soon disappeared, despite efforts by Longstreet to locate him during the Knoxville Campaign. His true identity was not established until more than 120 years afterwards.

Hazen, William Babcock (1830-1887). Born in Vermont, Hazen's family early relocated to Ohio, where he grew up and formed a close friendship with James A. Garfield. An 1855 West Point graduate, he served in the infantry in the Pacific Northwest and Texas, where he was so severely wounded in battle with the Comanches in 1859 that he did not return to active duty until 1861. Meanwhile having been promoted to captain, he taught tactics at West Point until October 1861, when he was appointed colonel of the *41st Ohio*. He subsequently commanded the *19th Brigade, 4th Division, Army of the Ohio* during the second day's fighting at Shiloh and in the advance on Corinth. At Perryville he commanded his brigade in Crittenden's *II Corps*. At Stones River he commanded the *2nd Brigade, 2nd Division, Left Wing*. Promoted to brigadier general of volunteers in April 1863, he commanded a brigade through the Tullahoma Campaign, at Chickamauga, at Missionary Ridge, and during the Atlanta Campaign. In August 1864 he took command of the *2nd Division, XV Army Corps* and led it during the March to the Sea and in the Carolina Campaign. He commanded *XV Corps* May-August 1865, and in July 1866 was appointed colonel of the 38th Infantry. He transferred to the 6th Infantry in 1869, while being breveted a major general for war service In 1870 Hazen served as an observer with the German armies during the Franco-Prussian War. Promoted brigadier general in the Regular Army in 1880, Hazen became Chief Signal Officer and head of the Weather Bureau, posts which he held until his death. Responsible for dispatching A.G. Greeley's ill-fated Arctic Expedition, Hazen's criticism of Secretary of War Robert Lincoln's failure to authorize a timely relief effort earned him a court martial, headed by Winfield Scott Hancock. The resulting presidential reprimand did nothing to harm Hazen's career, since public sentiment was overwhelmingly on his side, as was that of all experts on arctic exploration. His Civil War memoirs were published as *A Narrative of Military Service* in 1885. Hazen was an outspoken critic of sloth and corruption, sparing neither subordinate nor superior. Ambrose Bierce wrote of him, "General W.B. Hazen, a born fighter...was the best hated man that I ever knew, and his very memory is a terror to every unworthy soul in the service....He was aggressive, arrogant, tyrannical, honorable, truthful, courageous, a skilled soldier, a faithful friend, and one of the most exasperating of men. Duty was his religion...."

Heg, Hans Christian (c. 1829-1863). A native of Norway, Heg emigrated to the U.S. as a young man and settled in Wisconsin. He essayed his chances during the California Gold Rush, but shortly returned to Wisconsin and became one of the state's prison commissioners. On the outbreak of the Civil War he resigned from the prison commission to raise a regiment of Scandinavians which became the *15th Wisconsin.* At the head of his regiment he fought at Island Number 10, Perryville, and Murfreesboro, after which he was given command of a brigade in the *1st Division, XX Corps,* which he led during the Tullahoma campaign and at Chickamauga where he was mortally wounded on the first day.

Hindman, Thomas Carmichael, Jr. (1828-1868). A native of Tennessee, he served in the 2nd Mississippi during the Mexican War, and then practiced law in his adopted state. In 1854 he removed to Arkansas, publishing a newspaper and dabbling in the state's rather violent brand of politics (along with his friend Patrick Cleburne he was once wounded during a politically-motivated ambush). Elected to Congress as a pro-slavery man in 1858, he was an ardent secessionist, and in May of 1861 was appointed colonel of the 2nd Arkansas. Named a brigadier general later that year, in early 1862 he commanded what amounted to a division at Shiloh. Shortly promoted to major general, he was assigned command in Arkansas to help stem a Federal offensive there. Suffering a strategic defeat at the Battle of Prairie Grove (7 December 1862), he was subsequently transferred. He served for a time on the Court of Inquiry looking into the loss of New Orleans. He was then assigned to the Army of Tennessee in July 1863, where he was given a division, and for a time a larger command, with which he did poorly. In this capacity he had the usual personality clashes with Braxton Bragg, but performed so well at Chickamauga –where he was wounded—that the latter gave him what was formerly Breckinridge's Corps after Missionary Ridge. He returned to division command when John B. Hood joined the Army of Tennessee in early 1864. He commanded his division throughout the Atlanta Campaign, until wounded at Kennesaw Mountain. Although upon recovery he sought command, he was thereafter inactive in the war. Briefly a resident in Mexico after the war, he shortly returned to Arkansas and plunged into Anti-Reconstruction politics, until murdered in 1868.

Hotchkiss, Jedediah (1828-1899). A native of New York, Hotchkiss settled in Virginia in the 1840s and founded a school. When the Civil War began, he volunteered as a cartographer, and served on the staff of Brigadier General Robert S. Garnett and later Robert E. Lee in [West] Virginia in 1861. Ill with typhoid for a time, in March 1862 he joined T.J. Jackson's staff in the Army of the Valley as a captain and Chief Topographical Engineer. He took part in Jackson's Valley Campaign, and later served on the staff of Second Corps in the Antietam, Fredericksburg, Chancellorsville, Mine Run, and Wilderness Campaigns, and during Early's Valley Campaign in 1864. A major at the end of the war, after it he was active in business affairs and veterans organizations. A brilliant cartographer and topographical engineer, Hotchkiss, certainly the best of Jackson's staff officers, was of critical importance in assisting in Jackson's most notable successes; at Chancellorsville, for example, it was he who discovered the trail that permitted Jackson's flank march.

Humphreys, Benjamin Grubb (1808-1882). Born in the Mississippi Territory, Humphreys entered West Point in 1825, but was dismissed for rioting on Christmas Eve of 1826. He took up planting and the law in his native state. An anti-secessionist, he nevertheless raised a company for the 2nd Mississippi at the outbreak of the Civil War, rising to command of the regiment by November of 1861. He led the regiment in all the battles of the Army of Northern Virginia (except Second Manassas) through Gettysburg, after which he succeeded to the command of Barksdale's brigade. Promoted to brigadier general, he led the brigade at Chickamauga, Knoxville, and the Wilderness, under Longstreet, and in the Shenandoah under Early, until wounded at Berryville in September 1864. He subsequently commanded a military district in Mississippi. After the war he entered politics as a moderate, becoming the state's first elected post-war governor, but was driven from office by radical elements. He thereafter became a planter and insurance broker.

Johnson, Bushrod Rust (1817-1880). Born to a Quaker family in Ohio, he graduated from West Point in 1840, with William T. Sherman and George H. Thomas. He served in the Florida War and along the Rio Grande during the opening operations of the Mexican War. After a short time as a subsistence commissary to Winfield Scott's army at Vera Cruz, he resigned from the service (in the midst of the war) and took up an academic post. By 1855 he was superintendent of the University of Nashville, while remaining active in the state militia of both Tennessee and Kentucky. When the Civil War broke out he entered Tennessee service as an engineer officer. Shortly passing into Confederate service, he was promoted to brigadier general in January of 1862 and commanded a division at Fort Donelson. Upon surrender of the fort he was able to elude captivity, and was assigned a brigade in Polk's Corps, which he lead at Shiloh, where he was lightly wounded. He commanded a division in the rear guard during Beauregard's retreat from Corinth later that year, but shortly reverted to brigade command. He led his brigade at Perryville and Murfreesboro, and during the Tullahoma Campaign. At Chickamauga he commanded a provisional division which saw some of the heaviest fighting.

He later commanded a division at Knoxville, under Long-street, and in the trenches before Richmond and Petersburg (it was on his front that the mine was exploded in the "Battle of the Crater") until their evacuation. His division was virtually annihilated at Sayler"s Creek. After the war he served for a time as chancellor of the University of Nashville.

Johnston, William Preston (1831-1899). The son of Con-federate General Albert Sidney Johnston, Preston W. Johnston had attended the Western Military Institute before taking up the law in Kentucky. At the outbreak of the Civil War he entered Confederate service as a major in the 2nd Kentucky Cavalry, transferring shortly to the 1st Kentucky Cavalry as lieutenant colonel, seeing combat at Danesville, Kentucky, in early 1862. In May of 1862 he was promoted colonel and became an aide-de-camp to Jefferson Davis. In this capacity he was at Seven Pines, made a tour of inspection of the Western Theater to investigate the situation there after Shiloh (where his father had been killed), becoming involved in an unseemly attempt to blame the Confederate defeat on Pierre G.T. Beauregard, thereby relieving his father of re-sponsibility. Johnston thereafter served on Davis' staff, and was a constant presence whenever the armies were operating near Richmond. Briefly jailed at the end of the war, he spent some time in Canada before returning to the U.S. to become a college professor and eventually a university president.

Jones, David Rumph (1825-1863). A native of South Caro-lina, Jones graduated from West Point in 1846. Service in Mexico brought him a brevet captaincy. However, despite marriage to a niece of Zachary Taylor, he was still only a first lieutenant when he resigned in February 1861. He served as a major and aide-de-camp to Pierre G.T. Beauregard at the bombardment of Fort Sumter (an inaccurate legend has it that he hauled down the American flag after the fort's surrender). Promoted to brigadier general in June 1861, he commanded a brigade at First Bull Run, and others through the summer, fall, and spring of 1861-1862. Promoted to major general in April 1862 (to date from March 10), he led a division in John Magruder's command during the opening phases of the Peninsular Campaign, and then in the First Corps, Army of Northern Virginia, fighting in the Seven Days, at Second Bull Run, South Mountain, and Antietam. Shortly afterwards a heart condition caused him to give up his command, and he died January 15, 1863. An able officer, Jones seems to have had a good eye for staff talent, selecting both Osmun Latrobe and Raphael J. Moses for his staff, both of whom later served Longstreet. An easy going man, his nickname was "Neighbor."

Kelly, John Herbert (1840-1864). A native of Alabama, he resigned from West Point when his state seceded and entered Confederate service. In September 1861 he was appointed a major in the 14th Arkansas Battalion, but shortly was transferred to the 9th Arkansas Battalion, which he led at Shiloh. Promoted to colonel of the 8th Arkansas, he led his regiment at Perryville, Murfreesboro (where he was severely wounded), and through the Tullahoma Campaign. At Chickamauga he commanded a brigade. Shortly promoted to brigadier general–the youngest in the Confederate Army at the time—he was mortally wounded at Franklin on September 2, 1864, while commanding a division of Joseph Wheeler's Cavalry Corps.

Kershaw, Joseph Brevard (1822-1894). A native of South Carolina, Kershaw, an attorney, served as a volunteer officer in the Palmetto Regiment during the Mexican War. Returning to his profession, he entered politics, served in the state legislature, attended the South Carolina "secession convention," and shortly volunteered for military service. Made colonel of the 2nd South Carolina in April of 1861, he served at Morris Island and at First Bull Run. Appointed a brigadier general in February of 1862, he commanded his brigade during the Peninsular, Second Bull Run, Antietam,

Fredericksburg, Chancellorsville, and Gettysburg Campaigns, then went west with Longstreet to fight at Chickamauga and Knoxville, accumulating one of the most distinguished records of any brigade in the war. He assumed command of McLaws' division when the latter was relieved by Longstreet. He commanded his division in the Wilderness, Spotsylvania, Cold Harbor, Petersburg and Cedar Creek, being promoted to major general in May, 1864. Captured at Sayler's Creek, he was briefly imprisoned. After the war he returned to South Carolina to practice law, entered politics, serving as a state senator and judge.

Latrobe, Osmun. Served as a staff officer successively in Robert Toombs' brigade, D.R. Jones' division , and, shortly before Antietam, to Longstreet's corps, rising from brigade commissary to corps chief of staff, a post which he assumed after Sorrel received a brigade. He was a very capable officer, with considerable initiative.

Law, Evander McIvor. (1856-1920). A native of South Carolina, he graduated from The Citadel in 1856 and became a teacher, helping to found a military high school in Tuskegee, Alabama. When the Civil War broke out, he recruited a company for the 4th Alabama, of which he was shortly promoted to lieutenant colonel. Severely wounded at First Manassas, Law was elected colonel of the regiment the following October, and led it in the Seven Day's battles, from which he emerged as a brigade commander. He commanded his brigade at Second Manassas and Antietam. Promoted brigadier general, he led his brigade at Fredericksburg, Gettysburg, during the Suffolk Expedition, at Gettysburg, and took it to Georgia in September of 1863. At Chickamauga he assumed command, of Hood's division when the latter was jumped to an effective corps commander. Reverting to brigade command, he led his brigade at Knoxville, the Wilderness, Spotsylvania, and North Anna, and commanded two brigades at Cold Harbor, where he was wounded. He later commanded forces in South Carolina, fighting at Bentonville, and surrendered with Joseph Johnston. After the war he was a writer, journalist, and educator, helping to create the Florida public school system.

Liddell, St. John Richardson (1815-1870). A native of Mississippi, he entered West Point in 1833, but was expelled in less than a year, apparently for some breach of discipline. He became a planter in his native state until the outbreak of the Civil War, when he volunteered. He served variously as an aide-de-camp to William J. Hardee and a confidential courier to Albert Sidney Johnston, before being given command of a brigade as a colonel shortly after Shiloh. Promoted brigadier general in July 1862, he led his brigade at Perryville, Murfreesboro, and during the Tullahoma Campaign, during which he distinguished himself by his stubborn defense of Liberty Gap. During the defensive operations around Chattanooga his brigade formed part of a small reserve division, which he commanded at Chickamauga, before reverting to brigade command during Bragg's investment of Chattanooga. Relieved of duty after the Federal breakout from Chattanooga (during which he was on leave), he was given command of a subdistrict in northern Louisiana, and served in the Red River Campaign. In July 1864 he was given a territorial command on the Gulf Coast. After the war he resumed planting, but was murdered by a personal enemy while on a steamboat on the Black River. His reminiscences were published as *Liddell's Record*.

Long, Armistead Lindsay (1825-1891). A native of Virginia, Long graduated from West Point in 1850 and served in the artillery until May 1861, when he was assigned as an aide-de-camp to Brigadier General Edwin V. Sumner, his father-in-law. Long resigned from the Army in June 1861, and entered Confederate service as a major of artillery. For a time he served as a staff officer in [West] Virginia, but was shortly transferred to Robert E. Lee's staff in South Carolina.

When Lee became commander of the Army of Northern Virginia in mid-1862, Long became his military secretary as a lieutenant colonel. He was shortly transferred to command the artillery of Second Corps, in which assignment he served to the end of the war, rising to brigadier general in September 1863. After the war he was for a time chief engineer to a Virginia canal company, but became completely blind in 1870. Thereafter until his death he devoted himself to writing, including a notable biography of Lee.

Long, Eli (1837-1903). A native of Kentucky, Long graduated from the Frankfort Military School in 1855, and was commissioned in the regular army the following year. Early in the Civil War he became a captain in the *4th Cavalry*. Wounded at Murfreesboro, he was appointed colonel of the *4th Ohio Cavalry*, a hard luck outfit which he soon managed to turn into an outstanding command, leading it during the Tullahoma Campaign. Given a brigade, he performed well against Joseph Wheeler during the Chickamauga Campaign, and later during the Atlanta Campaign, earning a promotion to brigadier general. He commanded a division during the Nashville Campaign and on Wilson's Raid in the Spring of 1865. Wounded five times during the war, Long held brevets in every rank in both the volunteer and regular armies up to and including major general. After the war he continued in the service, retiring as a major general in 1867, settling in New Jersey and practicing law.

Lytle, William H. (1826-1864). A native of Ohio, Lytle practiced law until the outbreak of the war with Mexico, when he volunteered as a second lieutenant in the *2nd Ohio* and rose to captain before being mustered out. Returning to the law, Lytle was twice elected to the state legislature and in 1857 was appointed major general of the Ohio militia by Governor Salmon P. Chase. He was named colonel of the *10th Ohio* and led it at Carnifex Ferry, [West] Virginia, September 1861, where he was wounded. He commanded the *17th Brigade* at Perryville, where he was again wounded and captured as well. Exchanged and promoted to brigadier general in November 1862, he led *1/3/XX* during the Tullahoma Campaign and at Chickamauga, where he was killed on September 20 opposing the advance of Patton Anderson's Mississippians. An accomplished poet, Lytle is known for his epic "Anthony and Cleopatra," published in 1858, which begins with the famous line, "I am dying, Egypt, dying...."

McNair, Evander (1820-1902). Born in North Carolina, but resident in Mississippi from infancy, McNair, a merchant, served in Jefferson Davis' Mississippi Mounted Rifles during the Mexican War. After the war he became a merchant in Arkansas. On the outbreak of the Civil War he helped raise the 4th Arkansas and was elected its colonel. He led the regiment at Wilson's Creek and Pea Ridge, where he was promoted to brigade command, led a brigade in central in Kentucky in mid-1862, was promoted to brigadier general later that year, and commanded his brigade at Murfreesboro, Jackson, and Chickamauga, where he was wounded. His brigade was shortly transferred to the Trans-Mississippi, and he led it in Sterling Price's Missouri Raid. He lived quietly after the war.

Mahone, William (1826-1895). A native of Virginia, he graduated from VMI in 1847, and later taught in a military high school while studying engineering. He subsequently served as an engineer for several railroads, and by the outbreak of the Civil War he was president and superintendent of the Norfolk and Petersburg. Appointed colonel of the 6th Virginia, he took part in the capture of the Norfolk Navy Yard, commanded Norfolk until it was recaptured by Union forces in early 1862, and directed the construction of defenses at Drewry's Bluff, below Richmond. Transferred to the Army of Northern Virginia, he served in every one of its battles from Seven Pines through Appomattox, save for Antietam, during which he was recovering from wounds, meanwhile rising to major general. After the war he returned to railroading, creating the Norfolk and Western, while entering politics, serving in the US Senate.

Manigault, Arthur Middleton (1824-1886). A native of South Carolina, he served in the Palmetto Regiment during the war with Mexico, and afterwards became a rice planter. On the eve of the Civil War he supervised the construction of the Confederate batteries at Charleston and served as an aide-de-camp to Beauregard during the bombardment of Fort Sumter. Named colonel of the 10th South Carolina, he served for a time as a district commander in his home state, before going west with his regiment to join Beauregard's army at Corinth. He led the regiment during Bragg's Kentucky Campaign, and a brigade at Murfreesboro, and was promoted to brigadier general in mid-1863. Continuing in brigade command, he led it during the Tullahoma Campaign, at Chickamauga and Missionary Ridge, during the Atlanta Campaign, and at Franklin, where he was wounded so seriously as to preclude further service. He wrote *A Carolinian Goes to War*.

Martin, John Alexander (1839-1889). A native of Pennsylvania, by the time he was 19 Martin had purchased a newspaper which he successfully published for many years. Resident in Kansas when the Civil War broke out, he took part in the organization of the *8th Kansas* and was made lieutenant colonel in October 1861. He succeeded to regimental command in February 1862, and served with a battalion of the regiment in Halleck's Corinth Campaign and at Perryville, before being assigned as Provost Marshal at Nashville, where the balance of the regiment joined his battalion. Assigned to the *3rd Brigade* under Col. Hans Heg, *1st Division, XX Army Corps,* Martin led the regiment through the Tullahoma Campaign and at Chickamauga, where, on the afternoon of September 19, Martin succeeded to brigade command when Col. Heg was mortally wounded.

Reverting to regimental command after the battle, Martin led the *8th Kansas* at Chattanooga, where it took part in the storming of Missionary Ridge on November 25, 1863, and, after the regiment enjoyed a brief furlough home, in the Atlanta Campaign from July 1864. Breveted a brigadier general of volunteers in March 1865, after the war Martin entered politics and was elected governor of Kansas in 1885, dying in office.

McCook, Alexander McDowell (1831-1903). A native of Kentucky, he became the highest ranking of the celebrated seventeen "Fighting McCooks of Ohio," being the brother of Daniel McCook, Jr., and Robert L. McCook, and a cousin of Edward M. McCook. By profession a lawyer, in April 1861 he was commissioned colonel of the *1st Ohio Volunteers*, and led the regiment at First Bull Run. Promoted brigadier general of volunteers in September 1861, he led the *2nd Division, Army of the Ohio*, at Shiloh, and was made a major general in July 1862. He commanded *I Corps, Army of the Ohio*, at Perryville, and the *Right Wing* at Stones River. In the reorganization of January 9, 1863, his wing was redesignated the *XX Corps*, which he led through the Tullahoma Campaign and at Chickamauga. At Chickamauga, McCook left the field after the disaster to the Federal right had dissolved large segments of his command. Although exonerated by a court of inquiry convened at his request, he was not again assigned to field duty, ending the war as commander of the *District of East Arkansas*. Transferring to the Regular Army after the war, he was promoted to lieutenant colonel of the 26th Infantry in 1867, and subsequently breveted brigadier general and major general in the Regular Army. In 1896 he represented the United States at the coronation Tsar Nicholas II. He retired shortly after the Spanish-American War, during which McCook, a Major General in the Regular Army, held only administrative assignments. Brigadier General John Beatty characterized

McCook as "a chucklehead" and a "blockhead," finding it "astonishing...that he should be permitted to retain command of a corps for a single hour." McCook was one of many senior officers in the Civil War who were not up to the level of command to which they were assigned. He had the misfortune of having his inadequacies illuminated by the crisis on the Federal right at Chickamauga, a battle which became the graveyard of several military careers.

Mitchell, John Grant (1838-1894). A native of Ohio, Mitchell was practicing law there when the Civil War broke out. He volunteered and was commissioned a first lieutenant in the *3rd Ohio*. Rising to captain, he saw service with his regiment in [West] Virginia, Tennessee, and northern Alabama. In September 1862 he became lieutenant colonel of the *113th Ohio*, rising to colonel in May 1863. Ill during the Tullahoma Campaign, he did not rejoin his regiment until the opening stages of the Chickamauga Campaign. Placed in command of *2/1/Reserve*, he led that through the Battle of Chickamauga. Although he missed the Battle of Chattanooga, he served thereafter as a brigade commander in the *Army of the Cumberland* until the end of the war, rising to brigadier general of volunteers in January 1865, and acquiring a brevet for major general of volunteers in March of that year. After the war he practiced law in Columbus.

Moses, Raphael J. A former civilian, he served as a staff officer for Robert Toombs' brigade, and later D.R. Jones' division, before Longstreet made him a commissary officer on his own staff. He served with Longstreet until the Spring of 1864, when he was assigned as Chief Commissary for Georgia.

Oates, William Calvin (1835-1910). A native of Alabama, as a young man Oates earned his living as a house painter, then read law. He edited a newspaper and practiced law for several years whilst dabbling in local politics. On the outbreak of the Civil War he recruited a company which became part of the 15th Alabama, of which he was soon named colonel. During the war he led his regiment ably and courageously in 27 engagements in the Shenandoah Valley, Northern Virginia, Tennessee, and around Richmond, but most notably at Gettysburg, where his attempt to storm Little Round Top was frustrated by Joshua Chamberlain's *20th Maine*. He accompanied his regiment west with Longstreet, and fought at Chickamauga, arguably having a negative effect on Confederate success in the battle, and later served in East Tennessee. In August of 1864 he lost his right arm in the fighting around Richmond, but returned to duty and remained with his regiment until Appomattox. After the war, Oates resumed his profession in Alabama, becoming quite prosperous, and entered state politics. He served in the state legislature and a delegate to a state constitutional convention. In 1880 he entered the House of Representatives, where he became an outspoken segregationist, nativist, and anti-immigrant. He served in the House until 1894, and for a time held the equivalent of the filibuster championship, speaking for eight days. In 1894 he became governor of Alabama, and in 1898 President William McKinley made him a brigadier general of volunteers and gave him a brigade, in which assignment he proved so boorish towards a black battalion under his command that he was transferred to another brigade. He saw no active service during the Spanish-American War, and afterwards practiced his profession until his death.

Pendleton, Alexander Swift (1840-1864). The son of William N. Pendleton, sometime clergyman and sometime Chief of Artillery of the Army of Northern Virginia, "Sandie" Pendleton was very well educated for the times, being a graduate of Washington College and master's student at the University of Virginia. A pre-war resident of Lexington, Virginia, where his father had a parish, Pendleton, a professor at Washington College, was acquainted with T.J. Jackson, then a professor at VMI, through a literary society to which they both belonged. He entered the Confederate Army as a second lieutenant of engineers in May 1861, and almost immediately was appointed to Jackson's staff at Harper's Ferry. Shortly before First Bull Run, Jackson made Pendleton brigade chief of ordnance. Thereafter, Pendleton served on Jackson's staff until the latter's death, missing only the Second Bull Run Campaign, when he was on sick leave. Pendleton was effectively Stonewall's chief of staff from Dabney's resignation in mid-1862 until November 1862, when he was replaced by the far less suitable Charles J. Faulkner. When Richard S. Ewell succeeded to command of Jackson's Second Corps, he made Pendleton chief-of-staff again. He served in this capacity until December 1863, when Jubal Early requested his services for his proposed Shenandoah Valley Campaign. Pendleton served thereafter under Early, taking part in the "Raid on Washington" and the disastrous Shenandoah Campaign that followed. Shortly after the Third Battle of Winchester, Pendleton was mortally wounded at Fisher's Hill.

Perry, William Frank (1835-1901). A native Georgian, he was self-educated, practiced law and became Alabama's first superintendant of public instruction. Serving as the president of a female college in Alabama in 1862, he enlisted as a private in the 44th Alabama when war broke out, being elected major a short time thereafter. Promoted to colonel after Sharpsburg, he led the regiment at Gettysburg and commanded Law's Brigade during the 20th at Chickamauga. He led the regiment at Knoxville, Wilderness, Spotsylvania, and Cold Harbor, after which he took command of Law's brigade until the end of the war. He was repeatedly recommended for promotion to brigadier general by Longstreet and was finally commissioned to that rank in early 1865.

After the war, he returned to teaching, and was a professor of English and philosophy at the time of his death.

Pitcher, Thomas Gamble (1824-1895). A native of Indiana, Pitcher graduated from West Point in 1845 and served in the Infantry. Winning a brevet in Mexico, he served in the 8th Infantry from 1849 until the outbreak of the Civil War, rising to captain and depot commissary at Fort Bliss, El Paso, on the eve of the Civil War. His only active combat service during the war was at Cedar Mountain, during the Second Bull Run Campaign, when he was wounded commanding a battalion of skirmishers. Promoted brigadier general of volunteers in March 1863 (to rank from the previous November), he spend the rest of the war as provost marshal of, first, Vermont, and later Indiana. Mustered out of the volunteer service in 1866, he became colonel of the 44th Infantry and Superintendent of West Point. For several years Governor of the Soldiers' Home in Washington, D.C., he retired in 1877 for reasons of health.

Preston, William (1816-1887). A native Kentuckian, he received a law degree from Harvard in 1838 and took up the practice of law. He served as lieutenant colonel of the 3rd Kentucky during the Mexican War. After the war he served for a time in both houses of the state legislature, was elected to Congress in 1853, and became Minister to Spain in 1858. On the outbreak of the Civil War he returned to the United States. He served as a staff officer to his brother-in-law Albert Sidney Johnston until the latter's death at Shiloh. Appointed a brigadier general April 14, 1862, Preston commanded a brigade at Murfreesboro and another under Buckner in East Tennessee in the Spring of 1863. When Buckner's forces were ordered to join Bragg, Preston assumed command of a provisional division, which he led at Chickamauga. In 1864 he was appointed Confederate Minister to Imperial Mexico but was unable to reach his post and spent the rest of the war in the Trans-Mississippi. After the war he briefly lived abroad, before returning to the practice of law in his home state.

Ransom, Robert, Jr. (1828-1892). A native of North Carolina, he graduated from West Point in 1850 and served in the cavalry until he resigned in January 1861. He entered Confederate service as a cavalry captain in the Spring of 1861, rose to colonel of the 1st North Carolina Cavalry in October of that year, and brigadier general the following March. He commanded an infantry brigade in North Carolina for a time, one in Longstreet's First Corps from August to November 1862, and a division November 1862-Janaury 1863. From January 1863 he commanded various brigades in Virginia and North Carolina, rising to major general in May. He then commanded divisions in the Department of Richmond and in that of West Virginia and Tennessee, a cavalry division in East Tennessee, and, from April to June 1864 the Department of Richmond. In June 1864 he was given a cavalry division in the Valley, taking part in the Battle of Monocacy and the attack on Washington. Ill health caused him to be relieved of duty in August 1864. He served thereafter on courts martial duty. After the war he was a civil engineer. His elder brother was Confederate Brigadier General Matt W. Ransom

Reynolds, Joseph Jones (1822-1899). Born in Kentucky, he later relocated to Indiana. He graduated from West point in 1843, along with U.S. Grant, and was posted to the artillery. He served on garrison duty for a time, and was later assigned as an instructor at West Point. After eight years at the Academy, he served briefly in the Indian Territory, before resigning to teach mathematics and engineering at Washington University in St. Louis. He was commissioned colonel of the *10th Indiana* April 25, 1861, and was promoted to Brigadier General of Volunteers less than a month later. He commanded under Rosecrans in [West] Virginia in mid- and late-1861, but resigned from the service in January 1862 to tend to business following his brother's death. While out of the service he was active in recruiting and training Indiana volunteers, and was reappointed a brigadier general in September 1862, and promoted to major general the following month. Assigned a division under Thomas, he was detached to guard the Louisville and Nashville Rail Road at the time of Stones River. He led his division through the Tullahoma Campaign and commanded the *4ʰ Division, XIV Corps*, under Thomas, at Chickamauga. On November 10, 1863, Thomas named him chief-of-staff of the *Army of the Cumberland*, and he served n that capacity through the Battle of Chattanooga. In January 1864 he was assigned to command *XIX Corps* in the *Department of the Gulf*, and from November 1864 to April 1866 he commanded the *Department of Arkansas*. After the war he remained in the Regular Army, earning a brevet as brigadier general of regulars for Chickamauga and major general for Missionary Ridge. He became colonel of the 26th Infantry in 1866, and of the 3rd Cavalry n 1870. During Crook's Sioux Expedition during the winter of 1875-1876, Reynolds captured Crazy Horse's encampment on the Powder River, but withdrew without pressing the fight against some Indians who were in a nearby woods. Subject to an investigation for this, he resigned from the army in 1877.

Robertson, Felix Huston (1839-1928). A native-born Texan, the son of Jerome Bonaparte Robertson, he entered West Point in 1857, and resigned upon the secession of Texas in January 1861. Entering Confederate service, he was present as a second lieutenant of artillery at the bombardment of Fort Sumter, commanded a battery at Shiloh, and distinguished himself at Murfreesboro, where he was promoted to major. Commander of the Artillery Reserve at Chickamauga, he commanded Wheeler's horse artillery during the Atlanta Campaign, rising to brigadier general by mid-1864, and subsequently served for a time as Wheeler's chief-of-staff before commanding a cavalry division. Severely wounded at Buckhead Creek in November 1864, he saw no further active service. After the war he practiced law in Texas. The only native-born Texan to attain a generalcy in the Confederacy, he was also the last Confederate general to die.

Robertson, Jerome Bonaparte (1815-1891). Born in Kentucky, he removed to Texas in 1836, shortly after securing a degree in medicine from Transylvania University. He served in the Army of the Republic of Texas for a time, and then practiced his profession. In 1861 he became a captain in the 5th Texas Infantry, rising to colonel by mid-1862. He led the regiment during the Seven Days and at Second Bull Run, where he was wounded, rising to brigadier general in November 1862. Taking command of the Texas Brigade he led it at Fredericksburg, Gettysburg, where he was again wounded, and at Chickamauga, and Knoxville. In early 1864 he was removed from command by Longstreet after he clashed with Micah Jenkins, his division commander. Robertson returned to Texas and commanded a reserve corps there until the end of the war. The father of Felix Huston Robertson, after the war he returned to his profession and served for a time as Texas superintendent of immigration.

Sorrel, Gilbert Moxley. (1838-1901). A native of Georgia, in 1861 he was working as a bank clerk, serving as a private in a militia company. He was present at the bombardment of Fort Sumter, and later took part in the capture of Fort Pulaski. Shortly before First Bull Run, he traveled to Virginia, and served as a volunteer aide-de-camp to Longstreet at First Bull Run. So impressed was Longstreet the he secured Sorrel a commission and appointment as assistant adjutant general on his staff. Sorrel rose to chief of staff of Longstreet's First Corps, and served in all of its actions until the October 1864. At the Wilderness he led the counter attack that almost collapsed the Union *II Corps*. Promoted to brigadier general in October 1864, he was given command of a brigade in the

Third Corps. He was wounded at Antietam and Petersburg, and again at Hatcher's Run, in February 1865. The war ended before he could return to duty. After the war he was a merchant in Savannah for a time, and was later connected with a steamship company. Considered by some the best staff officer in the Confederate Army, his *Recollections of a Confederate Staff Officer* is a valuable memoir of the war.

Spears, James Gallant (1816-1869). A native of Tennessee, he was largely self-educated, and became a lawyer. A Douglas Democrat and staunch Unionist, he was a delegate to the anti-secessionist Tennessee conventions held in Knoxville and Greenville in May and June 1861. After the secession of Tennessee he was declared a traitor by the Confederate government, and fled to Kentucky, where he organized the Unionist *1st Tennessee Infantry*. Appointed lieutenant colonel of the regiment September 1, 1861, he led it in the fights at Wildcat Mountain (October) and Logan's Crossroads (January 1862). Promoted to brigadier general in March 1862, he led a brigade of East Tennessee Unionist troops, occupied the Cumberland Gap in June 1862, and later fought against Bragg's rear guard after Stones River. Spears' brigade was on detached duty and later guarding lines-of-communication during Rosecrans' Tullahoma Campaign and the advance on Chattanooga. The brigade arrived in Chattanooga at noon on September 20. He later led the brigade during the relief of Knoxville. Like many East Tennesseans a staunch Unionist, but pro-slavery man, Spears' outspoken criticism of the Emancipation Proclamation eventually earned hi a court martial and he was dismissed from the service on August 30, 1864. He returned to his home and concentrated on the revival of his family fortune.

Steedman, James Blair (1817-1883). A native of Pennsylvania, Steedman served in the Texas Army during the Mexican War. He later served as a member of the Ohio legislature, was a "forty-niner" during the California gold rush, and became publisher of the *Toledo Times*. A Douglas Democrat, he became colonel of the *14th Ohio* in April, 1861, and led it at Philippi, [West] Virginia. Promoted brigadier general of volunteers in July 1862, he commanded a brigade at Perryville, on line-of-communications duty during Stones River, and in the Tullahoma Campaign. In August 1863 he was given command of the *1st Division, Reserve Corps*, which he led with conspicuous courage and ability at Chickamauga, during the desperate fight on the right of the Horseshoe-Missionary Ridge line on the afternoon of September 20. He commanded the post of Chattanooga from October 1863 through May 1864, meanwhile rising to major general of volunteers in April 1864. Although he continued in rear echelon assignments, during the battle of Nashville he commanded an *ad hoc* force. Resigning from the Army in August, 1866, Steedman went on to become collector of internal revenue at New Orleans, a state senator in Ohio, and a newspaper editor and police chief in Toledo.

Stewart, Alexander Peter (1842-1908). A native of Tennessee, he graduated from West Point in 1842 and served in garrison and as a mathematics instructor at USMA until he resigned in 1845, to teach mathematics in Cumberland University and the University of Nashville. Although opposed to secession, he accepted a major's commission in 1861 and commanded the heavy artillery at Belmont, Missouri, and Columbus, Kentucky. Appointed a brigadier general in late 1861, he commanded a brigade at Shiloh, Perryville, and Murfreesboro. Made a major general in June 1863, he commanded a division during the Tullahoma Campaign, at Chickamauga, and at Missionary Ridge. Promoted to lieutenant general in mid-1864, he assumed command of Polk's Corps when the latter was killed at Pine Mountain, Georgia and continued in this post until the end of the war. After the war he engaged in business and academic pursuits, rising to Chancellor of the University of Mississippi, and served as a commissioner of the Chickamauga-Chattanooga National Military Park. His men called him "Old Straight."

Taliaferro, William Booth (1822-1898). A native Virginian from a prosperous old family, Taliaferro (the name is pronounced "Toliver'), who had served in the regular army during the Mexican War, rising to major, was a lawyer and politician in his home state on the eve of the Civil War. A major general in the state militia, he was present at the arrest of John Brown at Harper's Ferry in 1859. When the Civil War broke out, he briefly served in his militia capacity before volunteering for Confederate service, becoming colonel of the 23rd Virginia, and later commanded a brigade in [West] Virginia. Promoted brigadier general in March 1862, he led a brigade under Jackson in the Valley and during the Pensinsular Campaign, and commanded a division under Jackson briefly in mid-1862 and from later that year until February 1863. Having run afoul of Jackson's temper by siding with William W. Loring in the latter's personality clash with the former, he left the Army of Northern Virginia in early 1863. He thereafter commanded various brigades and districts in South Carolina, Georgia, and Florida until October 1864. In October 1864 he was given a brigade, and later a division, in Hardee's corps, served for a time in the Shenandoah Valley, and commanded a division at Bentonville. After the war he entered politics and served in the judiciary in his native state.

Taylor, Walter Herron (c. 1838-1916). A graduate of VMI, he was in banking when the Civil War broke out. He served initially in the Virginia militia, rising to lieutenant colonel, but in November 1861 was commissioned a captain in Confederate service. From May 1861 he was attached to Lee's personal staff, and remained so for the entire war, rising to lieutenant colonel and assistant adjutant general. An able organizer, he several times became involved in the fighting. Not present during Lee's meeting with Grant at Appomattox, after the war he wrote *Four Years with General Lee,* a memoir of the war, and *General Lee,* a biography of his former commander

Toombs, Robert A. (1810-1885). A native of Georgia, he became a attorney in his home state by the age of 20, and soon amassed considerable wealth while becoming important in politics, serving in the state legislature, the House of Representatives, and the Senate. A thorough believer in slavery and secession, he was a delegate to the Provisional Confederate Congress and was almost elected President of the Confederacy. He served as Confederate Secretary of State until July 1861, when he accepted a commission as a brigadier general. He commanded a brigade with some ability in the Peninsula, the Seven Days, Second Bull Run, and Antietam, where he was wounded. Failing to secure a promotion, he resigned in March 1863, and spent most of the next 18 months as a severe critic of the Davis Administration and the prosecution of the war. He later returned to active duty, and served during Sherman's March to the Sea and in the Carolina Campaign. After the war he fled abroad, not returning until 1867. He soon became an active player in Georgia politics, but, since he never applied for a formal pardon, held no public offices until his death.

Trigg, Robert Craig (1830-1872). A native Virginian, he graduated from VMI in the early 1850s and took up the law. At the outbreak of the Civil War he entered Confederate service, rising to colonel of the 54th Virginia in September 1861. Although never promoted higher than colonel, he several times served as a temporary brigade commander, notably in East Tennessee in mid-1863 and at Chickamauga, and saw service with his regiment during the Atlanta Campaign through to the end of the war.

Upton, Emory (1839-1881). A native of New York, Upton graduated from West Point in the May 1861 class. He spent the early months of the war as a training officer in Washington, D.C. He served as a staff officer at Blackburn's Run and First Bull Run, where he was wounded, then as a battery commander during the Peninsular Campaign. During the Antietam Campaign he commanded an artillery brigade in *VI Corps*, and was shortly promoted colonel of the *121st New York*, which he led at Fredericksburg. At Gettysburg he was in temporary command of *2/1/VI* for the first two days of the battle and during the pursuit. He was later given command of the brigade and led it through the operations in late 1863, at the Wilderness, and at Spotsylvania. During the battle of Spotsylvania on May 10, 1864, he executed a masterfully planned attack on the "Bloody Angle" that might have broken the Confederate lines had it been supported. Wounded, he returned to duty in time for Cold Harbor, served in the initial fighting around Petersburg, was promoted brigadier general of volunteers, took part in the relief of Washington during Jubal Early's "Raid," and then commanded his brigade in the Shenandoah, where he fought as a division commander at Opequon on September 19, 1864. Again wounded, he did not return to service until December. Transferred to Alabama, he was given command of the *4th Cavalry Division*, under James H. Wilson. By the end of the war he held six brevets (including major general in both the regular and volunteer service). After the war he was Commandant at West Point for a time, served on various commissions, and spend two years visiting foreign armies, which became the basis for his *The Armies of Asia and Europe* (1878). Aside from writing two tactical manuals, he also wrote *The Military Policy of the United States*, a rather militaristic demand for compulsory service and a large standing army, which was not published until 1903. Colonel of the 4th Artillery, he committed suicide at the age of 42 when he discovered that he had an incurable illness.

Van Derveer, Ferdinand (1823-1892). Born in Ohio, he practiced law until the outbreak of the Mexican War, when he served as a volunteer, rising to captain in the 1st Ohio, and distinguishing himself at Monterey. After the war he practiced his profession in his home state. In September 1861 he became colonel of the *35th Ohio*, and commanded it during the siege of Corinth and at Perryville. He commanded a brigade during the Tullahoma Campaign, at Chickamauga and Missionary Ridge (where he took part in the storming of the heights), and during the Atlanta Campaign, until Kennesaw Mountain, when he went on sick leave. Promoted brigadier general of volunteers in October 1864, he served to the end of the war in Alabama. After the war he resumed the practice of law in Ohio.

Venable, Charles Scott (1827-1900). A native Virginian, Venable received an unusually good education both in the U.S. and abroad, and embarked upon an academic career as a professor of mathematics and an astronomer. A lieutenant colonel of South Carolina militia, he was present at the bombardment of Fort Sumter. He shortly afterwards entered Confederate service a private in the 2nd South Carolina, but as soon commissioned. He appears to have come to Lee's attention when he was commander of the coast defenses of the Carolinas and Georgia. Shortly after Lee was appointed military advisor to Jefferson Davis he added Venable to his staff as a major. Venable served with Lee from then until Appomattox, rising to lieutenant colonel. After the war he resumed his academic career.

Walker, John George (1822-1895). A native of Missouri, Walker received a direct commission as a second lieutenant in the Mounted Rifles during the Mexican War, in which he was breveted for Molino del Rey, where he was wounded. Continuing in the Regular Army, he resigned as a captain in July 1861, and after some wait in December 1861, was commissioned a major of cavalry in the Confederate Regular

Army (to date from March!). Shortly promoted lieutenant colonel of the 8th Texas Cavalry, by early January 1862 he was a brigadier general. He commanded a brigade in North Carolina until mid-1862, and then one in the Army of Northern Virginia, serving in the Seven Days, until promoted to division command in the First Corps in August. He missed the Second Bull Run Camping, but did serve in the Antietam Campaign. Promoted to major general in November 1862, he was sent to the Trans-Mississippi, where he commanded various divisions, districts, and even a corps, serving in the Red River Campaign and on garrison duty. After the war he briefly lived in Mexico, before returning and becoming a U.S. consular agent in Latin America.

Whitaker, Walter C. (1823-1887). A native of Kentucky, he practiced law. During the Mexican War he served as a lieutenant in the 3rd Kentucky. He subsequently served in the state legislature. On the outbreak of the Civil War he proposed the legislation that ended Kentucky's "neutrality" and at the end of 1861 was commissioned colonel of the *6th Kentucky*. He led his regiment at Shiloh, Stones River, and during the Tullahoma Campaign. Promoted brigadier general of volunteers in June 1863, he commanded *1st Brigade, 1st Division, Reserve Corps* at Chickamauga. He led a brigade at Chattanooga, during the Atlanta Campaign, at Franklin, and at Nashville. Breveted major general of volunteers at the end of the war, he returned to the practice of law in his native state. Reputedly a hard drinking man in a hard drinking age, in later life he was for a time confined in a mental institution, but recovered sufficiently to return to the practice of law.

Wilcox, Cadmus Marcellus (1824-1890). Born in North Carolina, but raised in Tennessee, Wilcox graduated from West Point in 1846. After service in the war with Mexico, earning a brevet for Chapultepec, he remained in the Regular Army, authoring a rifle manual. He resigned in June 1861 and entered Confederate service, fighting at First Bull Run as colonel of the 9th Alabama. His entire war service was with what would become the Army of Northern Virginia, as a colonel, brigadier general (from October 1861), and major general (August 1863), while commanding successively a brigade and then a division. A capable officer, Wilcox several times displayed commendable initiative, notably at Fredericksburg. When Lee evacuated the defenses of Richmond and Petersburg, Wilcox commanded the rearguard. After the war he settled in Washington, D.C., and held a variety of government appointments.

Wilder, John T. (1830-1917). Born in New York, as a young man he relocated to Ohio, where he worked as a foundryman, and later to Indiana, where he established a small foundry. By the eve of the Civil War he was a successful businessman and a recognized expert in hydraulics. In May 1861 he raised a light artillery battery which was accepted for service as an infantry company in the *17th Indiana*, with Wilder as its captain. The following month he was promoted to lieutenant colonel. He served with the regiment in the [West] Virginia Campaign of 1861, and accompanied it to join the *Army of the Ohio* later that same year. When the regimental commander was promoted to brigadier general in March of 1862 he succeeded to command as a colonel. The regiment served at Shiloh on the second day, and took part in the Corinth Campaign. During the subsequent fighting in Kentucky, Wilder commanded Union forces at Munfordville, where both he and the regiment were captured. Exchanged, he was given a brigade in the *Army of the Cumberland*. With this brigade he took part in the pursuit of John Hunt Morgan, and so missed Stones River. In early 1863 Wilder convinced Rosecrans to mount the brigade, which was done on horses impressed in middle Tennessee. At the same time he arranged for it to be equipped with the Spencer repeating carbine, initially by helping his men to pay for their own. During the Tullahoma Campaign, Wilder's brigade seized the strategic

Hoover's Gap through the Cumberland Mountains and held it against a strong Confederate counterattack under William Bate, earning for it the nickname '*Lightning Brigade*.' Wilder and his brigade went on to raid Confederate supply depots and lines of communication in Tennessee. When Rosecrans began his drive on Chattanooga on August 16,1863, the "*Lightning Brigade*" led the advance, feinting upriver of the town while the bulk of the *Army of the Cumberland* crossed the Tennessee River well below the city, thereby flanking Bragg's position. The *92nd Illinois* of Wilder's brigade was the first Union unit to enter Chattanooga, on September 9, raising the U.S. flag over the town's most prominent hotel, the Cruchfield House.

At Chickamauga, Wilder's brigade successfully defended Alexander's Bridge during the meeting engagement on September 18, and rendered valuable service during the fighting on the 19th and 20th. Ordered off the field by Assistant Secretary of War Dana, Wilder and his command retired to Chattanooga. Subsequently the brigade was engaged in chasing and fighting Confederate cavalry under Joseph Wheeler, and took no direct part in the Battle of Chattanooga. Suffering from recurring bouts of typhoid fever, which he had contracted in 1862, Wilder who had been breveted a brigadier general of volunteers in August, resigned on October 4, 1864. After the war he settled in Tennessee, where he became a railroad and mining developer. Wilder exemplified the technical-minded citizen soldier whose ideas and application augured a change in the nature of battle.

Willich, August von (1810-1878). Born in Prussia, the son of a Napoleonic officer, Willich was orphaned at the age of three and raised by the theologian and philosopher Friedrich Schleiermacher. Receiving a military education, at eighteen he was commissioned in the Royal Prussian Army. During the revolutionary disorders that began in 1846, Willich became an adherent of Karl Marx and was swept up in the revolutionary fervor. Writing an impertinent letter to the king, he was court martialled, and upon his acquittal was permitted to resign from the army. He became a carpenter, but in 1848 served in the revolutionary army in Baden. When the revolution collapsed, he fled to Britain, but in 1852 migrated to the United States. Willich worked for a time as a carpenter at the Brooklyn Navy Yard, then on the U.S. Coast Survey until 1858, when he accepted the editorship of the Cincinnati *Deutscher Republikaner*, which he held until the outbreak of the Civil War. In 1861 he enlisted in the *9th Ohio*, and was shortly commissioned first lieutenant and adjutant, and soon afterwards was promoted to major. He fought with the regiment at Rich Mountain, [West] Virginia, in July 1861, and was shortly afterwards called back to Indiana to recruit and train the *32nd Indiana*, becoming it colonel on August 24, 1861. Willich commanded the regiment on the second day at Shiloh, and was appointed brigadier general of volunteers in July 1862. He commanded *1st Brigade, 2nd Division, Right Wing*, at Stones River, where he was captured on December 31, 1862. Returning to command in May, he led the brigade (redesignated *1/2/XX*) during the Tullahoma Campaign, playing a conspicuous role in the fighting at Liberty Gap, at Chickamauga, Chattanooga (where his brigade helped storm Missionary Ridge), and in the Atlanta Campaign, until he was wounded at Resaca. When he returned to duty he was given an administrative command at Cincinnati, but ended the war on duty in Texas. Breveted major general of volunteers in October 1865, he was mustered out in 1866. After the war he returned to Cincinnati, where he served as county auditor for two years. He returned to Germany shortly before the outbreak of the Franco-Prussian War. When the war broke out he offered his services to the Prussian Army, but was refused on the grounds of his advanced age. He remained in Berlin for a time, attending lectures on Marxism, but then returned to Ohio.

In his later years he devoted himself to the St. Mary's Shakespeare Club, which he had founded.

Wood, Thomas John (1823-1906). A native of Kentucky, Wood graduated from West Point in 1845, and won a brevet for gallantry while serving on Zachary Taylor's staff in Mexico. He subsequently served on the frontier and in Utah. At the outbreak of the Civil War, by then a major, Wood was serving as a mustering officer in Indiana. Shortly promoted to lieutenant colonel, he was appointed a brigadier general of volunteers in October 1861. He commanded the *6th Division, Army of the Ohio*, at Shiloh, during the siege of Corinth, and as part of the *II Corps* at Perryville. He led the *2nd Division, Left Wing*, at Stones River, where he was wounded, and, when the wing was redesignated, in *XXI Corps*, through the Tullahoma Campaign and at Chickamauga. In the latter battle, Wood executed Rosecrans' order that virtually brought that general's career to an end and cost the Union the battle. Wood himself was not censured for this, and in fact was awarded a brevet for gallantry. He subsequently commanded a division in the newly organized *IV Corps* at Chattanooga, during the Atlanta Campaign, in which he was wounded at Lovejoy's Station, and at Franklin. He commanded *IV Corps* at Nashville, and was promoted major general in early 1865. Although he continued in the Regular Army after the war, in 1868 he retired from active duty for disability from his wartime wounds, becoming a member of the Board of Visitors of USMA. He was the last living member of the USMA Class of 1845.

Wofford, William Tatum (1824-1884). A native of Georgia, Wofford, a lawyer, served as a captain in a battalion of Georgia mounted rifles during the Mexican War. Returning to his home state, he practiced his profession, entered politics, serving several years in the legislature, and edited a newspaper. An anti-secession delegate to the state secession convention in 1861, he nevertheless volunteered for service, becoming colonel of the 18th Georgia early in 1861. After a brief tour of duty in the Carolinas, the regiment was incorporated in Hood's Texas brigade during the Peninsular Campaign and the Seven Days. Wofford, as senior colonel, was several times in temporary command of the brigade, notably at Second Bull Run, South Mountain, and Antietam. The regiment was shortly transferred to Cobb's brigade, and Wofford assumed command of the brigade when Cobb was killed at Fredericksburg. Promoted to brigadier general in January 1863, Wofford commanded his brigade at Chancellorsville, Gettysburg, Knoxville, during the Overland Campaign, and in the Shenandoah, until January 1865. At that time Governor Brown of Georgia requested his services, and he held a district command until the end of the war. After the war he served briefly in the House of Representatives, but lost his seat to Radical Reconstruction. He thereafter was active in railroading, civic affairs, and served as a delegate to the state's anti-Reconstruction constitutional convention of 1877.

Bibliography

In the case of some published materials the contributors occasionally used different editions of the same work. When checking references, please refer to the edition specificied in the notes.

Archival Materials and Official Documents

Edward Porter Alexander Papers, Southern Historical Collection, University of North Carolina.

John B. Bachelder Papers, New Hampshire Historical Society

Henry L. Benning Papers, Southern Historical Collection, University of North Carolina.

Edward M. Boagni Collection, Baton Rouge.

Campbell-Colston Family Papers, Southern Historical Collection, University of North Carolina.

John F. H. Claiborne Papers, Southern Historical Collection, University of North Carolina.

Confederate States of America, War Department, *Regulation For the Army of the Confederate States*. New Orleans, 1861.

Coles, R.T., *History of the Fourth Regiment, Alabama Volunteer Infantry, CSA, Army of Northern Virginia*. Unpublished mss, Alabama Department of Archives & History, Montgomery.

Francis Warrington Dawson Papers, Duke University.

Henry Kyd Douglas Papers, Special Collections Library, Duke University, Durham, North Carolina.

Jubal Anderson Early Papers, Library of Congress

Faulkner, Charles J., Service Record, National Archives Record Section, Microcopy 331, Roll 91.

50th Alabama File. Chickamauga-Chattanooga National Military Park Library, Fort Oglethorpe, Georgia.

Franklin Galliard Papers, Southern Historical Collection, University of North Carolina

Thomas J. Gorge *Diary*, Department of Archives and History, Louisiana State University.

William Henry Harder Papers, Tennessee State Library and Archives, Nashville.

Jedediah Hotchkiss Papers, Library of Congress.

Thomas J. Jackson Papers, Library of Congress.

Samuel R. Johnston Papers, Virginia Historical Society

Thomas Butler King Papers, Southern Historical Collection, University of North Carolina-Chapel Hill.

Eli Long Papers, United States Army Military History Institute, Carlisle Barracks, Pennsylvania.

Augustus Baldwin Longstreet Papers, Duke University.

James Longstreet Papers, *The Century* Collection, New York Public Library.

James Longstreet File, Chickamauga/Chattanooga National Military Park Library, Fort Oglethorpe, Georgia.

James Longstreet Papers, Chicago Historical Society Library.

James Longstreet Papers, Duke University

James Longstreet Papers, Emory University.

James Longstreet Papers, Harvard University

James Longstreet Papers, The Historical Society of Pennsylvania.

James Longstreet Papers, The Henry E. Huntington Library.

Lafayette McLaws Papers, Southern Historical Collection, University of North Carolina.

Raphael J. Moses Manuscript, Southern Historical Collection, University of North Carolina, Chapel Hill

19th Illinois File, Chickamauga/Chattanooga National Military Park Library.

William P. Palmer Collection of Braxton Bragg Papers, Western Reserve Historical Society, Cleveland, Ohio.

Pendleton, Alexander, Service Record, National Archives and Records Service, Microcopy 331, Roll 196.

William N. Pendleton Papers, Southern Historical Collection, University of North Carolina, Chapel Hill

Benedict J. Semmes Papers, Southern Historical Collection, University of North Carolina, Chapel Hill.

Sorrel, G. Moxley, Service Record, National Archives and Records Service, Microcopy 331, Roll 233.

United States War Department, *Official Records of the Union and Confederate Armies in the War of the Rebellion.* Washington: Government Printing Office, 1880-1901.

Louis T. Wigfall Papers, Library of Congress.

Whitesdes, Edward G., *Diary, Civil War Times Ilustrated Collection,* United States Army Military History Institute, Carlisle Barracks, Pennsylvania.

Wilder, John T., "Statement of the Operations of My Brigade During the Battle of Chickamauga...," 17th Indiana File, Chickamauga-Chattanooga National Military Park Library.

Books, Dissertations, Personal Narratives, Diaries, and Articles

Alexander, Edward Porter, "Artillery Fighting at Gettysburg," in Johnson and Buel, *Battles and Leaders of the Civil War* (Reprint, New York: Thomas Yoseloff, 1956), III, 357-368.

_____, *Fighting for the Confederacy,* edited by Gary W. Gallagher. Chapel Hill: Duke University, 1989.

_____, *Military Memoirs of a Confederate: A Critical Narrative*. New York: Scribner's, 1907. Reprint. Bloomington: Indiana University Press, 1962.

Allan, William, "Letter from William Allan, of Ewell's Staff," *Southern Historical Society Papers*, IV (Aug. 1877), 76-80.

The Annals Of The War Written By Leading Participants North And South. Philadelphia: The Times Publishing Company, 1879. Reprint, Dayton, Ohio; Morningside House, 1988.

Bean, W.G., *Stonewall's Man: Sandie Pendleton*. Chapel Hill: University of North Carolina Press, 1959.

Bertram Wyatt-Brown, *Honor and Violence in the Old South*. New York: Oxford University Press, 1986.

_____, *Southern Honor: Ethics and Behavior in the Old South*. New York: Oxford University Press, 1982.

_____, *Yankee Saints and Southern Sinners*. Baton Rouge: Louisiana State University Press, 1985.

Bierce, Ambrose, *Ambrose Bierce's Civil War*, ed. William McCann. Washington: Renery Gateway, 1956.

Bigelow, John, Jr., *The Campaign of Chancellorsville*. New Haven: Yale, 1910.

Biographical Directory of the United States Congress, 1744-1989. Washington: Government Printing Office, 1989

Black, Robert C., III, *The Railroads of the Confederacy*. Chapel Hill: The University of North Carolina Press, 1952.

Borcke, Heros von, *Memoirs of the Confederate War For Independence*. Two volumes. New York: P. Smith, 1938.

Burke, W. S., and Roch, J. L., *The History of Leavenworth, the Metropolis of Kansas*. Leavenworth: The Leavenworth Times Book and Job Printing Establishment, 1880.

Busey, John W., and Martin, David G., *Regimental Strengths at Gettysburg*. Baltimore: Gateway Press, 1982.

Bushong, Millard Kessler, *Old Jube: A Biography of General Jubal A. Early*. Boyce, Va.: The Carr Publishing Company, Inc., 1955.

Cist, Henry M. *The Army of the Cumberland*. Reprint. Wilmington, North Carolina: Broadfoot Publishing Company, 1989.

Coddington, Edwin B., *The Gettysburg Campaign*. New York: Scribners, 1984.

Coffman, Edward M., *The Old Army: A Portrait of the American Army in Peacetime, 1784-1898*. New York and Oxford: Oxford University Press, 1986

Connelly, Thomas L., *Autumn of Glory: The Army of Tennessee, 1862-1865*. Two volumes. Baton Rouge: Louisiana State University Press, 1971.

_____, *The Marble Man; Robert E. Lee and IIis Image in American Society*. New York: Alfred A. Knopf, 1977.

Connelly, Thomas L., and Bellows, Barbara L., *God and General Longstreet: The Lost Cause and the Southern Mind*. Baton Rouge: Louisiana State University Press, 1982.

Connelly, Thomas L., and Jones, Archer, *The Politics of Command: Factions and Ideas in Confederate Strategy*. Baton Rouge: Louisiana State University Press, 1973.

Cozzens, Peter, *This Terrible Sound: The Battle of Chickamauga*. Urbana: University of Illinois Press, 1992.

Crute, Joseph H., Jr., *Units of the Confederate States Army*. Midlothian, Va: Derwent Books, 1987.

Cullum, George W., *Biographical Register of the Officers and Graduates of the U.S. Military Academy at West Point, N.Y.* Three volumes. Boston and New York: Houghton, Mifflin and Company, 1891.

Cumming, Kate. *Kate: The Journal of a Confederate Nurse,* ed. Richard B. Harwell. Baton Rouge: Louisiana State University Press, 1959.

Daniels, Josephus, *Tar Heel Editor*. Chapel Hill: University of North Carolina Press, 1939.

Davis, Jefferson, *The Rise and Fall of the Confederate Government*. New York: D. Appleton and Co., 1881.

Dawson, Francis W., *Reminiscences of Confederate Service, 1861-1865*. Baton Rouge: Louisiana State University Press, 1980.

Douglas, Henry Kyd, *I Rode With Stonewall*. Chapel Hill:University of North Carolina, 1940.

Early, Jubal A., *The Campaigns of Robert E. Lee: An Address by Lieut. Gen. Jubal A. Early before Washington and Lee University, January 19, 1872.* Baltimore: John Murphy & Co., 1872.

_____, *A Memoir of the Last Year of the War for Independence In the Confederate States of America.* New Orleans: Blelock & Co., 1867.

_____. "Leading Confederates on the Battle of Gettysburg; A Review by General Early," *Southern Historical Society Papers*, IV (Dec. 1877), 241-302.

_____, "Letter from Gen. J. A. Early," *Southern Historical Society Papers*, IV (Aug. 1877), 50-66;

_____, "Reply to General Longstreet's Second Paper," *Southern Historical Society Papers*, V (July 1878), 270-87.

Eckenrode, Hamilton J., and Conrad, Bryan, *James Longstreet: Lee's War Horse.* Chapel Hill: University of North Carolina, 1936.

Elam, W.C., "A Scalawag," *Southern Magazine*, 8 (April 1871).

Fishwick, Marshall William, *Virginians on Olympus: A Cultural Analysis of Four Great Men.* Richmond: n. p., 1951.

Foster, Gaines M., *Ghosts of the Confederacy: Defeat, the Lost Cause: and the Emergence of the New South.* New York: Oxford University Press, 1987.

Freeman, Douglas Southall, *Lee's Lieutenants: A Study in Command.* Three volumes. New York: Scribner's, 1942-1944.

_____, *R.E. Lee.* Four volumes. New York: Scribner's, 1934-1935.

Fuller, J.F.C., *Grant and Lee.* Bloomington: University of Indiana Press, 1957

Gallagher, Gary W., "The Army of Northern Virginia in May 1864: A Crisis of High Command," *Civil War History*, Vol 36, No 2 (June 1990), 101-118.

_____, "Scapegoat in Victory: James Longstreet and the Battle of Second Manassas," *Civil War History*, Vol 34, No 4 (October 1988), 293-307.

Bibliography

Goree, James Langston, V, ed., *The Thomas Jewitt Goree Letters*, Two volumes. Bryan, Texas: Family History Foundation, 1981.

Govan, Gilbert E., and Livingood, James W., *The Chattanooga Country, 1540-1976: From Tomahawks to T.V.A.* Third edition, Knoxville: The University of Tennessee, 1977.

Gow, June I., "Chiefs of Staff in the Army of Tennessee Under Braxton Bragg," *Tennessee Historical Quarterly*, Vol. 27, 4 (Winter, 1968), 341-360.

Gracie, Archibald, *The Truth About Chickamauga.* Dayton, Oh.: Morningside Bookshop, 1987.

Greezicki, Richard J., "Humbugging the Historian: A Reappraisal of Longstreet at Gettysburg," *Gettysburg Magazine*, No. 6 (January 1992).

Hagerman, Edward. *The American Civil War and the Origins of Modern Warfare.* Bloomington: University of Indiana Press, 1992.

Hallock, Judith Lee. *Braxton Bragg and Confederate Defeat.* Tuscaloosa: The University of Alabama Press, 1991.

_____. *James Longstreet in the West: A Monumental Failure.* Boulder: Ryan Place Publishers, 1995.

Hamlin, Percy Gatlin, ed., *The Making of a Soldier: Letters of General R.S. Ewell.* Richmond: Whittet & Shepperson, 1935

_____, *"Old Bald Head" (General R.S. Ewell): The Portrait of a Soldier.* Strausburg, Va.: Shenandoah Publishing House, Inc., 1940.

Harwell, Richard Barksdale, ed., *Kate: The Journal of a Confederate Nurse.* Baton Rouge: Louisiana State University Press, 1959.

Hattaway, Herman, "Clio's Southern Soldiers: The United Confederate Veterans and History," *Louisiana History*, XII (Summer 1971), 213-42.

Heitman, Francis B., *Historical Register and Dictionary of the United States Army from Its Organization, September 29, 1789, to March 2, 1903.* Two volumes. Washington: Government Printing Office, 1903.

Hennessy, John J., *Return to Bull Run.* New York: Simon & Schuster, 1992.

Hill, Daniel Harvey, "Chickamauga—The Great Battle of the West," in Johnson and Buel, *Battles and Leaders of the Civil War* (New York: Thomas Yoseloff, 1956), III, 638-662.

Hill, Jim Dan, *The Minuteman in Peace and War.* Harrisburg, Pa.: Stackpole, 1964.

Hittle, J.D., *The Military Staff: Its History and Development.* Harrisburg: Stackpole, 1944.

Hood, John B., *Advance and Retreat: Personal Experiences in the United States and Confederate States' Armies,* edited and with an Introduction and Notes by Richard N. Current. Bloomington: Indiana University Press, 1959.

Hotchkiss, Jedediah, *Make Me a Map of the Valley,* edited by Archie P. McDonald. Dallas: Southern Methodist University Press, 1973.

Hudson, F, "The Charleston and Knoxville Campaigns: History of the 59th Georgia Infantry Regiment," Pt II, *The Atlanta Historical Journal,* XXV, No. 3 (Fall 1981).

Imboden, John D., "The Confederate Retreat from Gettysburg," In Johnson and Buel, *Battles and Leaders of the Civil War* (New York: Thomas Yoseloff, 1956), III, 420-429.

Johnson, Robert Underwood, *Remembered Yesterdays.* Boston: Little, Brown, 1923.

Johnson, Robert Underwood and Buel, Clarence Clough, eds., *Battles and Leaders of the Civil War.* Four volumes. Reprint, New York: Thomas Yoseloff, 1956.

Jones, J. William, *Personal Reminiscences, Anecdotes, and Letters of Robert E. Lee.* New York: D. Appleton, 1874.

Keller, Morton, *Affairs of State: Public Life in Late Nineteenth Century America.* Cambridge: Harvard University Press, 1977.

Knight, Oliver Knight, *Life and Manners in the Frontier Army.* Norman: University of Oklahoma Press, 1978.

Krick, Robert K., "'I Consider Him a Humbug...'—McLaws on Longstreet at Gettysburg?" *Virginia Country's Civil War Quarterly*, Vol 5.

_____, "If Longstreet . . Says So, It is Most Likely Not True: James Longstreet and the Second Day at Gettysburg," in Gary W. Gallagher (ed.), *The Second Day at Gettysburg*. Kent, Oh.: Kent State University Press, 1993.

Lane, Lydia Spencer, *I Married a Soldier: or, Old Days in the Old Army*. Albuquerque: Horn & Wallu, 1964.

Lee, Fitzhugh, "Letter from General Fits. Lee," *Southern Historical Society Papers*, IV (Aug. 1877), 69-76.

_____, *General Lee*. New York: D. Appleton and Company, 1894.

_____, "A Review of the First Two Days' Operations at Gettysburg and a Reply to General Longstreet," *Southern Historical Society Papers*, V (April 1878), 162-94.

Lee, Susan P., editor, *Memoirs of William Nelson Pendleton*. Philadelphia: J. B. Lippincott Company, 1893.

Lewis, Lloyd, *Captain Sam Grant*. Boston: Little, Brown, 1950.

Liddell, St. John Richardson, *Liddell's Record*, edited by Nathanial C. Hughes. Dayton Ohio: Morningside Bookshop, 1985.

Livermore, Thomas L., *Numbers and Losses in the Civil War in America: 1861-1865*. Bloomington: Indiana University Press, 1957. Reprint, Millwood, N.Y.: Klaus, 1977.

Long, A.L., "Letter from A. L. Long, Military Secretary to General R. E. Lee," *Southern Historical Soceity Papers*, IV (Sept. 1877), 118-23.

_____, *Memoirs of Robert E. Lee: His Military and Personal History*. New York: J. M. Stoddart & Company, 1886.

Longstreet, Helen D., *Lee and Longstreet at High Tide: Gettysburg in Light of the Official Records*. Gainesville, Ga.: By the author, 1904.

Longstreet, James, "The Battle of Fredericksburg," *The Century*, XXXII (Aug. 1886), 609-626.

_____, *From Manassas to Appomattox*. Philadelphia: J. B. Lippincott and Co., 1896. Reprints, Bloomington: Indiana University Press, 1960.; Secaucus, N.J.: The Blue and Grey Press, 1988; New York: Mallard Press, 1991.

_____, "General James Longstreet's Account of the Campaign and Battle," *Southern Historical Society Papers*, V (Jan. 1878), 54-86.

_____, "General Longstreet's Second Paper on Gettysburg," *Southern Historical Society Papers*, V (June 1878), 257-69.

_____, "The Invasion of Pennsylvania," *The Century*, XXXII (June 1886), 309-15.

_____, "Lee in Pennsylvania," in *The Annals of the War Written by Leading Participants North and South* (Philadelphia: The Times Publishing Company, 1879), 414-26.

_____, "The Mistakes of Gettysburg," in *The Annals of the War Written by Leading Participants North and South* (Philadelphia: The Times Publishing Company, 1879), 619-33.

_____, "The Seven Days Fighting Around Richmond," *The Century*, XXX (July 1885), 470-74, 576.

_____, "Our March Against Pope," *The Century*, XXXI (Feb. 1886), 601-14

Lord, Walter, ed., *The Fremantle Diary*. Boston: Little, Brown & Co., 1954.

Lowe, Percival, *Five Years a Dragoon ('49 to '54) And Other Adventures on the Great Plains*. Norman, Ok.: University of Oklahoma Press, 1965.

Luvaas, Jay, and Nelson, Harold W., *The U.S. Army War College Guide to the Battle of Antietam*. New York: Perennial Press, 1988.

McCall, George B., *Letters From the Frontiers*. Philadelphia: J.B. Lippincott & Co., 1868.

McClellan, H.B., *I Rode With Jeb Stuart*. Bloomington: University of Indiana Press, 1958.

McLure, Alexander K., *Recollections of Half a Century*. Salem, Ma.: The Salem Press, 1902.

McMaster, Richard K., *Musket, Saber, and Missile: A History of Fort Bliss*. El Paso, Tx.: Complete Letter and Printing Service, 1963.

McMurray, Richard M. McMurry, *Two Great Rebel Armies: An Essay in Confederate Military History*. Chapel Hill: The University of North Carolina Press, 1989.

McWhiney, Grady, *Braxton Bragg and the Confederate Defeat*. New York: Columbia University Press, 1969.

_____, *Southerners and Other Americans*. New York: Basic Books, Inc., Publishers, 1973.

Manigault, Arthur M., *A Carolinian Goes to War*, edited by P. Lockwood Tower. Columbia, S.C.: The University of South Carolina Press, 1983.

Martin, P. T. Martin, "Recollections of a Confederate," *Confederate Veteran Magazine*, No. 15 (May 1907).

The Military Annals of Tennessee, John Berrien Lindsley, ed. Wilmington: Broadfoot Publishing, 1995.

Mills, W. W., *Forty Years at El Paso, 1858-1898*. El Paso, Tx.: Carl Hertzog, 1962.

Myres, Sandra L., "Frontier Historians, Women, and the 'New' Military History," *Military History of the Southwest*, XIX (Spring 1989).

_____, *Westering Women and the Frontier Experience, 1800-1915*. Albuquerque: University of New Mexico Press, 1982.

Oates, William C., "Gettysburg—The Battle on the Right," *Southern Historical Society Papers*, VI (Oct. 1878), 172-82.

_____, *The War Between the Union and the Confederacy and Its Lost Opportunities*. Dayton, Ohio: Press of Morningside Bookshop, 1985.

Owen, William Miller, *In Camp And Battle With The Washington Artillery*. Boston: Ticknoe and Company, 1885. Reprint, Gaithersburg, Md.: Butternut Press, n.d.

Perry, William F. "A Forgotten Account of Chickamauga." ed. Curt Johnson. *Civil War Times Illustrated*, September/October, 1993.

Pfanz, Harry W., *Gettysburg: Culp's Hill and Cemetery Hill*. Chapel Hill: The University of North Carolina Press, 1993.

_____, *Gettysburg: The Second Day.* Chapel Hill: University of North Carolina Press, 1987.

Piston, William Garrett, *Lee's Tarnished Lieutenant: James Longstreet and His Place in Southern History.* Athens, Ga.: University of Georgia Press, 1987

_____, "Lee's Tarnished Lieutenant: James Longstreet and His Image in American Society." Ph.D. dissertation, University of South Carolina.

Prucha, Francis Paul, *The Sword of the Republic; The United States Army on the Frontier, 1783-1846.* Lincoln and London: University of Nebraska Press, 1969.

Ratchford, James Wylie. *Some Reminiscences of Persons and Incidents of the Civil War.* Austin: Shoal Creek Publishers, 1971.

Riley, Glenda, *Women and Indians on the Frontier, 1825-1915.* Albuquerque: University of New Mexico Press, 1984.

Robertson, James I., *General A.P. Hill: The Story of a Confederate Warrior.* New York: Random House, 1987.

Robertson, William Glenn, Shanahan, Edward P., Boxburger, John I., and Knapp, George E., *Staff Ride Handbook for the Battle of Chickamauga, 18-20 September 1863.* Fort Levenworth: Combat Studies Institute, 1992.

Ross, Fitzgerald, *Cities And Camps of the Confederate States,* edited by Richard Barksdale Harwell. Urbana: University of Illinois Press, 1958.

Rowland, Dunbar, *Jefferson Davis, Constitutionalist.* Ten volumes. New York: J.J. Little & Iver Company, 1923.

Roberton, Dr. William Glenn; Lieutenant Colonel Edward P. Shanahan; Lieutenant Colonel John I. Boxberger; and Major George E. Knupp. *Staff Ride Handbook for the Battle of Chickamauga: 18-20 September 1863.* Fort Leavenworth, Kansas: Combat Studies Institute, 1992.

Sanger, Donald Bridgman, *The Story of Old Fort Bliss.* El Paso, Tx.: Buie Company, 1933.

Sanger, Donald Bridgman, and Hay, Thomas Robson, *James Longstreet: Soldier, Politician, Officeholder, and Writer.* Two volumes. Baton Rouge: Louisiana State University Press, 1952.

Shaver, Lewelleyn A. *A History of the Sixtieth Alabama Regiment: Gracie's Alabama Brigade.* Montgomery, Alabama: Barrett and Brown, 1867.

Scott, Robert Garth, *Into the Wilderness With the Army of the Potomac.* Bloomington, Il.: University of Indiana Press, 1988.

Sears, Stephen W., *To the Gates of Richmond.* New York: Ticknor & Fields, 1992.

Shaver, Lewellyn A., *A History of the Sixtieth Alabama Regiment. Gracie's Alabama Brigade.* Montgomery, Alabama: Barrett & Brown, 1867. Reprint, Gaithersburg, Md.: Butternut Press, n.d.

Smith, James Power, "With Stonewall Jackson," *Southern Historical Society Papers,* Vol 43, (1920).

Sorrel, G. Moxley, *Recollections Of A Confederate Staff Officer,* edited by Bell Irvin Wiley. Jackson, Tennessee: McCowat-Mercer Press, 1958. Reprint, Dayton, Oh.: Press of Morningside Bookshop, 1978

Stallard, Patricia Y., *Glittering Misery: Dependents of the Indian Fighting Army.* San Rafael: Presidio Press, 1978.

Taylor, Walter H., "The Campaign in Pennsylvania," in *The Annals of the War Written by Leading Participants North and South* (Philadelphia: The Times Publishing Company, 1879), 305-318.

_____, *Four Years With General Lee,* edited by James I. Robertson, Jr. Bloomington: Indiana University Press, 1962.

_____, "Memorandum from Colonel Walter H. Taylor," *Southern Historical Soceity Papers,* IV (Aug. 1877), 80-87.

_____, "Second Paper by Col. Walter H. Taylor, of Lee's Staff," *Southern Historical Society Papers,* IV (Sept. 1877), 124-39.

Tennesseans in the Civil War. Nashville, Tn: Civil War Centennial Commission, 1964.

Thiam, Raphael P., comp., *Notes Illustrating the Military Geography of the United States, 1813-1880.* Washington: Adjutant General's Office, 1881. Reprint, Austin and London: University of Texas Press, 1979.

Thomas, Emory M., *Bold Dragoon: The Life of J.E.B. Stuart.* New York: Harper & Row, Publishers, 1986.

Tucker, Glenn, *Chickamauga, Bloody Battle in the West.* Dayton, Ohio: Morningside Bookshop, 1976.

_____, *High Tide at Gettysburg.* Indianapolis: Bobbs-Merrill, 1958.

_____. *Lee and Longstreet at Gettysburg.* Indianapolis: Bobbs-Merrill, 1968.

Vandiver, Frank E., *Mighty Stonewall.* New York: McGraw-Hill, 1957.

Wade, John Donald, *Augustus Baldwin Longstreet: A Study of the Development of Culture in the South.* Athens: The University of Georgia Press, 1969.

Walters, J.B., "General William T. Sherman and Total War," *Journal of Southern History,* Vol 14, No. 4 (November, 1948).

Warner, Ezra J., *Generals in Blue: Lives of the Union Commanders.* Baton Rouge: Louisiana State University Press, 1964. Reissued, 1981.

_____, *Generals in Gray: Lives of the Confederate Commanders.* Baton Rouge: Louisiana State University Press, 1959. Reissued, 1981.

Weigley, Russell F., *History of the United States Army.* New York: Macmillan, 1967.

Wert, Jeffry D., *General James Longstreet: The Confederacy's Most Controversial Soldier—A Biography.* New York: Simon & Schuster, 1993.

Wilcox, Cadmus M., "General C. M. Wilcox on the Battle of Gettysburg," *Southern Historical Society Papers,* VI (September 1878), 97-124.

Wilhelm, Thomas, *A Synopsis History of the Eighth U.S. Infantry and the Military Record of Officers Assigned to the Regiment From Its Organization July, 1838, to Sept. 1871.* New York: Eighth Infantry Headquarters, 1871.

Williams, Samuel C., *General John T. Wilder, Commander of the Lightning Brigade.* Bloomington, In.: Indiana University Press, 1936.

Wilson, Charles Reagan, *Baptized in Blood: The Religion of the Lost Cause.* Athens, Ga.: University of Georgia Press, 1980.

Wise, Jennings C., *The Long Arm of Lee.* Reprint, New York: Oxford University Press, 1959.

Wolseley, Garnett, "An English View of the Civil War," *The North American Review*, May 1889, 538-63; July 1889, 30-43; August 1889, 164-81; September 1889, 278-92; Oct. 1889, 446-59; Nov. 1889, 594-606; December 1889, 713-27.

Wyeth, John A., *With Sabre and Scalpel.* New York: Harper and Brothers Publishers, 1914.

Utley, Robert M., *Frontiersmen in Blue; The United States Army and the Indian, 1848-1865.* Lincoln and London: University of Nebraska Press, 1967.

Interviews

Ogden III, James, Park Historian, Chickamauga-Chattanooga National Military Park. Interviewed by the author. Fort Oglethorpe, Georgia. March 9, 1993.

Ogden III, James, Park Historian, Chickamauga-Chattanooga National Military Park. Consultation with the author. April 1, 1994.

Newspapers

Washington National Intelligencer
Washington Post

Maps

Map of the Battlefield of Chickamauga published by the Chickamauga and Chattanooga National Park Commission. Compiled and drawn by C.E. Betts, C.E., Park Engineer, 1896.

Chickamauga Battlefield Location Map for Monuments, Markers, and Plaques. Department of the Interior, U.S. Geological Survey, 1934.

Index